FACES OF TRADITION IN CHINESE PERFORMING ARTS

ENCOUNTERS: EXPLORATIONS IN FOLKLORE AND
ETHNOMUSICOLOGY
Ray Cashman and Michael Dylan Foster, Editors
A *Journal of Folklore Research* Book

FACES OF TRADITION IN CHINESE PERFORMING ARTS

Edited by Levi S. Gibbs

Indiana University Press

This book is a publication of

Indiana University Press
Office of Scholarly Publishing
Herman B Wells Library 350
1320 East 10th Street
Bloomington, Indiana 47405 USA

iupress.indiana.edu

© 2020 by Trustees of Indiana University

All rights reserved
No part of this book may be reproduced or utilized in any form or by any means, electronic or mechanical, including photocopying and recording, or by any information storage and retrieval system, without permission in writing from the publisher. The paper used in this publication meets the minimum requirements of the American National Standard for Information Sciences—Permanence of Paper for Printed Library Materials, ANSI Z39.48-1992.

Manufactured in the United States of America

Cataloging information is available from the Library of Congress.

ISBN 978-0-253-04583-6 (pbk.)
ISBN 978-0-253-04586-7 (web PDF)

1 2 3 4 5   25 24 23 22 21 20

Contents

	Acknowledgments	vii
	Introduction: Faces of Tradition in Chinese Performing Arts / Levi S. Gibbs	1
1	Grasping Intangible Heritage and Reimagining Inner Mongolia: Folk-Artist Albums and a New Logic for Musical Representation in China / Charlotte D'Evelyn	17
2	Chinese Singing Contests as Sites of Negotiation among Individuals and Traditions / Levi S. Gibbs	41
3	Dynamic Inheritance: Representative Works and the Authoring of Tradition in Chinese Dance / Emily E. Wilcox	64
4	Collecting Flowers, Defining a Genre: Zhang Yaxiong and the *Anthology of Hua'er Folksongs* / Sue Tuohy	94
5	From Field Recordings to Ethnographically Informed CDs: Curating the Sounds of Yunnan for a Niche Foreign Market / Helen Rees	125
	Glossary of Selected Chinese Terms and Phrases	155
	Index	169

Acknowledgments

First and foremost, I would like to thank Ray Cashman for his tireless efforts, patience, and insightful feedback throughout the process of seeing this edited volume to fruition. I am also grateful to Janice E. Frisch, Gary Dunham, Rachel Rosolina, and David Miller at Indiana University Press and Pete Feely at Amnet for seeing through the volume's production. Thanks also to Eileen Allen for creating the index. This volume began as a panel that I chaired at the 2013 American Folklore Society Annual Meeting, for which Sue Tuohy generously served as discussant. Thanks to Emily Wilcox for securing permission from Siqintariha for the wonderful cover photo, and to Michael Dylan Foster for providing valuable support early on in the project. Thanks also to Hilary Warner-Evans, Kristina Downs, Marisa Wieneke, and Ray Cashman for their careful editing work and to the anonymous reviewers of the individual chapters for their valuable comments and suggestions. Lastly, I want to thank Helen Rees for patiently providing helpful feedback along the way.

FACES OF TRADITION IN CHINESE PERFORMING ARTS

Introduction
Faces of Tradition in Chinese Performing Arts

Levi S. Gibbs

Traditions are not static; they constantly adapt past practices to new circumstances (Toelken 1996). While a performance tradition may appear to be a monolithic institution, like a city viewed from an airplane, upon closer inspection one sees the people who inhabit and shape that city. Each performance tradition is populated by individuals who debate what and who belong, how the tradition should develop, and how to represent the tradition as a whole. In an ever-changing world, these artists and scholars choose paths between continuity and change.[1] Their choices revolve around particular areas of cultural production where traditions and individuals interact, such as those explored in this edited volume: CD albums, singing competitions, representative works, textual anthologies, and ethnographic videos. These symbolically powerful sites are where emblematic objects are formed, presented, and critiqued, where artists and scholars seek to "traditionalize" their performances, collections, and selves, endowing each "with a dimension of traditional authority" and making their mark on a tradition's landscape (Bauman 2004, 27; cf. Hymes 1975). The works they produce win acclaim, are forgotten, or fall somewhere in between; if individuals and their works do win approval, both may go on to become powerful "faces of tradition" that transform the topographies of the traditions they represent and provide inspiration for future artists and scholars.

In this edited volume, the authors explore five case studies in which individuals and their creations have become "faces" of Chinese performance traditions.[2] Rather than concentrating on the hegemony of broad traditions or the creativity of individual variations, we look for a balanced view of the push and pull between continuity and change. By exploring each of our five extended examples, we see how multiple voices meet and play in and around these pivotal discursive sites.

When a CD is published or a "representative work" of Chinese dance is added to the contemporary canon, individual artists and their styles are validated, and yet that validation extends to other individuals as well—choreographers, TV producers, critics, scholars, editors, and so on. In addition, we often see how a bid to traditionalize may lead to a ripple effect of mutually reinforcing outcomes: winning a contest may strengthen an artist's association with a representative work and lead to the production of a CD album, which may then influence how scholars and producers write and organize future anthologies.

What, then, are the benefits of looking at Chinese case studies of performance traditions, and why now? China's opening up following economic reforms in the late 1970s and early 1980s has led to increased access for researchers, and each of the authors in this edited volume has conducted extensive fieldwork there. Through interviews and participant observation, we have come to know many of the players involved and how these traditions have changed over time. As in other places around the world, performance traditions in China are often presented as representing particular territories and ethnic groups, as well as the nation as a whole, and yet each of us has seen firsthand how *individuals* negotiate the minutiae of steps involved in adapting, performing, interpreting, and representing repertoires and traditions. With the expansion of available media and documentation—newspaper/web articles, TV programs, CD albums, documentaries, and government-funded initiatives to designate and preserve intangible cultural heritage—we can bear witness to a growing number of bids to traditionalize, the dynamics of how each of those bids functions individually, as well as how multiple bids interact and often reinforce one another.[3] In the process of this examination, we gain insight into how individuals and those who surround them continue to negotiate their places in traditions and how those traditions are represented and cultivated.

Our approach fits into an emerging body of literature on the mutual relationship between individuals and traditions—a topic that has gained attention in recent years in the disciplines of ethnomusicology, folklore studies, and dance ethnography. Scholars of China have noted "an emergence of the individual" in the post-Mao era (Kipnis 2012, 3; cf. Yan 2009), and there have been increasing efforts by Chinese and foreign scholars to look at the role of individuals in performance traditions (cf. Zhang J. 2004; Xiao 2004; Tian 2004; Qiao 2010; Zhang C. 1985; Hung 1993; Stock 1996; Tuohy 2003; Jones 2004, 2007, 2009; Rees 2001, 2009, 2016; Yung 2008; Schein 2010; Gibbs 2018; Wilcox 2019). Similar endeavors have been seen in studies on Japan and South Korea (cf. Howard 2006a, 2006b; Tansman 1996; Hughes 2008), and elsewhere (cf. Danielson 1997).

In what follows, I introduce various approaches to the individual and tradition, together with associated concerns about representation and individual agency, all of which provide a background for a discussion of what I call "mechanisms of traditionalization." We hope that our examination of these mechanisms will inspire others to explore similar phenomena in a variety of geographical and temporal contexts. By concentrating on these discursive sites, we may transcend some of the pitfalls involved in focusing solely on traditions *or* individuals, continuity *or* innovation, and instead highlight the dynamic push and pull between them.

Approaches to Individuals and Traditions

Although research on any sort of tradition requires contact with at least one individual, in the final textual products, individuals may appear in a range of ways. The spectrum of possibilities extends from descriptions of anonymously populated traditions "not dealing at all with individuals" to works "dealing exclusively with one individual" (Ruskin and Rice 2012, 303). While most projects fall somewhere in between—dealing with at least some individuals—different factors may contribute to the visibility or invisibility of individuals in published works. This disparity may be due in part to disciplinary differences—Jonathan Stock and Helen Rees suggest a bifurcated approach in the focus on individuals in musicology and ethnomusicology, whereby the former has historically tended to emphasize biographies verging on hero worship, while the latter has often concentrated on shared musical activities at the expense of individuals (Stock 2001, 7; Rees 2001, 59).[4] Rees and Antoinet Schimmelpenninck point to a similar division they observed in China during the late twentieth century between local song collectors and urban-based scholars, suggesting that the former "usually know their informants personally and make many visits to their homes" and "are often meticulous about noting who sang what, and where, and when, in their mimeographs and publications" (Rees 2001, 44), while the latter "pay very little attention to the singers" (Schimmelpenninck 1997, 54).

The degree of focus on the individual can also vary depending on the creative genre in question. In her chapter in this volume, Emily E. Wilcox argues that the term "modern dance" refers to dances that are created by individual artists and assumed to have no connection to either historical or folk dance, while "traditional dance" is seen as being preserved from a historical tradition, its value stemming from the dance's presumed authenticity and continuity through time. Wilcox further posits that contemporary Chinese ethnic dance falls in between traditional and modern, due to the dialogic nature of its choreographic works. In Anthony Shay's research on various genres of state folk dance, he describes how the creative contributions of individuals are often overlooked. In *Choreographic Politics* (2002), Shay writes, "Because the dances purportedly originate with 'the people,' the characters of the founder-artistic directors and choreographers are often muted. Many individuals among the public largely believe the fiction that the choreographies they view on stage reflect actual dances as they would be experienced in a traditional field setting" (39, quoted in Wilcox, this volume, 88).

Among scholarly works that deal with individuals and traditions, we can outline three major approaches: (1) studies of particular traditions based on observations of individual actors within them (i.e., outlining the forest, if you will, with reference to the shared characteristics of individual trees); (2) studies that focus on an individual, attempting to place that individual within the tradition in which the individual participates (i.e., focusing on a unique tree, while showing how it fits into the forest that surrounds it); and (3) studies that emphasize how the two categories—individuals and traditions—mutually transform each other (i.e., looking at how the lifespans of individual trees contribute to the overall appearance of the forest and the other trees in it, as well as how the broader characteristics of the forest as a whole influence the nature and perception of individual trees).[5]

The first approach suggests that to understand a tradition, one must begin with the individuals who participate in it. This notion, perhaps, stems from the nature of fieldwork where one tends to encounter individuals first, and then go on to construct maps of larger circles of interaction, imagined and otherwise. For example, in order to move from engagements with individuals to an understanding of broader traditions, Albert B. Lord suggests starting with an individual singer and working outward to the singers who have influenced the individual, to the larger community, and eventually to the entire "language area" (1960, 49). In a similar vein, James Porter and Herschel Gower write, "Instead of generalizing about musical change from observation of a group as if it were homogenous, a more orderly methodology would set out to 'discover' the beliefs and knowledge held by individuals, working outward in concentric circles to compare performers' beliefs with those of nonperformers" (1995, 273). Works included in this approach look at how an individual's life experience enriches our understanding of a tradition (cf. Abrahams 1970; Newman 1995; Rees 2009). While this movement from individuals to an understanding of the group is inherent, in a sense, in most types of fieldwork, Stock points out that the "way of working at the data-gathering level" does not significantly change when we write more about individuals; rather, he argues, the trend toward inclusion of the individual is "largely a literary one" (2001, 6).

The second approach looks at how elements of tradition can help us to better understand the nature of an individual (cf. Sawin 2004). Scholars using this approach compare an individual with others in that person's social web in order to see what commonalities they share and what their unique points are. Along this line of thinking, Porter and Gower suggest, "Every singer must be discerned against a ground consisting of other singers in the same or a contiguous tradition; otherwise, the sense of a collective well of language, style, and idiom is lost" (1995, xlv). However, whether one is trying to better understand a particular individual or tradition, there is an underlying tension in attempting to define one with reference to the other. In her recent edited volume on women singers in global contexts, Ruth Hellier writes: "It is important to note that we are not attempting to engage generalizations and broad theorizations in relation to these unique women. Given the focus upon individual lives and specificity, such an undertaking would be problematic and would undermine the thrust of the project. Nevertheless, because these are biographical narratives of women singers there are obviously commonalities and recurrent strands, even as the diversity documented within these threads, themes, connections, and clusters serves to emphasize individual experiences" (2013, 25). The difficulty in striking a balance between acknowledging commonalities among individuals and making generalizations about culture extends to any attempt to describe either individuals or traditions. In writing about the Traveller tradition to which the singer Jeannie Robertson is said to belong, Porter and Gower note, "'Traveller culture'... cannot be reduced to a number of individual personalities, nor is it a homogeneous totality" (1995, xvii). Neither tradition nor the individual can exist in isolation, and as such, focusing the scholarly lens too closely on one or the other is problematic.

The third approach attempts to acknowledge and address this underlying tension by looking at how individuals and traditions mutually transform each other (cf. Porter and Gower 1995; Cashman, Mould, and Shukla 2011). In Lord's classic work, he writes, "The singer of tales is at once the tradition and an individual creator" (1960, 4). In a more recent edited volume that follows this line of thought, Ray Cashman, Tom Mould, and Pravina Shukla declare, "Tradition and the individual are inseparable" (2011, vi). The suggestion of "inseparability" has direct import on the artistic works produced by performers. Linda Dégh argues that for a story to be successful, it must combine elements of tradition and of the individual—essentially exhibiting both familiarity and creativity (1995, 75). Other scholars, in turn, highlight the contrasting influences of the traditional and the individual as forces pulling on the artist's work (Fiedler 1952). Although divergent, both of these notions highlight the mutual interaction between the two—summed up nicely by Henry Glassie: "History, culture, and the human actor meet in tradition" (2003, 193).

Within this interplay between individual and tradition, there emerges a sense that neither entity can define itself outside of a dialogic relationship with the other. In a chapter on "The Role of Tradition in the Individual" in the edited volume *The Individual and Tradition: Folkloristic Perspectives*, Ray Cashman writes: "The individual and tradition: in a very real sense, one does not exist without the other. Moreover, as things-to-believe-in both are in one sense completely inaccessible. We cannot witness, characterize, or perhaps even approach such things as the individual or tradition (or poetry, or love, or God) except through their instantiations, and we cannot appreciate either the individual or tradition without fully grasping their interdependence" (2011, 319). The notion that neither the individual nor tradition can be appreciated completely "without fully grasping their interdependence" calls us to look more closely at the instances of that engagement (319). In the chapters in this edited volume, we look to shine a light on those instances—the mechanisms through which individuals and traditions interact. Rather than focusing solely on (1) *individuals* as faces of particular traditions, or (2) *traditions* as summations of the creative expressions of both prominent and anonymous faces, here, we look at (3) the *specific processes* through which the relationships between individuals, works, and traditions are reconfigured.

We therefore explore how discourses surrounding CD albums, song competitions, representative works, textual anthologies, and ethnographic videos form continuous conversations about how to interpret each tradition and the players associated with it. Implicit in our approach is an acknowledgment of the fluidity of tradition. According to Richard Handler and Jocelyn Linnekin, there is no "essential, bounded tradition," but rather "tradition is a model of the past and is inseparable from the interpretation of tradition in the present" (1984, 276). Handler and Linnekin suggest that "the ongoing reconstruction of tradition is a facet of all social life, which is not natural but symbolically constituted" (1984, 276; cf. Hymes 1975, 353–54). The title of this volume—*Faces of Tradition*—alludes to such symbolic constitutions as it provides a visage for the range of complex exchanges involved in positioning various "faces" within and between traditions. Largely through exchanges such as those explored in this book, individuals and their works become faces and are authorized to represent traditions to a certain degree, thus enacting one of Dorothy Noyes's definitions of tradition, "the transfer of responsibility for a valued practice or performance" (2009, 233).

Scholars, Cultural Brokers, and Narrative Strategies

The framing of traditions and the placing of individuals within those traditions cannot be separated from the influence of scholars and cultural brokers—anthropologists, judges, educators, journalists, and so on. As the authors in this edited volume show through various examples, these individuals may influence how a tradition as a whole is imagined (cf. Tuohy 1988), as well as how an individual artist's representative status is repositioned within that tradition. By providing "fresh ears" and eyes, these intermediaries "provide new opportunities" for individuals to reformulate their places within broader traditions (Sawin 2004, 95). Scholars, audiences, and recording executives may all have a hand in encouraging artists to specialize in particular genres, leading to their eventual association with those genres (Sawin 2004, 173; Wald 2004). In the chapters that follow, we see a range of examples of such interactions. Yang Yucheng, the Inner Mongolian scholar who produced the CD album series described by Charlotte D'Evelyn, essentially refigured public notions of a tradition through the production of symbolic physical objects. Yunnanese performances recorded by Zhang Xingrong and Li Wei'er and published as ethnographic CDs and videos through the efforts of collaborators including Helen Rees have helped individual musicians and groups become more widely known, facilitating national and international tours. Zhang Yaxiong, the scholar Sue Tuohy discusses, created the first textual anthology of *hua'er* songs, which not only served as a face of that tradition but was also instrumental in establishing the field of *hua'er* studies. Various scholars I discuss, including Tian Qing and Qiao Jianzhong, have supported particular singers in competitions and by nominating them for "representative transmitter" status. In addition to refiguring the images of particular traditions and practitioners within them, scholars may also attempt to redefine particular traditions in relation to each other. To this end, D'Evelyn observes that Yang Yucheng's project can be seen as an attempt to distinguish Mongol folk traditions from other more commercialized "'fast food' (*kuaican*) musical options that exist in Inner Mongolia" (this volume, 36).

The work of scholars not only influences how a tradition is publicly conceived but also how the practitioners themselves think about the tradition. This happens through conversations between scholars and practitioners, the publication of articles and books discussing practitioners' works and the traditions with which they identify, and the promotion of practitioners' works in large-scale performance venues, including concert halls, universities, television shows, and compact discs. Such engagements can have a transformative effect on an artist, as noted by Porter and Gower in their work on the Scottish traditional singer Jeannie Robertson: "The projection of her repertoire into spacious halls developed from these contexts, while she also was pushed by scholars and apprentice singers to consider the aesthetic form and the significance of particular songs" (1995, 270). In these ways, scholars influence how traditions are interpreted and appreciated.

Another influential aspect of the scholarly enterprise includes "the narrative strategies employed when individuals are included in musical ethnographies" (Ruskin and Rice 2012, 302). Within these "narrative strategies" the contributions of individuals may be accentuated or deemphasized. Those strategies that emphasize individuality argue for the "hard agency" of "choosing," while those that view individuals as more passive components within a tradition reflect the "soft agency" of "following" (Ortner 2006; Sewell 1992; Bronner 1998, 10). Jesse Ruskin and Timothy Rice suggest that "within this web of individual choices, data from individuals may be used to support both convergent and divergent views of culture, providing evidence either of common cultural trends or different patterns, styles, etc. that compete within the tradition" (2012, 307–8). While certain narrative strategies, such as biography, place emphasis on choices made by individuals, in doing so they also speak to additional factors, including the influence of "prominent individuals" (Stock 2001, 10), the "representational stance" (12) with which we view a tradition, and the effects of that narrative on "refiguring culture" (14) with a "greater emphasis on individual role and agency" (5)—all of which should "encourage us to look more closely at the individuals with whom we work and at the ways in which we document this work" (15–16).

In his discussion of "the politics of representation in ethnographic writing" (2001, 5), Jonathan Stock suggests that by altering our "representational stance" (12) to reconceive "'culture' as a mosaic of individual decisions, evaluations, actions and interactions" (10), we can present traditions less as "cultural-average accounts" and more as they are negotiated on a micro level (7). By shifting our focus in this manner, we can reposition how individuals and traditions are portrayed in scholarly writing. That said, we recognize that the decisions made by individuals in these situations are never isolated from their contexts, and therefore, we first address one of the major underlying issues in the relationship between individual and tradition—that of agency.

Agency and the Individual

Stith Thompson famously asked, "What . . . is the relation of the individual to the tradition which he carries on—how compulsive is the tradition of his social group and how much freedom is there for the expression of individuality?" (1953, 592). By changing the degree with which individuals are represented in scholarly works, there has been a corresponding shift from essentializing depictions of bounded traditions (Handler and Linnekin 1984) to descriptions that look at ongoing issues of individual choice within a tradition. Hellier suggests that "by focusing on processes of decision-making and choices, we move away from the notion of 'constraints' towards 'tensions' and 'opportunities'" (2013, 25). According to Stock, this type of focus reflects new notions of culture that "place greater emphasis on individual role and agency" (2001, 5), offering "a reconceptualization of 'culture' as a mosaic of individual decisions, evaluations, actions and interactions; consequently a desire to draw attention to individual cultural agency" (10).

The issue of individual agency, however, brings with it potentially problematic notions of intentionality. The idea of intentions as "definite goals consciously held in the mind" (Giddens 1979, 56) can be complicated in several ways—they may be "after-the-fact rationalizations" (Ortner 2006, 135) or "straddle conscious and unconscious aspects of cognition and emotion" (Giddens 1979, 58). Furthermore, to focus on intentions "obscures the fact that most social outcomes are in fact unintended consequences of action" (Ortner 2006, 135; italics removed). Each of these factors forms potential criticisms for biographies that focus on one individual, even though they may contain a well-balanced combination of viewpoints. Sherry B. Ortner argues that "the social and cultural forces in play in any historical engagement are infinitely more complex than what can be learned from looking at actors' intentions" (2006, 132). Citing John and Jean Comaroff's view that "the 'motivation' of social practice" involves both "the (culturally configured) needs and desires of human beings" and "the pulse of collective forces" (1992, 36), Ortner raises concerns that "the close examination and analysis of the 'pulse of collective forces' . . . begin[s] to get slighted when the weight of analytic effort gets shifted to 'agency,' and that results in a deeply inadequate account of what was actually going on" (2006, 132). How, then, do we reconcile notions of individual agency with such collective forces?

Jiwei Ci adds helpful nuance to this discussion in *Moral China in the Age of Reform* by suggesting that there are multiple strategies of "power attribution and subjectivity constitution" in China leading to different sorts of agency (2014, 40). According to Ci, attempts to assert one's individualism—what he calls "*agency-through-freedom*" (2014, 40)—is just one tactic used by individuals. He suggests that another prominent strategy found in China is "*agency-through-identification*," whereby "power is attributed to . . . specific individuals who diffuse it . . . by making themselves appear as qualified mediators of a tradition or true representatives of a movement and hence as suitable loci of identification. Ordinary people identify with a tradition or community or movement through the more direct and tangible identification with its messengers or representatives" (2014, 94). Such identification bears witness to the roles of and interactions between the faces of tradition we explore in this book.

Ci's dialectic between freedom and identification connects to the underlying question raised by Stith Thompson: To what degree do traditions influence individual choices? As Simon Bronner notes, "Vehement argument can arise whether *following* tradition means unconsciously following a severe form of cultural authority or *choosing* from tradition that which one finds appropriate" (1998, 10; emphasis in original). Pierre Bourdieu looks for a happy medium between the two with his notion of *habitus* as "structuring structures" (1990, 53), and Ortner, reminding us that "individuals or persons or subjects are always embedded in webs of relations," suggests that "whatever 'agency' they seem to 'have' as individuals is in reality something that is always in fact *interactively negotiated*" (2006, 151–52; emphasis added). One can argue that it is only through this active negotiation that individuals position themselves in relation to others and to traditions at large. In this context, we can understand the mechanisms discussed below as points of intersection where the agency of individual performers, scholars, judges, and others meet in ongoing dialogues about how to define the nature of the particular tradition at hand.

Mechanisms of Traditionalization

The chapters in this edited volume examine various means through which individuals and their works have become faces of traditions, reshaping how those traditions are represented and understood. Charlotte D'Evelyn explores how singers' voices and song styles are made tangible through the publication of CD albums (*zhuanji*) in Inner Mongolia, canonizing individual performers and connecting their repertoires and localities to the traditions that surround them. Levi S. Gibbs discusses the role of televised singing competitions in branding singers, songs, and regions, and repositioning them within the professional hierarchy, regional traditions, and the national mediascape. Emily E. Wilcox looks at how "representative pieces" (*daibiaozuo*) developed by individual choreographers and dancers redefine Chinese culture as expressed through classical dance, while positioning stylistic schools within the broader field of Chinese dance. Sue Tuohy examines the role of scholars in constructing the "imagined tradition" of a regional song genre, while at the same time delineating the contents of its canon. Helen Rees writes about her involvement with ethnographic CD and video publications during a period of over twenty-five years working with Nimbus, Pan, Ode, and Apsara to publish Yunnanese materials (many recorded by Yunnanese scholars Zhang Xingrong and Li Wei'er), some of which have helped to facilitate tours and make a name for the individual musicians and groups involved.

Extending from studies of the life histories of individuals in relation to (1) social change, (2) the revision of existing theories, and (3) the individuals' positions within particular traditions, these chapters look at specific mechanisms in which individuals interact with and reconfigure traditions. As mentioned earlier, the "faces of tradition" of our title holds a double meaning—referring both to the individuals who come to represent traditions *and* to the mediums through which those individuals engage with and affect those traditions, including CD albums, ethnographic videos, representative works, anthologies, and awards in competitions. In the discursive spaces surrounding these media, individual agents and the objects associated with them are fused together as representatives of tradition. Wilcox observes that by creating "representative works" in dance, choreographers, along with the works they create, can become representatives of new stylistic interpretations of Chinese culture. In a similar vein, D'Evelyn posits in her work on the production of CD albums in Inner Mongolia that packaged CD albums offer one of many ways to capture the archival musical knowledge contained within each folk artist's memory, to ascribe value upon it "through researched appraisal as well as pomp and celebration," and to produce a physical package to contain and pass down the otherwise intangible riches of their musical past (this volume, 37). In each case, individuals and the objects associated with them (e.g., CD albums, ethnographic videos, representative works, awards, and anthologies) become points of reference for further engagements with the traditions they come to represent.

While each of these individuals makes use of elements of tradition in their own creations, the works they produce also provide inspiration for future works.

Claude Lévi-Strauss (1966) refers to the individual who selects and assembles elements of tradition as a *bricoleur*, characterized by Cashman, Mould, and Shukla as "a crafty recycler who constructs new possibilities out of available handed-down raw materials, meeting present needs" (2011, 4). For example, the "representative works" described by Wilcox are pieced together in a creative fashion from earlier material and these works, in turn, influence further choreographic innovation, new dance training curricula, and the establishment of various schools of style, thus molding future possibilities for the generations that follow (Wilcox, this volume). Likewise, the CD project examined by D'Evelyn produces symbolic objects that will continue to provide entertainment and research material beyond the lifespans of the artists. In this way, the objects created by these bricoleurs become material available for the assemblage of future bricoleurs.

At the same time, the various mechanisms explored in this edited volume are often interrelated. Awards in competitions can provide a means for a new piece to become a "representative work" that goes on to be taught and performed as part of the canon (cf. Wilcox, this volume). Such awards can also lead a singer to (1) become publicly associated with a particular song, (2) justify the future production of a solo album (*zhuanji*), and (3) become designated as a representative transmitter of intangible cultural heritage (cf. D'Evelyn, this volume; Gibbs, this volume). Scholars often play an integral role in these mechanisms as well, promoting individual artists in competitions, serving as judges in those competitions, nominating them as representative transmitters, and producing scholarship that justifies those nominations. While keeping in mind that these mechanisms are often interconnected, we highlight the individual workings of one particular mechanism in each chapter, looking at its role in multiple case studies. By doing so, we are able to see how a range of individuals—performers, choreographers, scholars, teachers, and judges—are involved in deciding which performers, pieces, and styles are promoted within broader traditions, thus complicating notions of individual agency.

Writing on fields of cultural production, Bourdieu notes that "each author, school or work which 'makes its mark' displaces the whole series of earlier authors, schools or works" (1993, 60), while at the same time, "the meaning of a work (artistic, literary, philosophical, etc.) changes automatically with each change in the field within which it is situated for the spectator or reader" (30–31). The "marks" made when a scholar produces a textual anthology, an ethnographic video, or a CD album, when a judge awards a prize to a singer, when a choreographer composes a dance—each of these actions has broader effects that not only reposition the places of individuals and their works in the broader field but essentially reconfigure the tradition as a whole. The "representative works" Wilcox discusses can serve to canonize an existing dance style or establish a new "school" within an existing dance style, and in doing so, influence what is understood to be a part of the Chinese cultural tradition. D'Evelyn notes that the celebration of one artist's work through a CD album not only fills in a gap in the canon of representatives from Inner Mongolia's far western region but also aligns with recent attempts by Mongols in Inner Mongolia to reconfigure the canon of traditional music in a way that emphasizes regional styles and artistic lineages over pan-ethnic representations.

While changes in the field appear to be affected by the creations of individuals, one may argue that there is pushback from the field itself, in the sense that the judges in competitions are often scholars and/or practitioners who have assumed their cultural authority through experience with the tradition as it has existed up until that point. When an award-winning musician or choreographer becomes a judge in future competitions, is that judge likely to perpetuate a sense of aesthetics similar to that with which the judge gained entry into the field? Framing this tension in practice theory, Ortner writes, "It is no doubt the case that playing the game tends to reproduce both the public structures of rules and assumptions, and the private subjectivity/consciousness/habitus of the players, and thus that playing the game . . . almost always results in social reproduction" (2006, 149). One might then ask whether these mechanisms—CD albums, contests, representative works, anthologies, ethnographic videos—not only allow individuals to influence traditions, but also influence those individuals through the process of engagement. That is to say, given that those mechanisms are already set in place within those traditions, do individuals' engagements with those mechanisms (including the techniques and repertoires they have adapted from earlier practitioners) implicitly carry with them an influence from the tradition toward the individual? While certainly agreeing with Jonathan Stock's assertion that "the personal, the idiosyncratic and the exceptional turn out to be the building blocks of the collective, the typical and the ordinary" (2001, 15), here we concern ourselves with the points at which "the personal" and "the collective" come into contact with each other. By focusing on specific mechanisms in which multiple individuals have negotiated their own presence in relation to broader fields, we hope to point to tangible ways in which individuals and traditions interact.

Dartmouth College
Hanover, New Hampshire

Notes

1. See Barre Toelken's (1996) "twin laws of folklore": *conservatism* and *dynamism*.
2. For general discussions of Chinese performance traditions, including song, dance, storytelling, opera, puppetry, instrumental music, and theater, see Colin Mackerras (1981, 1983, 1984, 2008, 2011), Victor Mair and Mark Bender (2011), Stephen Jones (1995), Qiao Jianzhong (1998), Fan Pen Li Chen (2007), and Frederick Lau (2008). Studies on particular Chinese performance traditions include Sue Tuohy (1988), Antoinet Schimmelpenninck

(1997), Mackerras (1997), Helen Rees (2000), Bender (2003), Jonathan Stock (2003), Jones (2004, 2007, 2009), Sara Davis (2005), Nancy Guy (2005), Joshua Goldstein (2007), Rachel Harris (2008), Jin Jiang (2009), Qiliang He (2012), Haili Ma (2015), and Ka-ming Wu (2015).

3. For more on the history of intangible cultural heritage preservation in China, see Rees (2012).

4. Similarly, in their study of book-length musical ethnographies, Jesse Ruskin and Timothy Rice find a "small number of books devoted in the main to a single named individual," which they suggest as evidence that "ethnomusicologists treat individuals more often as members of communities than as autonomous actors" (2012, 303).

5. This tripartite categorization is largely adopted from conversations with Ray Cashman, whom I wish to thank here.

References

Abrahams, Roger, ed. 1970. *Almeda Riddle: A Singer and Her Songs*. Baton Rouge: Louisiana State University Press.
Bauman, Richard. 2004. *A World of Others' Words: Cross-Cultural Perspectives on Intertextuality*. Oxford: Blackwell.
Bender, Mark. 2003. *Plum and Bamboo: China's Suzhou Chantefable Tradition*. Urbana: University of Illinois Press.
Bourdieu, Pierre. 1990. *The Logic of Practice*. Translated by Richard Nice. Stanford, CA: Stanford University Press.
———. 1993. *The Field of Cultural Production: Essays on Art and Literature*. Edited and with an introduction by Randal Johnson. New York: Columbia University Press.
Bronner, Simon. 1998. *Following Tradition: Folklore in the Discourse of American Culture*. Logan: Utah State University Press.
Cashman, Ray. 2011. "The Role of Tradition in the Individual: At Work in Donegal with Packy Jim McGrath." In *The Individual and Tradition: Folkloristic Perspectives*, edited by Ray Cashman, Tom Mould, and Pravina Shukla, 303–22. Bloomington: Indiana University Press.
Cashman, Ray, Tom Mould, and Pravina Shukla. 2011. "Introduction: The Individual and Tradition." In *The Individual and Tradition: Folkloristic Perspectives*, edited by Ray Cashman, Tom Mould, and Pravina Shukla, 1–26. Bloomington: Indiana University Press.
Chen, Fan Pen Li. 2007. *Chinese Shadow Theatre: History, Popular Religion, and Women Warriors*. Montreal: McGill-Queens University Press.
Ci, Jiwei. 2014. *Moral China in the Age of Reform*. New York: Cambridge University Press.
Comaroff, John L., and Jean Comaroff. 1992. *Ethnography and the Historical Imagination*. Boulder, CO: Westview.
Danielson, Virginia. 1997. *"The Voice of Egypt": Umm Kulthūm, Arabic Song, and Egyptian Society in the Twentieth Century*. Chicago: University of Chicago Press.
Davis, Sara. 2005. *Songs and Silence: Ethnic Revival on China's Southwest Borders*. New York: Columbia University Press.
Dégh, Linda. 1995. *Narratives in Society: A Performer-Centered Study of Narration*. Bloomington: Indiana University Press.
Fiedler, Leslie A. 1952. "Archetype and Signature: A Study of the Relationship between Biography and Poetry." *Sewanee Review* 60 (2): 253–73.

Gibbs, Levi S. 2018. *Song King: Connecting People, Places, and Past in Contemporary China*. Honolulu: University of Hawai'i Press.
Giddens, Anthony. 1979. *Central Problems in Social Theory: Action, Structure and Contradiction in Social Analysis*. Berkeley: University of California Press.
Glassie, Henry. 2003. "Tradition." In *Eight Words for the Study of Expressive Culture*, edited by Burt Feintuch, 176–97. Urbana: University of Illinois Press.
Goldstein, Joshua. 2007. *Drama Kings: Players and Publics in the Re-creation of Peking Opera, 1870–1937*. Berkeley: University of California Press.
Guy, Nancy. 2005. *Peking Opera and Politics in Taiwan*. Urbana: University of Illinois Press.
Handler, Richard, and Jocelyn Linnekin. 1984. "Tradition, Genuine or Spurious." *Journal of American Folklore* 97 (385): 273–90.
Harris, Rachel. 2008. *The Making of a Musical Canon in Chinese Central Asia: The Uyghur Twelve Muqam*. Aldershot, UK: Ashgate.
He, Qiliang. 2012. *Gilded Voices: Economics, Politics, and Storytelling in the Yangzi Delta Since 1949*. Leiden, Netherlands: Brill.
Hellier, Ruth, ed. 2013. *Women Singers in Global Contexts: Music, Biography, Identity*. Urbana: University of Illinois Press.
Howard, Keith. 2006a. *Creating Korean Music: Tradition, Innovation and the Discourse of Identity*. Perspectives on Korean Music, vol. 2. Aldershot, UK: Ashgate.
———. 2006b. *Preserving Korean Music: Intangible Cultural Properties as Icons of Identity*. Perspectives on Korean Music, vol. 1. Aldershot, UK: Ashgate.
Hughes, David W. 2008. *Traditional Folk Song in Modern Japan: Sources, Sentiment and Society*. Folkestone, UK: Global Oriental.
Hung, Chang-Tai. 1993. "Reeducating a Blind Storyteller: Han Qixiang and the Chinese Communist Storytelling Campaign." *Modern China* 19 (4): 395–426.
Hymes, Dell. 1975. "Folklore's Nature and the Sun's Myth." *Journal of American Folklore* 88 (350): 345–69.
Jiang, Jin. 2009. *Women Playing Men: Yue Opera and Social Change in Twentieth-Century Shanghai*. Seattle: University of Washington Press.
Jones, Stephen. 1995. *Folk Music of China: Living Instrumental Traditions*. Oxford: Clarendon.
———. 2004. *Plucking the Winds: Lives of Village Musicians in Old and New China*. Leiden, Netherlands: CHIME Foundation.
———. 2007. *Ritual and Music of North China: Shawm Bands in Shanxi*. Aldershot, UK: Ashgate.
———. 2009. *Ritual and Music of North China. Vol. 2, Shaanbei*. Farnham, UK: Ashgate.
Kipnis, Andrew B., ed. 2012. *Chinese Modernity and the Individual Psyche*. New York: Palgrave Macmillan.
Lau, Frederick. 2008. *Music in China: Experiencing Music, Expressing Culture*. New York: Oxford University Press.
Lévi-Strauss, Claude. 1966. *The Savage Mind*. Chicago: University of Chicago Press.
Lord, Albert B. 1960. *The Singer of Tales*. Cambridge, MA: Harvard University Press.
Ma, Haili. 2015. *Urban Politics and Cultural Capital: The Case of Chinese Opera*. Farnham, UK: Ashgate.
Mackerras, Colin. 1981. *The Performing Arts in Contemporary China*. London: Routledge Kegan Paul.
———, ed. 1983. *Chinese Theater: From Its Origins to the Present Day*. Honolulu: University of Hawai'i Press.

———. 1984. "Folksongs and Dances of China's Minority Nationalities: Policy, Tradition, and Professionalization." *Modern China* 10 (2): 187–226.
———. 1997. *Peking Opera*. Hong Kong: Oxford University Press.
———. 2008. "Music and Performing Arts: Tradition, Reform and Political and Social Relevance." In *The Cambridge Companion to Modern Chinese Culture*, edited by Kam Louie, 253–71. Cambridge: Cambridge University Press.
———. 2011. "Tourism and Musical Performing Arts in China in the First Decade of the Twenty-First Century: A Personal View." *CHINOPERL Papers* 30: 153–80.
Mair, Victor H., and Mark Bender, eds. 2011. *The Columbia Anthology of Chinese Folk and Popular Literature*. New York: Columbia University Press.
Newman, Katharine D. 1995. *Never Without a Song: The Years and Songs of Jennie Devlin, 1865–1952*. Urbana: University of Illinois Press.
Noyes, Dorothy. 2009. "Tradition: Three Traditions." *Journal of Folklore Research* 46 (3): 233–68.
Ortner, Sherry B. 2006. *Anthropology and Social Theory: Culture, Power, and the Acting Subject*. Durham, NC: Duke University Press.
Porter, James, and Herschel Gower. 1995. *Jeannie Robertson: Emergent Singer, Transformative Voice*. Knoxville: University of Tennessee Press.
Qiao Jianzhong. 1998. *Tudi yu ge: chuantong yinyue wenhua jiqi dili lishi beijing yanjiu* [Land and song: Research on traditional music culture and its geographical and historical background]. Ji'nan, China: Shandong wenyi chubanshe.
———. 2010. "Dashan de qingyun—Shi Zhanming he ta yanchang de Zuoquan min'ge" [The feeling of the mountains: Shi Zhanming and his Zuoquan folksongs]. *Renmin yinyue* (5): 42–43.
Rees, Helen. 2000. *Echoes of History: Naxi Music in Modern China*. New York: Oxford University Press.
———. 2001. "He Yi'an's Ninety Musical Years: Biography, History, and Experience in Southwest China." *World of Music* 43 (1): 43–67.
———, ed. 2009. *Lives in Chinese Music*. Urbana: University of Illinois Press.
———. 2012. "Intangible Cultural Heritage in China Today: Policy and Practice in the Early Twenty-First Century." In *Music as Intangible Cultural Heritage: Policy, Ideology, and Practice in Preservation of East Asian Traditions*, edited by Keith Howard, 23–54. Farnham, UK: Ashgate.
———. 2016. "Environmental Crisis, Culture Loss, and a New Musical Aesthetic: China's 'Original Ecology Folksongs' in Theory and Practice." *Ethnomusicology* 60 (1): 53–88.
Ruskin, Jesse D., and Timothy Rice. 2012. "The Individual in Musical Ethnography." *Ethnomusicology* 56 (2): 299–327.
Sawin, Patricia. 2004. *Listening for a Life: A Dialogic Ethnography of Bessie Eldreth through Her Songs and Stories*. Logan: Utah State University Press.
Schein, Louisa. 2010. "Flexible Celebrity: A Half-Century of Miao Pop." In *Celebrity in China*, edited by Louise Edwards and Elaine Jeffreys, 145–68. Hong Kong: Hong Kong University Press.
Schimmelpenninck, Antoinet. 1997. *Chinese Folk Songs and Folk Singers: Shan'ge Traditions in Southern Jiangsu*. CHIME Studies in East Asian Music, vol. 1. Leiden, Netherlands: CHIME Foundation.
Sewell, William H., Jr. 1992. "A Theory of Structure: Duality, Agency, and Transformation." *American Journal of Sociology* 98 (1): 1–29.

Shay, Anthony. 2002. *Choreographic Politics: State Folk Dance Companies, Representation and Power*. Middletown, CT: Wesleyan University Press.

Stock, Jonathan P. J. 1996. *Musical Creativity in Twentieth-Century China: Abing, His Music, and Its Changing Meanings*. Rochester, NY: University of Rochester Press.

———. 2001. "Toward an Ethnomusicology of the Individual, or Biographical Writing in Ethnomusicology." *World of Music* 43 (1): 5–19.

———. 2003. *Huju: Traditional Opera in Modern Shanghai*. Oxford: Oxford University Press.

Tansman, Alan M. 1996. "Mournful Tears and *Sake*: The Postwar Myth of Misora Hibari." In *Contemporary Japan and Popular Culture*, edited by John Whittier Treat, 103–33. Richmond, UK: Curzon.

Thompson, Stith. 1953. "Advances in Folklore Studies." In *Anthropology Today*, edited by A. L. Kroeber, 587–96. Chicago: University of Chicago Press.

Tian Qing. 2004. "Min'ge yu minzu changfa—zai Shanxi Zuoquan di er jie nanbei min'ge leitaisai xueshu yantaohui shang de fayan" [Folksongs and "national singing style"—A speech given at the scholarly conference of the Second National Chinese Folksong Competition held in Zuoquan, Shanxi]. *Yishu pinglun* (10): 8–13.

Toelken, Barre. 1996. *The Dynamics of Folklore*. Logan: Utah State University Press.

Tuohy, Sue. 1988. "Imagining the Chinese Tradition: The Case of Hua'er Songs, Festivals, and Scholarship." PhD diss., Indiana University, Bloomington.

———. 2003. "The Choices and Challenges of Local Distinction: Regional Attachments and Dialect in Chinese Music." In *Global Pop, Local Language*, edited by Harris M. Berger and Michael Thomas Carroll, 153–85. Jackson: University Press of Mississippi.

Wald, Elijah. 2004. *Escaping the Delta: Robert Johnson and the Invention of the Blues*. New York: HarperCollins.

Wilcox, Emily. 2019. *Revolutionary Bodies: Chinese Dance and the Socialist Legacy*. Berkeley: University of California Press.

Wu, Ka-ming. 2015. *Reinventing Chinese Tradition: The Cultural Politics of Late Socialism*. Urbana: University of Illinois Press.

Xiao Mei. 2004. "Guoyue san nü xing: chuancheng zhong de chuantong yu dangdai" [Three women in Chinese music: Traditional and contemporary in the midst of transmission]. In *Tianye pingzong* [Traveling in the field], edited by Xiao Mei, 356–90. Shanghai: Shanghai yinyue xueyuan chubanshe.

Yan, Yunxiang. 2009. *The Individualization of Chinese Society*. New York: Berg.

Yung, Bell. 2008. *The Last of China's Literati: The Music, Poetry and Life of Tsar Teh-yun*. Hong Kong: Hong Kong University Press.

Zhang Cuifeng. 1985. "The Autobiography of the Drum Singer Jang Tsueyfenq (as Told to Liou Fang)." Translated by Rulan Chao Pian. *Chinoperl Papers* 13 (1): 7–106.

Zhang Junren. 2004. *Hua'er wang Zhu Zhonglu—renleixue qingjing zhong de minjian geshou* [Zhu Zhonglu, king of Hua'er: The anthropology of a folksinger]. Lanzhou, China: Dunhuang wenyi chubanshe.

LEVI S. GIBBS is Assistant Professor of Chinese Literature and Culture in the Asian Societies, Cultures, and Languages Program at Dartmouth College. His research focuses on the social roles of singers and songs in contemporary China and the cultural politics of regional identity. He is author of *Song King: Connecting People, Places, and Past in Contemporary China*.

1 Grasping Intangible Heritage and Reimagining Inner Mongolia

Folk-Artist Albums and a New Logic for Musical Representation in China

Charlotte D'Evelyn

On July 16, 2010, I joined a group of scholars on the campus of Inner Mongolia University's Art College in Hohhot, China, to celebrate the release of solo album compilations for three Mongol folk musicians: Lu Badma (b. 1940), Modeg (b. 1930), and Idanjab (b. 1955). At the gathering, ethnic Mongol and Han officials and administrators gave speeches in praise of the accomplishments of these artists, describing the contributions each had made to the transmission of folk music in Inner Mongolia. The event ended with the ceremonial dedication and distribution of the first copies of the newly published CD albums, which were given the series label "Inner Mongolia Ethnic Music Classics—Great Masters Series" (hereafter the "Great Masters Series"). Rather than being created for commercial profit, these albums were intended to document the oral repertoire of a dying generation of folk musicians considered by scholars as the last transmitters of priceless oral heritage. Although these albums are available in many record stores in Inner Mongolia, the impetus for the project came primarily from new sources of government funding for cultural heritage documentation, which complements the interest of many urban Mongols in collecting and transmitting what they consider to be a fading musical past.

In the pages below, I offer a case study from my field research in Inner Mongolia to illustrate the changing politics of musical recognition for minorities in China today. I show how the CD album project mentioned above has served as one rallying point for urban Mongol scholars and performers to transform their cultural heritage from the intangible to the tangible, from the impermanent to the permanent. I highlight the long-song singer Lu Badma (henceforth, Badma) and her CD album compilation as an apt example of how minority actors creatively navigate and empower themselves within government heritage projects, even when those projects might otherwise seem top-down, monolithic, and disempowering to minority interests. While recognizing the enthusiastic role the Chinese government has played in sending Intangible Cultural Heritage (hereafter ICH) applications to UNESCO, I direct my attention in this chapter to the minority elites and folk artists who have benefitted from ICH recognition policies and the circumstances under which they have received that recognition.

I investigate the changes that have taken place in China in the past decade leading to an increased concern for sound preservation and emphasis on centering and celebrating those individuals who were once considered peripheral, idiosyncratic, and backward. I argue that the "Great Masters Series"—packaged with high-quality, glossy album boxes with liner notes and reproduced archival photographs—documents the relatively "untouched" sounds of the peripheries in a form that can be held, visualized, studied, and aurally consumed by scholars and local communities alike. Through each album endeavor, spearheaded by scholars and supported by the university and local governments, Mongol communities have rallied around the face of an artist, displayed on an attractively packaged album, as the communities have striven to recover the intangible sounds and practices of their cultural pasts.

Folk Artists in China

In *The Field of Cultural Production: Essays on Art and Literature*, Pierre Bourdieu argues that works of art gain meaning and value when such works achieve recognition within a particular cultural domain (1993, 8, 11). For Bourdieu, art begins as a neutral physical object, but acquires status when individuals—teachers, critics, publishers, and other agents—contribute to the production of knowledge about that art, thereby authorizing its importance. In the People's Republic of China (PRC), the process of defining cultural fields of value and producing knowledge about those fields has changed in tandem with the vicissitudes of the country's twentieth-century history. At different points in time, individuals have gained institutional or political power when they have found ways to integrate themselves into the artistic paradigm of the time.

From the 1940s until the 1960s, folksong policies in mainland China followed Mao Zedong's call for art to serve the masses (see McDougall 1980), a policy that ushered forth unprecedented efforts in China to collect repertoires of rural, orally transmitted folksongs (*min'ge*). Local village talents—musicians, folk singers, singer-storytellers, and dancers—gained recognition in this era through regional competitions and were recruited to participate in Soviet-style cultural work troupes (*wengongtuan*) or song and dance troupes (*gewutuan*). Despite the collectivist intentions of the communist project, the PRC was quick to recognize individual talent and make models out of communist exemplars who were willing to cooperate with the state project in exchange for recognition and, for many, life employment as government arts employees. As cultural workers, these amateur-turned-professional performers were called upon to spread official communist propaganda through a new genre of revolutionary song (*geming gequ*) that superimposed new lyrics upon recognizable local folk tunes collected from the countryside. Thus, the field of cultural production in the Mao era was dominated by themes of Marxist socialist realism and new willingness to recognize the value of rural folk music genres for their ability to spread party messages.[1]

In the post-Mao, economic reform era of the 1980s–90s, folksong collection and transcription efforts were renewed and published in the form of massive folksong collections, such as the *Zhongguo minjian gequ jicheng* (Anthology of Chinese folksong) (see Jones 2003; Yang Mu 1994). In the performance sphere, an increased focus on musical modernization (*xiandaihua*), professionalization (*zhuanyehua*), and stage orientation (*wutaihua*) resulted in government and popular support for "conservatory style" (*xueyuanpai*) compositions and standardized "national singing style" (*minzu changfa*).[2] Professional, conservatory-trained musicians considered rural "folk artists" (*minjian yiren*) to be "musically illiterate and technically inadequate" and criticized them for playing out of tune and being unable to read musical notation (Lau 1998, 49). Hence, until the early 2000s—outside of a handful of music scholars with interests in heritage protection—orally transmitted music of rural folk communities was useful only insofar as it could be cleaned up, systematized, and performed on the concert stage to spread messages of communism or social-artistic progress.

Representative Songs and Singers in Inner Mongolia

In Inner Mongolia, far from being excluded from this process, ethnic elites and artists have become involved as active participants in the construction and definition of fields of artistic value for local performing arts. Over the past seven decades, varied political and social agendas regarding the role of music in society have been passed down from the central government to the governing body of the Inner Mongolia Autonomous Region (IMAR), which has then passed on the torch of implementation to Mongol scholars, artists, and cultural leaders. These educated Mongol elites have played an important role in authorizing not simply works of art and music but also individual artists themselves, in the classification and production of knowledge about what it means to be Mongol in China.

During the Mao era, young, talented singers from the region were scouted to join regional song and dance troupes, including a local troupe category known in Mongolian as *Ulanmuchir* (Chin. *wulanmuqi*, Eng. "red branch") specifically charged with bringing socialism to scattered herders on the Inner Mongolian grasslands. Two examples of Mongol singers who emerged in this period include Lasurong and Dedema, Mongol superstars from the Mao era who remain household names today. It is tempting to represent minorities in China as victims of the political will of communist authorities; however, the reality is much more complicated. Despite ongoing political injustices and artistic misrepresentations, many minority individuals in China have been able to creatively adapt to political shifts and actively participate—on their own terms—in projects of ethnic identification, modernization, and history making (see Schein 2000; Baranovitch 2003; Litzinger 2000).

Lasurong (b. 1947), a Mongol from the Ordos region of Inner Mongolia, earned fame for his performance of the still widely popular "Zange" (Song of praise), featured in the film suite of *The East Is Red* (1964). He began his career in a local song and dance troupe and later moved to Hohhot for formal training and earned a music degree at the China Conservatory of Music in Beijing. Rather than focusing his studies on music of his home region, he studied with prominent singers and artists from the Shilingol and Horchin regions of Inner Mongolia who happened to be teaching in Hohhot and Beijing at that time. In his renowned performance of "Zange," Lasurong opens with an extended vocal melisma that shows off his virtuosic, Shilingol-flavored long-song technique that he learned and professionalized during his years as a conservatory student. Lasurong's adoption and professionalization of a singing style from a region outside his own may not seem overly significant, but they tell a story of Mao-era ethnic identification and homogenization that was satisfied with lumping all Mongols into a single consciousness. This strategy made it possible to mobilize Mongols as an (artificially) cohesive group toward Mao-era goals of national unification. Such political aims come out in the Mandarin lyrics of "Zange," which call for the people of the grasslands to "celebrate [their] liberation" under communism and for "brothers of every ethnic group" to "happily reunite" and "praise China's rise and prosperity." This song cemented Lasurong's role within the field of cultural value that required art to reflect and promote socialism and patriotism and enabled him to continue his musical career through some of the most challenging years of Inner Mongolia's history.

The female singer Dedema (b. 1947) achieved national fame in the 1980s for her solo performances of Mandarin-language pop songs that romanticize the Mongolian grasslands, such as "The Beautiful Grasslands Are My Home." Like Lasurong, Dedema took on professional musical training that distanced her from her birthplace and enlisted her in singing songs that would present standard, homogenized stereotypes of the Mongol people. She was raised in the far-western Alasha region of Inner Mongolia, a region that was largely unknown and unrecognized for its folksongs in the 1980s. Only later would Alasha achieve greater recognition under the strong-willed heritage efforts of Badma (see below), but during Dedema's time, the natural progression of her career as a singer led her to adopt the standardized *minzu changfa* (national singing style) that she had learned during professional training in Hohhot and later in Beijing at the China Conservatory of Music. In 1982, she was selected to join the Central Nationalities Song and Dance Troupe (*Zhongyang minzu gewutuan*), the top performing ensemble for minorities in China. Her complicit participation in the Chinese national system for musical training and state-sponsored musical performance enabled her to achieve tremendous power, status, and financial rewards. Her famous song "The Beautiful Grasslands Are My Home," discussed at length by Nimrod Baranovitch (2003, 2009, 2015), was created by the Mongol composer Altangaole (1942–2011) in 1977 and not only paved the way for an explosion of Mongol-flavored, Mandarin-language "grassland songs" (*caoyuan gequ*) in China but continues to be a popular choice for karaoke singing inside and outside of Inner Mongolia.

I offer Lasurong and Dedema as representative examples of Mongol singers who gained recognition during this period of PRC history because of their willingness to adapt their musical careers to the parameters of existing paradigms for ethnic representation. Like others who ascended as minority representatives during the 1950s–90s, Lasurong and Dedema both trained in the Chinese conservatory system, entered high-level professional performing ensembles, sang composed or newly arranged songs in Mandarin Chinese, and, most notably, gained recognition as representatives of the entire Mongol nationality. In terms of stylistic and lyrical content, the repertoire of songs they disseminated throughout their careers had very little in common with the local folksongs of their home regions of Ordos and Alasha. Instead, the music they sang was dominated by a standardized set of melodic figures and vocal ornaments and a professionalized method of vocal production that became recognizable throughout China as "Mongol stylistic flavors" (*Menggu weidao, Menggu fengge*). These flavors were used repeatedly in hundreds of thousands of grassland songs, as well as in instrumental compositions, such as the famous composition "Horse Race" for the *erhu* (Chinese two-string fiddle).

In television and stage performances in China, Chinese stereotypes continue to depict Mongols as a homogenous, colorful and simplistic grassland people while also often emphasizing musical professionalism, standardization, and ethnic unity. In this way, grassland songs continue to be a crucial avenue for Mongols in China to earn a living in late-night restaurant gigs or to ascend festival and national television stages. The cultural logics employed by songs such as "Beautiful Grasslands" fit well into the field of minority representations during the post-Mao eras. Songs depict Mongols as nonthreatening, domesticated herders living in a perpetual state of happy simplicity—in contrast to any lingering historical memories of Chinggis Khan and the Mongol hordes.[3] While such simplified, monolithic conceptions of Mongols in China still exist, they have been augmented and complicated by a new wave of national heritage concerns that have brought increasing attention to subethnic diversity and regional folksong variety in Inner Mongolia.

Intangible Cultural Heritage Preservation

Around the year 2001, coinciding with China's entry into the World Trade Organization and the first UNESCO convention for the safeguarding of Intangible Cultural Heritage (ICH), the Chinese government began recognizing and supporting music practiced by regional folk artists (*minjian yiren*). After decades spent revolutionizing old Chinese society and "developing" rural folksongs, the Chinese government shifted focus and recognized the opportunities for tourist revenue from cultural heritage, in addition to the international cultural cachet that comes with UNESCO designations of ICH. The years since 2001 have seen a reinvention and reconstruction of the orthodox government-supported field of cultural knowledge in China, including modes of understanding the value of its musical past. Professional musicians in China—including conservatory-trained and pop musicians—still achieve cultural authority and mainstream recognition. However, the addition of aging, rural, folk musicians to this field of respectability represents a great shift, indeed.

In her critical work on cultural heritage policies in China, Helen Rees writes, "Of late, local village folksongs and singers have found themselves in a most unexpected limelight. Marginalized for decades as "backward" (*luohou*), "coarse" (*cucao*), and "unscientific" (*bu kexue*) by China's obsession with technological and cultural modernization, today such folksongs form a cornerstone of the nation's recent embrace of UNESCO-style intangible cultural heritage protection" (2016, 3). Individuals who may have been marginalized in the past for imprecise technique and intonation and for their inability to read musical notation are now valorized as examples of cultural heritage unspoiled by outside influences. Previously considered unfit for the stage, they are now featured in concert galas, television documentaries, and university symposia, and recognized with official titles as "cultural transmitters" (*chuanchengren*) and "folksong kings/queens" (*min'ge wang*). Like the "national treasures" designations that have existed in Japan since 1950 and South Korea since 1962 (Rees 2012, 31), national recognition as a "cultural transmitter" in China accords folk artists with a small amount of government support each year and official certificates of recognition that are important as conversation pieces to display to friends and house guests (see Gibbs, this volume).

A crucial concept that has developed hand in hand with notions of cultural inheritance (*wenhua yichan*) in China over the past fifteen years is the term *yuanshengtai* (typically translated "original ecology," henceforth YST), which has come to refer to any product from a "pure" and "untouched" environment. Products that parade with the YST label include not only performing arts traditions but also consumables like milk, rice, or bottled water. The term is nearly unavoidable in China today and has been discussed at length by scholars as it relates to cultural tourism, changing representations of Chinese minorities, and concerns among scholars about the survival of cultural heritage outside of fading original cultural contexts (Yang Man 2009; Du 2015; Rees 2016).

In her thoughtful discussion of YST folksongs in China, Rees quotes a 2006 article by Chinese scholar Jia Shuying entitled "'Original Ecology' Hits the Youth Song Competition" (*'Yuanshengtai' chongji qing ge sai*)[4] which succinctly summarizes the changing attitudes in China toward conservatory training: "We [Chinese] have [now] entered a post-industrial age; people are starting to call for individuality, and society is beginning to need pluralism.... The conservatory style (*xueyuanpai*), which emphasizes technique and science, loses individuality and artistic essence" (Rees 2016, 57).

Rees also cites senior Chinese musicologist Qiao Jianzhong's definition of "original ecology folksongs" (*yuanshengtai min'ge*) that distinguishes the songs from "created works" (*chuangzuo zuopin*) sung in Mandarin and performed on the concert stage (Rees 2012, 2016). Newly created songs, popular in the 1980s and 1990s as discussed above, are sung by professionals trained in the "national singing style" (*minzu changfa*) and "conservatory style" (*xueyuanpai*), whereas YST folksongs are characterized by their "untouched" qualities and are typically sung in the contexts of rural daily life.

Suddenly, culture bureaus and professional musicians have started celebrating, rather than criticizing, the idiosyncrasies of local folk music, including the subtleties of free, uninhibited ornamentation and timbral variation, as well as internalization of vast oral repertoires. Such qualities have been recognized by scholars for decades but are only now finding respect and value in the nationally circulating field of cultural knowledge. Professional, conservatory-trained musicians are realizing they lack many of the skills of folk musicians, including their superior abilities to improvise and to learn music orally or memorize without the aid of written notation. From this vantage point, YST appears to be giving much-needed positions of legitimacy to formerly delegitimized folk artists.

Rees complicates this picture, however, noting that the term *YST* is now used so widely and as such a "hot-button" marketing term for music in China that it has become an empty signifier, often used to package traditional music into easy and palatable portions for mainstream consumption (2016, 75). For instance, *hoomii* ensembles in Inner Mongolia—based mostly on Tuvan models such as Huun Huur Tu that employ throat singing, Mongol instruments, and arranged folksongs—label themselves "original ecology folk bands" (*yuanshengtai zuhe*) and have achieved wide success in China and abroad. In private conversation, these "original ecology bands" admit that their repertoire counts as YST only in that they use traditional instruments and sing in indigenous languages (which include the Tuvan language) but that the style itself is quite modern and cosmopolitan.

Yet, aside from the futile complications of deciphering "real YST" from "fake YST" in China today, the widespread interest and investment in the "original ecology" brand in China today demonstrate the weight behind the term and willingness on the part of mainstream Chinese audiences to reconsider previous decades of attention to teleological notions of "cultural development" and "social progress" (*wenhua fazhan, shehui jinbu*). On my current fieldwork visits to China and Inner Mongolia, I find that I no longer have to argue with musicians about the merits of folk music in these regions compared to the so-called "genius" of European art music, arguments that I experienced during my first visits in the early 2000s. By 2009, I experienced nearly the opposite paradigm and witnessed rising enthusiasm for traditional musical heritage, particularly for traditions that could shed light on the musical past.

Du Chunmei notes there is an "explicit or almost automatic link between YST and authenticity" that, applied to Chinese minority cultures, confines minority people within a familiar straightjacket of trivialized and exoticized premodernity (2015, 553–56). YST singers such as Badma in Inner Mongolia are, indeed, celebrated for their connections to rural life and an assumed lack of exposure to the influences of modernization and globalization. Rather than seeing the YST project as necessarily limiting or disempowering, I have observed how this project has provided a framework for musicians, at least those fortunate enough to receive attention and resources, to participate in and locally implement the project on their own terms.

For the discussion below of Badma's long-song album *On the Vast and Fertile Plains of Alasha*, I take up Helen Rees's rhetorical urge to discover what is happening "on the ground" in China amidst "the avalanche of policies, procedures, regulations, projects, and concepts that have poured forth" from the Chinese government at the national and local levels since its engagement with ICH and UNESCO in the early 2000s (Rees 2012, 35). Rees queries whether these projects have led to the survival and transmission of traditional performing arts, as they claim to attempt, and whether grassroots efforts have filled in the gaps where government efforts and funding have left off. The "Great Masters" CD album series is one of many projects that eases local anxieties about disappearing folk heritage, and Badma's story illustrates how cultural heritage preservation efforts have been taken up with remarkable gusto and community support in Inner Mongolia. I examine the process of individual selection, recognition, documentation, and transmission that brought Badma from her hometown on the geographic and symbolic margins of Inner Mongolia to the center of institutional ICH funding efforts and academic enthusiasm.

Ethnic Nuance in Inner Mongolia

Contrary to most representations of ethnic Mongols on Chinese national television, Mongols are far from homogenous or united as an ethnic group. Linguistically and culturally diverse, Mongols live in and around an expansive region that spans more than 450,000 square miles north of the Great Wall bordering the Gobi Desert, southeast of the independent nation of Mongolia. Subethnic clan identification, using labels such as "Ordos Mongols" or "Ejinai Mongols," is a meaningful feature of Mongols' sense of self, even when they have been transplanted to a city center such as Hohhot.[5] Historian Christopher Atwood explains that subethnic identification in Inner Mongolia is often the first question that Mongols living in the city in China ask each other when they meet (2004, 245), a phenomenon that I experience frequently when I am doing fieldwork in Inner Mongolia.

Mongols' subethnic identities have generally been downplayed in Chinese national media in favor of representations that picture them as one of China's fifty-five colorful national minorities (*shaoshu minzu*). Musical representations of Mongols from the 1950s to the 2000s, such as those of Lasurong and Dedema described above, presented state-sanctioned images of China's Mongols as willing, cheerful citizens of the Chinese state. Dedema's subethnic identity as an Ejinai Mongol from Alasha is rarely mentioned when she is introduced on stage as a performer, and Lasurong has only recently begun to assert a stronger affiliation with the Ordos Mongols (and corresponding region) of Inner Mongolia.[6]

Today's *chuanchengren* (cultural transmitters), by contrast, retain intimate and vital identification with their home regions, villages, or subethnic groups when they appear on stage and on national television. For such *chuanchengren*, status and recognition depend on one's ability to transmit a regional lineage that has remained relatively unaffected by outside influences. Young artists from rural regions who move to the city to perform are often discouraged from receiving formal training for fear that such training will wash away the regional flavors of their hometown style and that this could disqualify them from *chuanchengren* status later in their careers.

Situating Alasha

This national climate—one that recognizes artists for their ability to transmit distinctive regional styles—represents a fascinating victory for regions on the periphery in China such as Alasha. Those regions considered the most isolated from modernization, globalization, and artistic professionalism gain more weight and significance in the media and the academy for having preserved and maintained "original ecology" (YST) environments and folk cultures. Underdeveloped and economically "backward" regions such as Alasha thus gain recognition and cultural capital precisely *because* of their lack of economic development. Regional governments in these locales have also become particularly savvy in their efforts to dedicate funds to support the documentation and protection of their regional cultures, hoping for such efforts to bolster tourism or provide greater regional and national visibility. The celebration and documentation of Badma as a folk artist from Alasha has the effect of "centering" Alasha within the field of local heritage recognition in Inner Mongolia.

Largely covered in sand dunes, Alasha is one of the most remote and least populated regions of Inner Mongolia. Inner Mongolia is widely discussed as a region on China's periphery (Bulag 2002b, 214; Bilik 2007; Bulag 2012), a conception that positions Alasha as a periphery on the periphery. Christopher Atwood describes how the Mongol princes of Alasha prior to the PRC period were relatively isolated from active political movements in eastern Inner Mongolia (2002; see also Bulag 2002b) and were relatively entrenched in an old-style feudalistic society centered on lama Buddhism. Welcoming Tibetan migration, the region has connections to the western branch of Mongols known as the Oirat. The region itself was the last league to join the Inner Mongolia Autonomous Region, formerly incorporated into the province of Ningxia.

Musically, Alasha exhibits features of a culture on the periphery of other recognized cultural centers. Scholars point out Alasha's musical connections and blending with the music cultures of Tibet, Oirat Mongols of Xinjiang, and Halh Mongols of Mongolia (the majority ethnic group there). Musical genres transmitted widely in Alasha include long song (Mong. *urtiin duu*, Chin. *changdiao*) and short song (Mong. *bogino duu*, Chin. *duandiao*). Folksinger and fiddler Badma has played a critical role in the promotion of Alasha as an important stylistic region for Mongol music over the past decade. Her work has drawn attention to the local flavor and uniqueness of Alasha long song, stylistic distinctions that highlight the panorama of musical diversity in Inner Mongolia. Alasha's position as an important long-song region is strengthened by its location in Inner Mongolia's "pastoral zone," a belt of steppe plateau grasslands that can support full herding (*quanmu*) economies. Indeed, long song is the musical form that Mongols believe best reflects and expresses the expansiveness of the grassland. A musicologist from Mongolia describes long song as "one of the most valuable and excellent riches of our people's arts" (Batzengel 1978, 51–52), a statement that echoes sentiments about this musical practice in Inner Mongolia. One of the first recognized "folksong kings" of Inner Mongolian long song is Lhajau (1922–2008), from Abag Banner in Shilingol (see Chao 2010), while one of the earliest celebrated "folksong queens" of long song is Bain Delger (b. 1945) from the Barga clan of Hulunbuir. These two widely celebrated and regionally distinct styles of long song ("central" and "eastern" styles, respectively) have only recently been joined by Alasha long song as a third "western" style.

In grassland settings, long songs are sung in the contexts of daily life for the sake of passing time, communicating across distances, evoking the contours and vastness of the natural landscape, or to calm animals while nursing or milking (see Yoon 2011, 2015). Important long songs are reserved for family feast occasions held in the yurt, known as *nair* (Mong.), and are often performed with horsehead fiddle or flute accompaniment. Musically, long songs evoke the open expansiveness of the grasslands through wide pitch range and extended rubato meter. Textually, songs paint poetic images of mountains, rivers, and other aspects of natural environment, describe beautiful and swift horses, or express love for one's homeland. Songs are considered "long" due to the length to which the notes are held rather than the length of time it takes to perform the songs.

A grassland sensibility, including the psychological and musical understanding of expansive, vast space, is considered an integral ingredient in proper performance of these songs. When they study long song, Mongol youth who were raised in the city are often criticized for their inability to appropriately express the aesthetic of the grassland due to fact that they grew up in crowded and fast-paced urban lifestyles. In this way, grassland pastoralism does not merely fuel a sense of symbolic cultural identity (see Williams 1996; Sanchez 2013; Baranovitch 2015); it is also understood as a necessary ecological resource for the smooth transmission and preservation of musical style.

However, lived experiences of grassland ecology are becoming increasingly rare as fewer and fewer Mongols live in fully herding regions (such as Shilingol and Hulunbuir mentioned above) and, even when they do, are forced to subsist within fenced-in plots of land and caps on livestock numbers (see Sneath 2003; Jiang 2004). Most of China's Mongols today have moved to urban city centers and many have been forcibly relocated due to grassland degradation and mining projects. While Mongols generally constitute the ethnic majority in pastoral regions, they constitute a very small minority of the population in Inner Mongolia's urban centers, where they are dwarfed by generations of Han Chinese immigrants. For instance, in the city of Hohhot, the capital of Inner Mongolia and my fieldwork base, ethnic Mongols make up less than 9 percent of the population, while Han Chinese make up nearly 88 percent.

The effects of city life and Han cultural influences (*Hanhua*) are felt intimately by Mongol musicians in cities such as Hohhot and Beijing, and many express a nostalgic longing for grassland ways of life that they either left behind, or in the case of urban-born Mongols, have never experienced at all. Dozens of heritage-minded Mongols in China, including music scholars, teachers, and performers, articulate several concerns for the continued survival of musical genres such as long song. They fear that city life is too fast paced and crowded and that the sonic quality of the grassland will be lost. They also fear that Mongol music has lost its cultural purity due to exposure to and influence from Han and Western influences. Additionally, they fear that their music has experienced too much "stagification" (*wutaihua*) in the city and has become detached from organic musical contexts in the grasslands. Such concerns coincide with current dominant discourses in China that value oral, folk heritage, yet these concerns also emerge organically from Mongols' observations of cultural losses after the Cultural Revolution stemming from fast-paced modernization, poor ability to sustain the Mongolian language, and urban relocation. Mongol musicologists in China who have been interested in musical documentation and transmission for many decades share these apprehensions. To address these perceived losses, scholars in Inner Mongolia, as in other regions of China, have applied the new stream of government funding toward ICH projects such as university symposia, concerts, heritage centers, and folk artist residencies.

At the forefront of heritage projects in Inner Mongolia is the leading Mongol musicologist Yang Yucheng (Mongolian name: Botolt, hereafter referred to as Professor Yang), faculty member at the Inner Mongolia University Art College in Hohhot. He established the Inner Mongolia Musical Heritage Inheritance Station (*Neimenggu yinyue chuancheng zhan*) in 2009 on the campus of his university. Among the wide variety of ongoing projects encompassed by the Inheritance Station, Professor Yang has spearheaded the creation and distribution of high-quality album compilations that feature old archival recordings combined with new, high-quality studio recordings made on-site at a newly built studio on the Art College campus. As a rural-turned-urban scholar, Professor Yang is well integrated into folk music communities and has intimate knowledge of those communities and isolated musical talents across Inner Mongolia. He invites his artist contacts from the countryside to serve long-term residencies at his university, during which time they serve as master teachers to transmit their knowledge to college and middle school students and undertake frequent visits to the recording studio to slowly and comprehensively document their musical repertoires and oral histories, the latter of which are channeled into the detailed album liner notes.

The collection of audio recordings has been a mainstay of scholarly activity in the PRC, even during the Mao years (1949–1976). Audio recordings from the 1950s until the 1990s, however, focused on either recomposition for the stage or publication in the form of notated transcriptions in volumes such as the 1964 "Survey of Chinese Music" and the massive, multivolume "Anthology of Chinese Music" project (see Yang Mu 1994; Jones 2003). By contrast, the "Great Masters Series" album project represents a very different priority and use of audio recordings. Rather than simply housing the recordings in the archives, the tracks are collected into solo albums to highlight the work and heritage embodied by each individual artist. The albums do not presume to group music by musical genre, but rather the albums are organized by the lineages inherited by the artist themselves. Each artist is framed as representative of the musical landscape of that artist's home region but also appreciated as an individual. Unlike previous recording projects that tended to spotlight a single musical genre and emphasize stylistic unity rather than individuality, Professor Yang's albums spotlight individual folk artists and cultural transmitters, celebrating individual accomplishments and personal styles. In today's climate, folk artists are seen as fulfilling an important role as repositories of a past that is destined to disappear if their knowledge is not made accessible to future generations.

Recognizing Badma

On the Fertile and Vast Alasha Grasslands: Mongolian Long Song Master Badma is one of five albums so far in the "Great Masters Series" that highlights long-song singers. The album not only positions Badma squarely in a canon of recognized long-song "kings and queens" in Inner Mongolia, but it also serves a mechanical purpose in the preservation and reproduction of tradition into a tangible form. Inside the smooth and high-quality CD case is a booklet of liner notes in Mongolian, Chinese, and English, featuring a forward by the venerated Mongol scholar Ulanji, a detailed biography of the artist, song lyrics and their translations, historical photographs of the artist and of the Alasha grassland environment, and an afterword by one of her new student-disciples. As with all of the albums in the Inner Mongolia Ethnic Classics series, Badma's album is an archival-quality product, parallel to albums produced by Smithsonian Folkways in terms of the well-researched liner notes and its function as a scholarly documentation effort.

Badma's album consists of tracks taken both from old archival recordings and from recordings made while she was in residence at the Art College of Inner Mongolia University in 2009. The quality and style of musical accompaniment of the tracks vary somewhat widely, but the broad and strong, chesty vocal timbre of Badma's singing remains consistent even between her early career recordings and more recent ones. The clearest difference between Badma's early recordings and the recent recordings made under the direction of Professor Yang is the choice of instrumental accompaniment for the long-song selections. Comparing the long-song tracks of this album, the early recordings feature large ensemble accompaniment, while the more recent recordings feature accompaniment by a single horse-head fiddle (*morin huur*). As composers and scholars in Inner Mongolia have shifted toward a greater interest in how music sounded in its "original" environment, the trend has been to return to the sophisticated simplicity of the solo *morin huur* as an accompanying instrument. Unencumbered by the need to precisely follow a score and to coordinate with an entire ensemble of musicians, the *morin huur* player is free to follow the singer in a more natural way and to offer personal embellishments to ornament the melodic line.

Badma herself was born in Alasha Banner in 1940 and grew up in a herdsman family. Her father, an ethnic Tibetan, was well educated and recognized in Alasha as a living Buddha. Her maternal side of the family identifies as Hoshud Mongols and consists of a long line of famous folksingers. Badma's earliest musical exposure came from her mother and aunt, whose singing she imitated at a very young age. Soon after, she began learning the horse-head fiddle from her maternal grandmother, who taught Badma using her own left-hand bowing technique—an atypical hand for bowing the instrument, even when players happen to be left-hand dominant as are Badma and her grandmother. Badma became a well-known performer during her twenties and performed at occasional herder gatherings in the local villages near her home. She began her career in an amateur cultural workers troupe (*wengongtuan*) and joined a local Ulanmuchir traveling ensemble in the early 1960s. Her performance career was halted suddenly in the mid-1960s during the Cultural Revolution, when she decided to return home to take care of her family.

This interruption in her performance career prevented Badma from receiving professional musical training, an unexpected but perhaps fortunate twist of fate that has facilitated her recognition as a cultural transmitter today. Having never been integrated into the professional singing world during what would have been the peak years of her vocal career, Badma is considered to have better preserved the "original ecology" (YST) musical flavors of Alasha. Today she is recognized for preserving the "original flavor" (*yuanweir*) of Alasha folksongs in ways that others such as Dedema, the nationally famous Mongol singer from Alasha described above, cannot.

While Badma's albums, concerts, and teaching endeavors are always associated and entitled with the identifying marker of Alasha, Dedema, having gained her fame in a much earlier era, is identified simply as a singer of the Mongol ethnic group generally. This broader identification coincides with her standardized vocal style, influenced by both China's national singing style (*minzu changfa*) and popular ballad style (*tongsu yinyue*), as well as the lack of geographic specificity in the lyrics of the grassland songs she sings. Another important singer from Alasha is Altantsetseg (b. 1955), a singer who gained great prominence both as a professional singer and for her stylistic connection to the Alasha region. She has received awards in numerous song competitions, including first prize in the National Young Singer's Competition (*Quanguo qingnian geshou shengyue bisai*) in 1979 and first prize in the National Minorities Song Competition (*Quanguo shaoshu minzu shengyue dasai*) in 1982. Today, Altantsetseg is a professor of long song and master's thesis advisor to a new generation of young professional singers. Nevertheless, it was not Altantsetseg, but Badma who was conferred with the title of "cultural transmitter" on the first list of IMAR-level representatives in 2008 (*Diyipi zizhiquji feiwuzhi wenhua yichan xiangmu daibiaoxing chuanchengren*). Although there are rampant disagreements and contestations over ICH lists such as this one, due to the fact that they are subject to the whims of political connections and personality conflicts, it is worth exploring Badma's inclusion, as well as Altantsetseg's exclusion, from the list as a method of illuminating the field of cultural knowledge that operates in China and Inner Mongolia today.[7]

I argue that Badma's recognized cultural-transmitter status as the "best representative of Alasha long song style" in Inner Mongolia (Ulanji 2010) stems from four main qualities: First, her birth year of 1940 links her to the pre-PRC era (pre-1949), a period before music in Inner Mongolia experienced radical changes and strong outside influences. Having inherited her musical practices from her own family members, she is considered an important resource for accessing Mongols' musical past. In addition to being recognized as a transmitter of her family's musical lineage, she also received the title of a "first-generation queen of long song" in 2007, a title that positions her as one of the oldest documented and traceable singers in Inner Mongolia. In his liner notes to Badma's album, the respected senior Mongol musicologist Ulanji describes Badma as a "living repository of treasured folksongs" (2010) and joins many other scholars and leaders in Inner Mongolia in emphasizing her importance as an archive of Alasha heritage and a conduit for Mongols to access the musical past of this region.

Second, Badma's lack of professional training is understood—within the field of cultural production of the early 2000s—as a style free from outside conservatory influences such as bel canto vocal production. While Altantsetseg's professionalism has earned her recognition abroad and in song competitions and has given her respect as a full-time university professor, this professionalism detracts from her YST credibility. Badma's upbringing in the isolated desert region of Alasha is frequently mentioned, as in the following excerpt from the liner notes of another of her solo albums, *Three Saintly Graces of Alasha*: "She is from a place on the distant Gobi steppes and has traveled through the holy land of folksong on the back of a camel. She went from an ordinary herder to become an elevated folk singer known around the world (*chengwei mingyang sifang de minjian gechangjia*)" (Baoyin 2009; transl. from Mandarin by the author). This excerpt not only depicts Badma's solitude in a vast, empty region—clearly one that fails to acknowledge the presence of villages and cities in Badma's homeland—but it also mentions her transition from "ordinary herder" to "elevated folk singer," a statement that emphasizes how today's climate has enabled her to ascend the stage without any schooling or training, due to her YST background.

Third, Badma has distinguished herself as a heritage ambassador in the Alasha musical community, as is evident in her leadership efforts and dissemination of Alasha music through published books and recordings. In 2003 she established the Alasha Folksong Society (*Alashan min'ge xiehui*) and in 2007 worked with the association to publish a major collection of Alasha long-song transcriptions in a volume entitled *A Collection of Alasha Mongolian Folksongs*. Included among them were more than one thousand transcriptions of folksongs from Hoshud, Torghud, and Halh musical styles, representing each of the subethnic Mongol clans of Alasha. This publication was crucial in bringing attention to Alasha as an important "stylistic color region" (*fengge secaiqu*) of Inner Mongolia, particularly within a climate that favored musical diversity and local flavors over musical standardization.[8] Unlike Altantsetseg, who has resided outside of her home region for decades, Badma still maintains her primary residence and social network in Alasha. Her recognized status as a "pioneer in the protection and transmission of long song" (Ulanji 2010; transl. from Mandarin by the author) has much to do with her ability to maintain local connections and sensitivities while still maintaining an interest in connecting with Mongols living outside her region.

Fourth, Badma exhibits a refreshing quality of in-betweenness and musical idiosyncrasy that is a hallmark of folk culture at the borderlands. Not only is it difficult to put Badma into a single category (she is both a singer and a fiddler; she is both Tibetan and Hoshud Mongol; she sings in Hoshud, Torghud, and Halh styles), but it is also Badma's nonconformity with the recognized musical center (i.e., the musical academy in Hohhot) that imparts a degree of YST flavor to her style. Her lack of conformity to musical standards, particularly in aspects of vocal production and horse-head fiddle technique, demonstrates how she has retained aspects of her YST regional and family lineage without being affected by modernization or professionalization.

As mentioned above, musical reformers in China in the Mao and post-Mao eras endeavored to create stage-worthy performance methods for vocal and instrumental music traditions. Reformers saw a need to systematize the diversity of scattered folk styles, techniques, and methods—often seen as backward and "unscientific"—into a unified package that could be taught uniformly in the conservatory setting, performed with precision, and designed to entertain audiences on the concert stage. In Inner Mongolia, musical reformers for traditions such as long song and the horse-head fiddle focused on the elimination of regional disparities and technical variations, which were widespread before the Mao era. Musical features of regional long songs were eventually documented, analyzed, and crystallized into canonical color regions beginning in the 1990s (Ulanji 1998). For singers training in the academy, teachers incorporated aspects of breathing and bel canto vocal production used in European opera into long-song vocal technique to strengthen the volume, tonal focus, and consistency of singers' vocal outputs. Teachers began using pianos or keyboards to accompany singers while they learned new pieces, a practice that emphasizes conformity to the Western equal-tempered system. Although Badma does sing with precise intonation, gained through years performing with large ensemble accompaniment, her vocal technique is quite unique among long-song singers in Inner Mongolia and has an open, chest-produced sound that, while relaxed, has a certain amount of grittiness typically eliminated by professional singers in favor of a focused, nasal-cavity-produced sound.

The horse-head fiddle is another useful example of the elimination of regional musical diversity for the sake of universally agreed-upon standards. Using one uniformly constructed instrument required adaptations of local variation in tuning and technique (see D'Evelyn 2014). For the horse-head fiddle, such standardization meant that musicians could perform on stage together, even if they came from opposite ends of Inner Mongolia. Badma, however, plays on an early twentieth-century, locally built (rather than factory-produced), skin-faced instrument and is one of the last remaining players to use her left hand to bow the instrument rather than the right hand. Scholars and other musicians are quick to mention the uniqueness and even oddity of her technique, but they also seem to respect the logics of local folk practices, which in this case meant using the bow with whichever hand felt more comfortable to the player instead of conforming oneself to arbitrarily rigid requirements. It is perhaps this uniqueness in Badma's vocal and fiddle techniques that intrigues many urban Mongol scholars today, who see these characteristics as comprising Badma's trademark and the special heritage passed down to her by her family members.

Urban Performance and Transmission

On July 15, 2010, the Inner Mongolia University Art College and Secondary Art School put on a tribute concert to Badma that featured performances by university and middle school students Badma had taught during her residency in Hohhot. The concert was an energetic event that included performances by a large youth chorus and an ensemble of long-song singers and horse-head fiddlers she had taught at the university. The audience applauded enthusiastically and filled the campus concert hall beyond its full capacity, with students and parents occupying the aisles. During section breaks in the concert, the lights were dimmed and a video was played with previously recorded statements by dozens of high-profile Mongol and Han scholars and university officials praising Badma and thanking her for her contributions to preserving ethnic Mongol heritage. Toward the very end of the concert, Badma herself took the podium and voiced her priorities for the future of the Alasha music, which involved a strong desire for preservation and transmission to young generations and her thanks to the university for helping her bring her visions to reality.

The concert brings to mind several questions about the future of Inner Mongolia's musical heritage and its reliance on a powerful field of cultural value surrounding cultural transmitters such as Badma. First, in the process of providing support and celebration for one surviving heritage lineage, such as that of Badma, is it possible the natural idiosyncrasies of her style become formalized as *the* Alasha flavor rather than one of *many* Alasha flavors? Or, perhaps in the opposite circumstance, in the process of learning Alasha folksongs, did the students absorb Badma's flavorful vocal style at all, or are they simply producing the melody and lyrics of her songs while retaining the standard conservatory style of vocal production in which they were trained?

Second, what is the future of YST music in the city? Does indigenous musical knowledge become lost in translation when sounds that were previously part of the participatory processes of work and ritual are packaged as a product on the stage (or on a CD album)? To borrow Rees's phrasing, when a YST folksong is brought to the stage or screen "is it still an original ecology folksong under these circumstances, when the originating environment and context are so drastically changed?" (2009, 62).

Third, will the students in the newly established "Alasha folksong transmission major" continue singing and transmitting these folksongs beyond their time as students at the academy? Will these songs remain relevant to Mongols even after government support for this heritage wanes? And do Mongols have the resources and capabilities to continue maintaining and supporting their musical past, which most see as valuable and worth preserving, as the "original ecologies" for that music are rapidly disappearing and transforming? I pose these questions above to complicate the cultural heritage dynamics in Inner Mongolia today, dynamics regarding preservation and change, which Mongols themselves recognize as relevant, problematic, and often paradoxical.

Cultural heritage collection and documentation projects like the "Great Masters Series" appear to alleviate some, but not all, of the stress of musical preservation and future transmission. Although recordings capture performance within the artificial and impersonal context of the recording studio, they provide a record for future generations to inherit a single moment of sonic history produced by a folk artist. Taken for what it is—an imperfect and incomplete, but valuable piece of sound history—these albums, along with the high-quality documentation provided within, offer one of many strategies to deal with the gradual passing of folk artists and the challenges of transmitting folk heritage in the modern world.

Far from a government-directed project imposed from above, the CD series emerged from efforts on the part of scholars in Inner Mongolia to preserve and document cultural heritage, aided significantly by regional and national government funding. Arbiters of the field of cultural production for Mongol music in China, as discussed above, include university professors, regional government officials, cultural bureau officers, and artists themselves. A national discourse focused on preservation and transmission of ICH has provided urban Mongol elites, such as university professors, administrators, officials, and young cosmopolitan performers, with the attention, funding, and empowerment to take on what they see as much-needed projects to collect and document their traditional music. The approach is anything but unidirectional and monolithic and appears as a negotiation between individuals on various levels of academic and cultural bureau leadership. In my experience, the outcome of ICH endeavors in Inner Mongolia is a surprising mix of top-down initiatives combined with nuanced, critically oriented visions and debates about the best methods for preserving and transmitting ICH.

Those individuals with community resources, such as the Mongol scholar Professor Yang, have greater ability to mobilize local artists and are generally willing to put in the work to make the projects happen. Shaping which traditions and artists receive funding and recognition can be worth the great cost in time and effort. For Yang, these recording projects have become a viable way for him to address his own anxieties about disappearing grassland culture and the need to recognize and celebrate the distinctiveness of Inner Mongolia's regional cultures and the individuality of its folk artists. In a 2009 article in which he reviews a folksong collection project undertaken by Badma in Alasha, Professor Yang notes: "As with any form of regional Intangible Cultural Heritage, Alasha folksongs are facing a serious problem of decline and withering. The great majority of pieces have already been lost, and the number of cultural transmitters are decreasing day by day. The natural environment and cultural contexts that folksongs rely upon for survival have been destroyed; the musical lives of traditional Mongolian herdsmen are experiencing rapid changes" (Botolt 2009, 7; transl. from Mandarin by the author).

Professor Yang's "loss mentality" is a large driving force in his work. He operates with a great sense of urgency, noting how "cultural transmitters are decreasing day by day" (*chuanchengren shuliang riyi jianshao*) (7). His agenda is not merely scholarly analysis of Mongol music but active engagement in its preservation. Moreover, even though he is rarely visible at the forefront of projects such as the CD album series, Professor Yang is the primary authority involved in the selection and framing of folk artists within the mission of the Inner Mongolia Musical Heritage Inheritance Station. In this way, he exercises tremendous power over the production of knowledge about and representations of Mongol cultural heritage in Inner Mongolia.

Conclusion

This chapter has highlighted various methods and contexts of heritage preservation in Inner Mongolia since the early 2000s. The "Great Masters Series" of CD albums is one powerful way scholars and artists have made the intangible

tangible amidst anxieties about the loss of original cultural environments. In our conversations, Yang Yucheng distinguishes his recording project as a meaningful way for Mongols to connect to their folk heritage. He contrasts this preservation-and heritage-oriented endeavor with the vast array of commercialized, "fast food" (*kuaican*) musical options that exist in Inner Mongolia, which he sees as a means for momentary enjoyment but not lasting value. The albums generated through the "Great Masters Series" and the accompanying "Famous Experts Series," "Genre Series," and "Regional Style Series" each serve not simply as sound archives to preserve the musical past but function as visible emblems of Professor Yang's efforts to reorient the field of Mongol music in China from fleeting and insubstantial *kuaican* (fast food) to lasting and valuable *yichan* (inheritance).

Badma's album, as the only album in the series thus far featuring an artist from Alasha, serves an important role in characterizing and differentiating the Alasha "color region" of long song in Inner Mongolia. In the context of contemporary scrambles for recognition, nested in the politics of heritage designation in Inner Mongolia today, minority actors such as Badma who live in isolated cultural peripheries have received unprecedented attention and appreciation. In a similar manner to Professor Yang, Badma has discovered her own way to harness recognition and to fit herself into the state system of artistic promotion. She has negotiated government bureaucracy, academic symposia, banners with cheerful slogans, and other formalities that comprise an unquestioned part of artistic activities in the People's Republic of China. Exhibiting a fluctuating center-periphery status, Badma is a singer from a remote homeland, as well as a fiddler with a rare and unusual bowing technique, yet at the same time she has been brought to the center of the ICH movement, filling in a missing heritage link in the panorama of long-song styles in Inner Mongolia, and becoming a recognized figurehead in efforts to transmit her own traditions through teaching and publication projects.

The "Inner Mongolia Ethnic Music Classics—Great Masters Series" has provided a rallying point for the redefinition of knowledge and value of the folk musical past in Inner Mongolia. Although the activities described in this chapter are part of a greater nationwide trend to value intangible cultural heritage and original ecology culture, the energy with which endeavors to transmit musical heritage have been embraced by local actors in Inner Mongolia—including urban scholars, university officials, musicians, and rural folk artists—demonstrates how much cultural value has been ascribed to these traditions and the individuals who transmit them. For ethnic Mongols such as Professor Yang and Badma who seek to make musical heritage accessible and relevant to changing urban lifestyles, packaged albums offer one of many ways to not only render tangible each folk artist's musical knowledge and memory but also to ascribe that musical knowledge with value through researched appraisal as well as pomp and celebration.

Further studies are necessary to observe the trickle-down effect of the "Great Masters Series" and to study how the albums have been received among various audiences across Inner Mongolia and China. I can briefly attest to the albums' circulation, having heard one of the albums on a road trip in the distant Hulunbuir region of Inner Mongolia and having another two of the albums gifted to me (in pirated form) by one of my Mongol friends in Beijing. I expect future studies to observe whether the next generations of Mongols in China, including those training as "transmission majors" at the Inner Mongolia University Art College, take up heritage endeavors as enthusiastically as their predecessors. It is also the job for future studies to look critically at projects such as the "Great Masters Series" as bordering on museumification and time-capsulization of folk culture and eventually ending up as part of a canon of "original ecology folksongs" in China.

My concern here in this study is not to question the methods or assumptions behind these heritage projects but rather to reveal the circumstances that led to the reevaluation and decentering of Mongol music in China, which now offer a pathway for musicians such as Badma, from the most remote and often ignored regions of Inner Mongolia, to be valued and recognized by grassroots and state heritage programs. Such energetic efforts in Inner Mongolia to preserve musical heritage in a physical package reveals just how much the climate has changed from the Mao era through the 1980s, to a climate that sees rural, unprofessional music from unknown lands as worthy of being handled, grasped, and displayed for future generations.

Skidmore College,
Saratoga Springs,
New York

Notes

1. Stephen Jones (2003) argues that folksong collection projects begun in the Mao era are significant as some of the first efforts to document and give attention to music of illiterate peasants, formerly considered uncouth and uncultured throughout Chinese history.

2. A style that combines aspects of regional folksong vocal production with European bel canto vocal support and vibrato.

3. See Dru Gladney (1994) and Louisa Schein (2000) for discussion of how such representations of minority cultures as "backward Other" function as a means for the Han Chinese to better understand their own majority identity.

4. Jia Shuying's article can be found in the sixth issue of the 2006 volume of *Yishu pinglun*.

5. Throughout history, mobile pastoralists came in and out of this vast steppe territory south of the Gobi and north of the Great Wall until the twenty-some clans settled into

territorial divisions designated during the mid–Qing Dynasty (1644–1911). The Manchu Qing implemented an administrative system of leagues and banners that roughly fixed territorial boundaries with clan names, and these clan-place-based subethnic designations are still used today (see Atwood 2004). Although numerous changes in territorial administration have taken place since the Qing period (see Bulag 2002a), Mongols refer to their clan identities according to the old league or banner name of their home regions. Prominent subethnic groups of Mongols in Inner Mongolia include the Ujumchin Mongols of Shilingol League, Barga Mongols of Hulunbuir League (now Hulunbuir City), the Horchin of Hinggan League (distributed across today's Tongliao City and Xing'an/Hinggan League), Tumed Mongols of Hohhot City, and Ordos Mongols of Ih-Juu League (now Ordos City).

6. It is notable that Lasurong's vocal training in the 1960s was conducted primarily with long-song teachers from Shilingol, and he frequently serves as a judge for long-song competitions outside the Ordos region, demonstrating the de-emphasis on regional affiliation among Mongols of Lasurong's generation.

7. As I mentioned above, those artists who gain cultural transmitter status receive a certificate and a small amount of government funding each year, but the main draw for inclusion on the list is the status it accords. I have found that disagreements about who receives official recognition and status have become a constant feature of my private conversations with musicians about ICH in Inner Mongolia.

8. The term *color region (fengge secaiqu)* was coined by senior Chinese musicologist Qiao Jianzhong to refer to the major stylistic regions of music in China (see Han 1989, 107).

References

Atwood, Christopher P. 2002. *Young Mongols and Vigilantes in Inner Mongolia's Interregnum Decades, 1911–1931*. Boston: Brill.

——. 2004. *Encyclopedia of Mongolia and the Mongol Empire*. New York: Facts on File.

Baoyin Batu. 2009. "Xinling de fozu bansuizhe gesheng—zhuming min'ge gehou Lu Badema" [The spirit of the Buddha following the sound of the voice: Celebrated female folksinger Lu Badma]. Liner notes for *Ende sansheng—zhuming minjian yishujia Lu Badema* [Three saintly graces: Musical album for celebrated folk artist Lu Badma], by Badma. China Musicians' Audiovisual Press 7-88079-811-0, compact disc.

Baranovitch, Nimrod. 2003. "From the Margins to the Centre: The Uyghur Challenge in Beijing." *The China Quarterly* 175 (September): 726–50.

——. 2009. "Compliance, Autonomy, and Resistance of a 'State Artist.'" In *Lives in Chinese Music*, edited by Helen Rees, 173–212. Urbana: University of Illinois Press.

——. 2015. "Ecological Degradation and Endangered Ethnicities: China's Minority Environmental Discourses as Manifested in Popular Songs." *Journal of Asian Studies* 75 (1): 181–205.

Batzengel. 1978. "Urtyn Duu, Xöömij, and Morin Xuur." In *Musical Voices of Asia: Report of the Asian Traditional Performing Arts, 1978*, edited by Richard Emmert and Yuki Minegishi, 52–53. Tokyo: Heibonsha.

Bilik, Naran. 2007. "Names Have Memories: History, Semantic Identity, and Conflict in Mongolian and Chinese Language Use." *Inner Asia* 9 (1): 23–39.

Botolt [Boteletu]. 2009. "Hanhai zhan miaoyin min'ge shu xinpian—ping daxing min'geji 'Alashan Menggu min'geji'" [Exhibiting the sublime sounds of the desert, a new collection of folksongs: A review of the large-scale folksong compilation *An Anthology of Alasha Mongolian Folksongs*]. *Zhongguo yinyue* [Chinese music] (2): 1–9.

Bourdieu, Pierre. 1993. *The Field of Cultural Production: Essays on Art and Literature*. Edited by Randal Johnson. New York: Columbia University Press.

Bulag, Uradyn Erden. 2002a. "From Yeke-Juu League to Ordos Municipality: Settler Colonialism and Alter/Native Urbanization in Inner Mongolia." *Provincial China* 7 (2): 196–234.

———. 2002b. *The Mongols at China's Edge: History and the Politics of National Unity*. World Social Change. Lanham, MD: Rowman and Littlefield.

———. 2012. "Seeing Like a Minority: Political Tourism and the Struggle for Recognition in China." *Journal of Current Chinese Affairs* 41 (4): 133–58.

Chao, David. 2010. "Urtiin Duu: The Mongolian Long Song in Mongolia and China." PhD diss., University of California, Los Angeles.

D'Evelyn, Charlotte. 2014. "Driving Change, Sparking Debate: Chi Bulag and the Morin Huur in Inner Mongolia, China." *Yearbook for Traditional Music* 46: 89–113.

Du Chunmei. 2015. "Manufacturing Naxi's Original Ecological Culture in Contemporary China." *Asian Ethnicity* 16 (4): 549–67.

Gladney, Dru C. 1994. "Representing Nationality in China: Refiguring Majority/Minority Identities." *Journal of Asian Studies* 53 (1): 92–123.

Han, Kuo-Huang. 1989. "Folk Songs of the Han Chinese: Characteristics and Classifications." *Asian Music* 20 (2): 107–28.

Jiang Hong. 2004. "Cooperation, Land Use, and the Environment in Uxin Ju: The Changing Landscape of a Mongolian-Chinese Borderland in China." *Annals of the Association of American Geographers* 94 (1): 117–39.

Jones, Stephen. 2003. "Reading between the Lines: Reflections on the Massive 'Anthology of Folk Music of the Chinese Peoples.'" *Ethnomusicology* 47 (3): 287–337.

Lau, Frederick. 1998. "Little Great Tradition: Thoughts on Recent Developments in Jiangnan Sizhu." *ACMR Reports: Journal of the Association for Chinese Music Research* 11: 45–66.

Litzinger, Ralph A. 2000. *Other Chinas: The Yao and the Politics of National Belonging*. Durham, NC: Duke University Press.

McDougall, Bonnie S. 1980. *Mao Zedong's "Talks at the Yan'an Conference on Literature and Art": A Translation of the 1943 Text with Commentary*. Ann Arbor: Center for Chinese Studies, University of Michigan.

Rees, Helen. 2009. "Use and Ownership: Folk Music in the People's Republic of China." In *Music and Cultural Rights*, edited by Andrew Weintraub and Bell Yung, 187–218. Urbana: University of Illinois Press.

———. 2012. "Intangible Cultural Heritage in China Today: Policy and Practice in the Early Twenty-First Century." In *Music as Intangible Cultural Heritage: Policy, Ideology, and Practice in the Preservation of East Asian Traditions*, edited by Keith Howard, 23–54. Burlington, VT: Ashgate.

———. 2016. "Environmental Crisis, Culture Loss, and a New Musical Aesthetic: China's Original Ecology Folksongs in Theory and Practice." *Ethnomusicology* 60 (1): 53–88.

Sanchez, Jamie N. 2013. "Cultural Colonialization: The Displacement of Mongolians in Inner Mongolia." *SPECTRA: The Aspect Journal* 2 (2). https://spectrajournal.org/SPECTRA/article/view/269/186.

Schein, Louisa. 2000. *Minority Rules: The Miao and the Feminine in China's Cultural Politics*. Body, Commodity, Text. Durham, NC: Duke University Press.

Sneath, David. 2003. "Land Use, the Environment and Development in Post-Socialist Mongolia." *Oxford Development Studies* 31 (4): 441–59.
Ulanji. 1998. *Mengguzu yinyueshi* [A musical history of the Mongol nationality]. Hohhot, China: Neimenggu renmin chubanshe.
———. 2010. Liner notes for *Furao liaokuo de Alashan—Mengguzu changdiao dashi Badema yanchang zhuanji* [Rich and vast Alasha—Vocal album of Mongolian long-song master Badma], by Badma. Great Masters Series. Inner Mongolia Culture and Video-Audio Press 978-7-88324-186-7, compact disc.
Williams, Dee Mack. 1996. "The Barbed Walls of China: A Contemporary Grassland Drama." *Journal of Asian Studies* 55 (3): 665–91.
Yang Man. 2009. "The Yuanshengtai Movement: Remaking of Chinese Ethnic Minority Identity." MA thesis, University of Hawai'i at Manoa.
Yang Mu. 1994. "Academic Ignorance or Political Taboo? Some Issues in China's Study of Its Folk Song Culture." *Ethnomusicology* 38 (2): 303–20.
Yoon, Sunmin. 2011. "Chasing the Singers: The Transition of Long-Song (Urtyn Duu) in Post-Socialist Mongolia." PhD diss., University of Maryland.
———. 2015. "Survival of the Fittest: The Urtyn Duu Tradition in Changing Mongolia." *Smithsonian Folkways Magazine*, summer. http://www.folkways.si.edu/magazine-summer-2015-survival-of-the-fittest-the-urtyn-duu-tradition-in-changing-mongolia/article/smithsonian.

CHARLOTTE D'EVELYN is an ethnomusicologist and faculty member in the Music Department at Skidmore College. Her research focuses on fiddles, regional folk song, and the politics of heritage in Inner Mongolia. She is active as a performer and student of the Chinese erhu, Mongolian horse-head fiddle, and höömii (throat singing).

2 Chinese Singing Contests as Sites of Negotiation among Individuals and Traditions

Levi S. Gibbs

WHEN I ARRIVED with three Chinese scholars at the remote home of the renowned ethnic Mongol *manhandiao* singer Qi Fulin in the summer of 2010, he quickly began to lay out award certificates from various singing competitions on his *kang* (brick bed) for us to photograph.[1] Qi's ritualistic manner suggested that this was how he showed "experts" from the outside who he was—these awards were his résumé, his "paper trophy case," his status in the world (English 2005, 20).[2] The awards represented how he had become a face of tradition—the outcome of a series of liminal events where Qi and others negotiated how *manhandiao* should look and sound. In contests, Qi's choices between continuity and change were publically validated or rejected, and the results of those interactions positioned Qi in relation to other *manhandiao* singers and on the national stage.

In this chapter, I suggest that large-scale singing competitions in China elevate professional folksingers, songs, singing styles, and localities in the national mediascape while creating narratives connecting contestants to other more established singers in mutually beneficial ways. I will focus mainly on professional folksingers from northern Shaanxi Province and Shanxi Province whose careers have caught my attention during fieldwork and research since 2002. While the examples I cite are anecdotal, these narratives of individuals participating in competitions show us how artists and others interact with performance traditions and reflect upon those interactions.

The image of Qi Fulin laying out his awards highlights a trope shared by contemporary professional folksingers in China—singers can build their professional identities by participating in and winning contests. Prizes serve as "instrument[s] of cultural hierarchy" and can affect a singer's rank and pay grade (English 2005, 54).[3] For singers in rural peripheries, contests often act as stepping stones from the local to the regional/provincial to the national. Encircled by audiences and expert judges, competitions offer singer-contestants popular approval from the common folk (*laobaixing*) and the intellectual/political elite (in the guise of the judges, officials, and other luminaries who comment on performances). Since the 1950s in mainland China, countless stories have told of peripheral singers coming to the center to participate in contests and galas, and meeting the likes of Mao Zedong, Zhou Enlai, Deng Xiaoping, and others (cf. Huo 2006; Schein 2010; Zhao 2010). Postcontest praise from political and cultural luminaries (including famous writers) and a singer's success become part of the narrative of a singer's rise to fame. Winning contests can lead to contracts for CD albums, appearances on TV and film, and even membership in song and dance troupes.

Televised singing competitions have become ubiquitous in recent years in the global mediascape. Competitions, similar to artists, form lineages complete with progenitors and progeny. The *Eurovision Song Competition* (ESC), which started in 1956, led to Britain's *Pop Idol*, which, in turn, inspired "over 30 versions worldwide, such as *American Idol, Deutschland sucht den Superstar* (in Germany), *South African Idol, Australian Idol,* and *Malaysian Idol*" (Meizel 2007, 159). In an introduction to an edited volume on global adaptations of the *Idol* format, Joost de Bruin and Koos Zwaan write, "The goal of *Idols* shows is to involve a nation (or a region consisting of several different nations) in a quest for a popular music idol who can be admired by all" (de Bruin and Zwaan 2012, 1). In China, large-scale song galas and songwriting contests emerged in the 1950s and early 1960s (cf. Wong 1984) and reemerged after the end of the Cultural Revolution through the likes of the 1980 National Selection of Rural Amateur Performers (*Quanguo nongcun yeyu yanchu diaoyan*) held in Beijing, the biennial All-China National Young Singers' Television Competition (*Quanguo qingnian geshou dianshi dajiang sai*) started in the 1980s, and MTV competitions in the early 1990s. These all led to a flood of televised competitions in the new millennium, including *Starlight Highway* (*Xingguang dadao*), *Super Girl* (*Chaoji nüsheng*), *Happy Boy* (*Kuaile nansheng*), *Dream China* (*Mengxiang Zhongguo*), and the *Red Song Contest* (*Honggehui*), to name a few.[4] Along with these competitions, there has also been a rise in contests showcasing "original ecology" (*yuanshengtai*) singing styles since 2002, discussed below (cf. Gorfinkel 2012; Rees 2016).

Competitions can serve as "display events" that maintain or disrupt social, political, and/or cultural hegemony (Stillman 1996; Abrahams 1981). Scholars have described how competitions often reinforce particular identities. Philip Bohlman (2004) shows how the *Eurovision Song Competition* promotes European nationalism (cf. Raykoff and Tobin 2007). Shzr Ee Tan (2005, 83) describes how *Sing Singapore*, Singapore's "biennial, government-sponsored, mass-song competition," contributes to "fostering a pan-national identity among its multiracial citizens of Chinese, Malay, Indian and Eurasian origins." Shelley Brunt

(2007) stresses the role of Japan's *Red and White Song Contest* (*Kōhaku Utagassen*) in "shaping Japanese cultural identity" (Shin and Kim 2006, 128). In China, scholars describe how the *Red Song Contest* promotes a "red" spirit—referring both to China's revolutionary past and a present-day "positive state of mind in the new age of Socialist construction" where the singing of "red songs" can provide "spiritual nourishment" (*jingshen shiliang*) (Xiong and Li 2011, 97; Zhang 2008, 257).[5] In a similar vein, Hui Xiao suggests that the 2005 *Super Girl* TV competition, composed entirely of female contestants and produced in a format similar to *American Idol*, promoted "the state agenda of building a 'harmonious society'" (2006, 60) in a finale "resonat[ing] with the image of a greater happy China celebrated every year by the CCTV Spring Festival Eve Gala" (64). Just as group singing enables individuals to connect to a larger whole (Blacking 1967; Small 1998), competitions offer a sense of unity by allowing multitudes to join together in acclaiming winners.

At the same time, singers' performances in competitions refigure the performance traditions they represent. When singers win contests, they elevate their status in the hierarchy of singers while "traditionalizing" their vocal styles, songs, and the places they represent—increasing their impact in the field of their performance tradition and within the national mediascape (Bauman 2004; Hymes 1975). In Pierre Bourdieu's discussion of the French literary field, he notes, "Each author, school or work which 'makes its mark' displaces the whole series of earlier authors, schools or works" (1993, 60). One could argue that singers and songs also "make their mark" through performances in competitions. Seen in this light, singing contests serve as liminal spaces where singers, judges, and audiences negotiate elements of continuity and change. Amy Kuʻuleialoha Stillman has noted how Hawaiʻian hula competitions "have provided the stage for creativity that has transformed the tradition" (1996, 357). Following the rise of celebrity culture in China and elsewhere, winning singers become "implicat[ed] ... in the processes through which cultural identity is negotiated and formed" (Turner 2004, 4). When a professional folksinger wins a contest in China, the singer, song, vocal style, and region represented become more prominent within the tradition (e.g., *manhandiao*, Zuoquan folksongs, northern Shaanxi folksongs) and in the national performancescape (Bender 2010, 120; cf. Thurston 2013, 168). When multiple song genres compete in a competition, the winner stands to reach a larger portion of national or transnational audiences. In Anthony Fung's study of China's attempt "to 'sinicize' MTV's brand," he notes how the CCTV-MTV (China Central Television–Music Television) Music Awards in 2004 strove to increase the prominence of Chinese singers in a field also including Asian pop stars and globally acclaimed singers (2006, 78–79).

Although singers stand to increase their visibility by participating in competitions, the televised illusion of individuals competing against each other overlooks all of the people involved in bringing those individuals to the stage—officials, scholars, teachers, managers, patrons, choreographers, and others—as well as the production costs of such displays. Backup dancers, costumes, training, entrance fees—all of these things add up. In many competitions, not only are individuals competing, but regions and traditions are as well. Large-scale competitions serve as sites for "regional entanglement" where each locality strives for national prominence and the stakes are high (Qian and de Kloet 2016, 293). The cultural prize "brings together an unusually wide range of cultural 'players'—artists, critics, functionaries, sponsors, publicists, journalists, consumers, kibitzers—providing all of them with an occasion in which they feel they have a certain stake and hence a certain obligation to assert their interests" (English 2005, 51). Singers' "celebrity" becomes "a product of complex cultural and economic processes," with each contestant a potential "celebrity-as-commodity ... produced and consumed in multiple contexts, for different reasons and with diverse effects" (Jeffreys and Edwards 2010, 6–7). Local officials support singers to advertise their regions. Music scholars seek to further the careers of their protégés. Media personalities such as TV show hosts endeavor to benefit by advancing singers' careers. No singer is an island unto her- or himself.

Implications of Judging

What, then, is the role of judges in such contests? By accepting or rejecting a performance, judges decide what aspects they feel should or should not be "traditionalized" in the performance tradition's accepted canon of songs, singers, and styles (Bauman 2004; Hymes 1975). Each performance is observed against previous expressive events, "invok[ing] an intertextual field ... constituted by the past performances that provide a standard for the comparative assessment of the performance now on view" (Bauman 2004, 9). As Richard Schechner notes, performance is "never for the first time" (1985, 36). A judge's praise or condemnation is often in reaction to a performance's "associational resonances" (Bauman 2004, 9; cf. Foley 1991, 1995). The value of particular resonances may change over time, following social trends. In China, folksingers once rejected for using nonconservatory-trained vocal styles were later praised for the same styles. Although the styles remained the same, the singers and songs were now judged differently in terms of the associated meanings they conjured up for listeners.

To win contests, singers often attempt to strike a balance between maintaining and disrupting the status quo—mastering techniques, styles, and repertoires of which the judges will approve, while setting themselves apart from other contestants in order to insert themselves in the pool of established singers. When I attended the multiday, regional finals of the *Red Song Contest* in Xi'an in 2012, I noticed that many contestants chose from a small pool of popular songs. Perhaps each hoped to sing a particular song "better" than the others and receive the adulation of the judges. Surely, the national performancescape needed singers who could perform these songs in a compelling way. It could be that the singers and their coaches saw mastering these songs as a means to advance careers—after all, other singers had become famous singing these songs. By choosing a piece from the "standard" repertoire of red songs, it seems, these singers attempted to perpetuate the field, while prominently positioning themselves (cf. Bourdieu 1993).

Performance is "a key means of boundary construction and maintenance" for groups, and festival performances such as singing contests "declar[e] difference between copresent individuals" (Noyes 2003, 13). Each singer seeks to endow his or her performance "with a dimension of traditional authority," hoping to join the group of established singers recognized as faces of tradition (Bauman 2004, 27; cf. Hymes 1975). For that to happen, judges and audience members weigh the singer's performance diachronically against past performances in the tradition, as well as synchronically against the performances of other contestants. The diachronic and synchronic contexts of the performance form a "double grounding" (Bauman 2004, 149) for the judges to determine which singer-contestant is best suited to extend "traditional authority" (27) forward into the present and future.

A competition's traditionalizing effect depends in part on judges' identities and the public nature of the event, together representing elite and popular approval. The judges' identities authorize competitions, adding weight to the competitions' power to traditionalize winning performances. The judges are introduced at the beginning of the event and have name cards prominently displayed on the table in front of them. Considered privileged experts with a refined sense of the quality of performers' work, the judges' role is "to assert authority... in an attempt to control the power of interpretation and safeguard the boundaries of genre" (Tuohy 1999, 42). Praise from a famous judge—singer, scholar, or professional music critic—has greater potential to elevate a singer's status and the competition as a whole than that of a less famous judge.

The judges also mediate popular support. Their table sits between the audience and the performers. Shots of the judges deliberating are invariably flanked by audience members in the background. Facing the performance together, the audience and judges critique the performers' artistic competency—the audience through applause and cheers, the judges through analysis and decisions. The symbolic placement of the judges between audience and performer suggests that the judges are gatekeepers of popular approval—a refracted lens through which the audience interprets the performance, a valve constraining and encouraging audience support for the performance. Representing elite power, scholarly knowledge, and professional expertise, judges have a dominating voice in determining the prizes awarded and the performers, repertoires, and styles seen to receive "popular support" in a competition (cf. Bourdieu 1993).

Individual judges may be associated with various groups, and a judge's approval can represent the approval of those groups. Bourdieu discusses "three competing principles of legitimacy" in fields of cultural production—other artists, the elite, and the popular (Bourdieu 1993, 50–51). Certain judges may represent a nexus between the three—for example, senior singers holding positions of power in professional associations while at the same time claiming to be representatives of the "common people" (*laobaixing*) via their folksinger personae.[6] Praise from such a judge symbolically points to the approval of a broad range of audiences.

By focusing on the role of competitions in individual singers' careers, we can see how singers—in conversation with judges and supporting individuals—weigh choices between continuity and change, embody and localize transformations in performance traditions, and choose which repertoires, styles, and singers are worthy of becoming the faces of a tradition.

Traditionalizing Singers and Styles

Qi Fulin's awards validated him as a singer, highlighting his style as representative of the *manhandiao* tradition and promoting that style on regional and national stages. For decades, singers have advanced their careers by participating in contests, although the rate of advancement and the particular players involved have changed over time with the rise of celebrity culture, satellite television, and the internet. In what follows, I offer two examples—an older singer and a younger singer—who advanced their careers through national contests with the assistance of other supporting individuals, including scholars, government officials, and, more recently, TV hosts.

Known as "Folksong King of Western China" (*Xibu gewang*) and "King of Northern Shaanxi Folksongs" (*Shaanbei min'ge wang*), Wang Xiangrong (b. 1952) won a string of contests beginning in 1977—local, regional, and finally the 1980 National Selection of Rural Amateur Performers, where he met leaders including Deng Xiaoping (1904–1997) (Zhao 2010, 5).[7] Also in attendance at the national competition was the celebrated writer Ding Ling (1904–1986), who had lived in northern Shaanxi during the revolutionary period, and who, as quoted by Miao Meng, praised Wang's singing by saying, "Having left northern Shaanxi several decades ago, today we heard real northern Shaanxi folksongs once more!" (Miao 2008, 73). Wang's success in Beijing led to his first music video and to his being hired by the Yulin Folk Arts Troupe in 1983, which paved the way for additional opportunities to perform on television, film, and abroad (cf. Gibbs 2017).

While Wang's success in the national competition had a clear impact on the growth of his career, a closer look reveals other people invested in Wang's success. Before and after the national competition in Beijing, various scholars "discovered" Wang and prepared him for performances on the stage.[8] One senior scholar I interviewed remembered showing Wang how to carry himself properly onstage at the beginning of Wang's career in the early 1980s. Wang Xiangrong also credited a regional official with opening the way for him to participate in the 1980 competition that served as a turning point in his career (Nan 2003; Gibbs 2013, 47). Wang's rise to prominence, in turn, brought attention to the regions he represented—Yulin Prefecture and northern Shaanxi Province.[9] While Wang's example shows how competitions can raise a singer's status and expand his or her audience, it also problematizes the illusion of individual singers competing in contests by highlighting how contestants are assisted by other people behind the scenes. Wang's case also shows how winning national contests can bring increased attention to a singer's region—an issue I will discuss further below.

While Wang's ascendance to fame took many years, the rise of televised singing competitions in China has sped up the process for younger singers. When Wang described the situation of professional folksingers in mainland China in the 1980s, he said, "Even if you sang for ten years, people still wouldn't know you. They could only hear your voice [e.g., in films and TV dramas], but they wouldn't know who was singing and what he looked like. Even if you wanted to find out more about [the singer], you wouldn't know where to begin looking" (Gibbs 2013, 280). Wang contrasted the relative invisibility of singers in the 1980s with the overnight fame younger generations of singers in the new millennium have achieved, in large part due to the rise of regional satellite channels in the 1990s and, more recently, the internet. A "heightened emphasis on the visual" has been seen across the creative industries in China, with similar phenomena noted among younger generations of writers and other professionals around the turn of the twenty-first century (Yang X. 2011, 11; cf. Edwards and Jeffreys 2010).

In the realm of professional folksingers, this rapid rise to fame is exemplified by the case of the "Folksong Prince" (*min'ge wangzi*) Abao (b. 1969, real name Zhang Shaochun), who gained national attention by winning a bronze medal in the 2004 CCTV Western China TV Folksong Competition and became a national media personality after participating in the TV singing competition *Starlight Highway* in 2005 (Rees 2016, 67; Wu T. 2006).[10] Abao's iconic *Starlight Highway* performance of the revolutionary northern Shaanxi folksong "The Wild Lilies Bloom a Brilliant Red" (*Shandandan kaihua hongyanyan*) rocketed him to fame among a fan base accustomed to pop singers (Cai 2005). Similar to Wang Xiangrong's 1980 Beijing contest victory, Abao's 2005 *Starlight Highway* success was seen as a turning point in his career. Abao went from performing with a traveling troupe and singing rock music at KTV (karaoke) establishments to appearing on the 2005 CCTV Spring Festival Gala and later serving as a judge on TV singing competitions, including *Starlight Highway* (Wu T. 2006; Cai 2005).

Similar to Wang, Abao's rise involved the support of surrounding individuals. In recent years, in addition to scholars and officials, TV show hosts and established singers have also provided younger singers with crucial support to advance their careers, styles, and repertoires. Singers and scholars I interviewed in Shaanxi Province inevitably cited *Starlight Highway* host Bi Fujian's role in Abao's rise to fame. The power of "Old Bi" was so great that one article asked, "How Many People Have Been Raised to Stardom by *Starlight Highway* and Bi Fujian?" (Liu and He 2012). Such a question raises issues of agency in the rise of celebrity culture. Whether a singer's fame stems from "true" talent or media hype is a distinction between what Chris Rojek calls "*achieved* celebrity," which "derives from the perceived accomplishments of an individual in open competition," and "*attributed* celebrity," which "is largely the result of the concentrated representation of an individual as noteworthy or exceptional by cultural intermediaries" (2001, 18; italics in original). In the introduction to an edited volume on celebrity culture in China, Elaine Jeffreys and Louise Edwards write, "In the case of boy bands, girl bands, and reality shows, media commentators and consumers may dismiss such entertainers as "phonies" whose temporary celebrity is an effect of artificial and commercially motivated media promotion (Turner 2004: 56–8). However ... real celebrity is defined as being independent from rather than a product of media processes" (2010, 6).

The tension between talent and hype sometimes results in conflicting biographies of singers—stories focusing on a singer's poor upbringing and years of traveling to learn folksongs compete with other narratives painting the same individual as an urban karaoke singer who got a break and performs a "pseudo-folk" hybrid. Conflicting depictions of the validity of contests embody a similar tension. On the one hand, accusations of bribery attempt to discredit the winners of contests. On the other hand, descriptions of a contest's fierce competition and luminary judges serve to boost the status of the winners. Both tensions—involving the integrity of singer and contest—are at play when discussing which events have authority to traditionalize worthy talent (Bauman 2004).

The rise of "overnight fame" has led some of the singers I interviewed to suggest that the majority of singers are more or less equally talented and that what matters most are one's connections. A younger singer I spoke with in Xi'an in 2011 said that if Bi Fujian had promoted *him* instead, *he* would have become as famous as Abao. This idea that one's social network matters more than one's vocal talent resonates with ethnographic studies of northern Shaanxi where locals explain success and social stratification as resulting from social connections rather than "chance or hard work" (Liu 2000, 161–64). The singer I spoke with would often repeat the phrase "friends equal wealth" (*pengyou jiushi caifu*), suggesting the broader one's social network, the "richer" one becomes.

Abao's *Starlight Highway* victory can also be seen as a public confirmation of his high-pitched singing style. Abao's life story is filled with earlier struggles against "experts" who failed to recognize his talent, criticizing his singing technique as "not scientific" (*bu kexue*) (Wu Y. 2005, 5–6).[11] His winning of *Starlight Highway* could be seen as an indication that trends had changed. Abao's style has been described in various ways. In one article, Abao is quoted as saying, "Being born in the countryside and traveling to the city to perform, my folksongs have added in many popular elements. City people are unable to sing songs as 'rustic' (*tu*) as those I sing, while country people are not as able as I am to sing with a 'pop feel' (*tongsu weir*). I have kneaded them together and formed my own style" (Cai 2005, 26). At times, Abao has described his singing style as "original ecology" (*yuanshengtai*)—referring to a trend of non-conservatory-trained folksong styles discussed below that coincided with Abao's ascension in the mid-2000s (cf. Rees 2016). The article about Abao combining "rustic" and "pop" styles concludes with a quote from him tying his rise to the fate of "original ecology" folksongs: "My hope is that 'original ecology' folksongs can have a place at the table in the field of Chinese songs (*Zhongguo getan*)" (Cai 2005, 26). Nevertheless, I spoke with several northern Shaanxi folk music scholars who felt Abao had changed the flavor of the songs—a process one scholar referred to as the "Abao phenomenon" (*Abao xianxiang*), perhaps denoting the mixture Abao himself attests to of "rustic" and "pop" (Liu et al. 2010, 255). Another senior scholar I interviewed was so outraged by Abao's characterization of northern Shaanxi folksongs that the scholar had repeatedly written to television executives imploring them to curb Abao's ubiquitous presence on national TV.

The fact that Abao's rise coincided with a growing desire for *yuanshengtai* folksongs and singers reinforces the idea that competition judges award vocal styles based on how they hope to refigure the field of singers. The rising popularity of yuanshengtai folksongs has been tied to a perceived authenticity of local/regional Han and ethnic cultures, and may be connected to what Chen Jie (2008) has termed the "third wave" of the consumption of *minzu* culture, which emerged in the 2000s (cf. Rees 2016). A string of competitions promoting yuanshengtai vocal styles previously rejected by popular media and music conservatories alike resulted. These included the 2002 First National Chinese Folksong Competition (*Shoujie Zhongguo nanbei min'ge leitaisai*) in Xianju, Zhejiang Province, the 2004 Second National Chinese Folksong Competition in Zuoquan, Shanxi Province, the 2004 CCTV Western China TV Folksong Competition (*CCTV xibu min'ge dianshi dasai*), and "the establishment of an 'original ecology' category" for the 2006 running of the All-China National Young Singers' Television Competition, among others (Tian 2004; Feng 2004; Cui Y. 2013; Rees 2016, 61). The meteoric rise of several singers appears to have coincided with this trend. Just as Abao and certain other Han professional folksingers transitioned from singing pop and/or rock styles in the 1980s and 1990s to "original ecology" folksongs in the 2000s, certain ethnic minority singers made a similar transition from pop songs to folk and ethnic songs during the same period. For example, the extremely popular

Miao singer A You Duo (b. 1977) started her career singing pop songs in restaurants before switching to Miao songs sung in Mandarin and the Hmu dialect of Miao once she became recognized—a choice that led her to win a series of prizes, including several at the national level (Schein 2010, 159). Whether or not scholars agree with Abao's designation as a yuanshengtai singer, his success in competitions points to a refiguring of the field of Chinese professional singers to include a larger portion reflecting the yuanshengtai aesthetic.

Branding Singers and Songs

In addition to validating singers and styles, competitions can fuse songs and singers in synergistic ways. In a study of popular music celebrities, P. David Marshall notes how "recordings tend to sanctify particular performers' renditions of particular songs," adding, "a song, in essence, becomes a sign of the performer" (Marshall 2006, 199). A similar effect, I would suggest, occurs with certain contest-winning song performances. For example, Abao's highly-stylized, high-pitched, prize-winning *Starlight Highway* performance of the revolutionary northern Shaanxi folksong "The Wild Lilies Bloom a Brilliant Red"—originally written in the 1970s—became an iconic image later emulated by other singers in the years that followed. Abao's performance not only provided a "model of winning" for later contestants, but each performance of the song by another singer reminds audiences of Abao's iconic performance.

The year after Abao won *Starlight Highway*, the show's host dubbed another contestant from the countryside—this time, a mountainous region in Hunan—the "female Abao" (*nü Abao*), suggesting a similar narrative of advancement from rural anonymity to national stardom (Lu 2007). Similar to her namesake, the "female Abao" Li Yu had struggled to have her talents appreciated. During the competition, *Starlight Highway*'s host asked her to sing an *a cappella* version of the song that made Abao famous the previous year, which she sang two notes higher than Abao (Lu 2007, 32). Calling Li Yu another "version" of Abao emphasized the similar path she followed to raise her status as a singer. At the same time, Li Yu's emulation of Abao's success can be seen as further boosting Abao's status. One might argue that Abao's and Li Yu's successes were mutually beneficial.

Other singers since then have attempted to emulate Abao's rise to success, often by performing the same song on the same show. The now-famous female northern Shaanxi singer Wang Erni (b. 1985) sang the same song on *Starlight Highway* in 2007 and later relocated to Beijing for frequent performances on national television. Wang Erni's performance on *Starlight Highway* inspired another female singer from the same region, the "Song Phoenix" (*ge fenghuang*) Cui Miao (b. 1986), who sang the same song on the same show two years later in 2009 and received a similar boost in fame.[12]

Abao's iconic performance of "The Wild Lilies Bloom a Brilliant Red" also appeared in other performance genres—highlighting the power of Abao's brand and the connection of that brand with the song. During a skit on the 2009 CCTV Spring Festival Gala, the prominent *xiangsheng* (Chinese crosstalk) comedian Xiao Shenyang impersonated Abao performing the song. When a Yan'an English teacher (Wen Shilong) who had made his name singing English renditions of northern Shaanxi folksongs had the opportunity to perform on a Chinese Spring Festival Gala performance televised across the country on a regional satellite TV channel based in Zhejiang Province, he chose to sing the song in English, translating the title line as "Wild Morning Star Lillies [sic] Are Blooming With Red Brilliance."[13] Wen's performance undoubtedly built on the song's association with the success of Abao, Li Yu, Wang Erni, Cui Miao, Xiao Shenyang, and others (Kang 2013; ZSSX 2009).

In certain cases, singers become associated with contest-winning songs for decades. One older singer, the "*Xintianyou* Song King" (*Xintianyou gewang*) Sun Zhikuan (b. 1958) from Shenmu County in northern Shaanxi Province, gained notoriety in 1986, winning the Golden Peacock Cup Award in a national competition for his rendition of "Tears Fall on the Desert Brush" (*Lei dandan pao zai shahaohao lin*), which he learned from the eminent teacher of northern Shaanxi folksongs Bai Bingquan (Bai 2005, 115). This song became one of Sun's hits for years to come, and he was still performing the song when I saw him sing at a gala in 2012. Sun's case suggests a strong correlation between participating in singing competitions and establishing an artist's "representative pieces" (*daibiaozuo*), the phenomenon Emily Wilcox explores in chapter 3.

A more recent example of the branding of singer and song is the case of a younger singer from northern Shaanxi, Li Zhengfei (b. 1980), who won a drinking song contest sponsored by a regional liquor company in 2001 and later became a spokesman for the company.[14] One might argue that Li's position as a spokesman helped to synergistically advertise both the liquor brand and Li Zhengfei as a singer. (His photo appeared in advertisements for the brand's liquor inserted in menus at northern Shaanxi-style restaurants in Xi'an, as I observed in early 2012.) When I attended a provincial arts gala performance in Xi'an in 2011, the piece Li performed was suitably entitled "Drinking Song" (*Jiuqu*). The examples of Sun Zhikuan and Li Zhengfei reinforce the idea that competitions "brand" performers, and, perhaps to a certain extent, the performance traditions they represent as well.

The Grouping of Success

In addition to winning awards and gaining exposure, singer-contestants benefit from the connections competitions offer—words of praise from esteemed judges, opportunities to develop master-disciple relationships with senior singers, and the chance to be grouped together with other established singers in future concerts. James F. English notes, "The prize serves the function of what economists call 'communication': it brings disparate players into informed contact with one another so that mutually beneficial transactions may (in theory) take place among them" (2005, 51). As sites where traditionalization is highlighted, competitions offer opportunities for "disparate players" to reformulate their relationships (51).

Similar to Ding Ling's praise for Wang Xiangrong after the national competition in 1980, when Wang later served as a judge at the regional semifinals of the 2012 *Red Song Contest* in Shaanxi Province, he offered praise to a younger male contestant. Assuming the role of honored adjudicator at the center of the judges' table, Wang called the young folksinger over after the singer's performance, stood up for all to see and said loudly (while at the same time creating a photogenic moment for the event's photographers), "This kid's not bad"—a phrase that undoubtedly became part of the lore surrounding the younger singer ever since. The powerful effect of Wang Xiangrong's phrase on the younger singer's career points to the roles of individual judges in raising the statuses of less established singers and deciding the future directions of the song traditions represented.

Judges who are senior, respected singers sometimes take talented singer-contestants under their wings as "disciples" (*tudi*)—an association that benefits the careers of both singers. Singing competitions are often viewed as liminal spaces where junior and senior artists can establish "vertical" relationships. For example, after successful performances in several competitions, Wang Erni became a disciple of Wang Kun (1925–2014), one of the original singers of the revolutionary model opera *The White-Haired Girl* (*Baimao nü*) (Cui J. 2013; Wang F. 2014). One of Wang Xiangrong's disciples, Zhou Jinping, met Wang at a contest "where Wang was judging and Zhou won first prize" (Gibbs 2013, 76). The "Shepherd Song King" Shi Zhanming (b. 1973) tells a similar story of meeting and "formally pa[ying] respects to Wang Xiangrong as a teacher" at a gala performance following Shi's success in a national contest in 2002 (Wang B. 2010, 5). Certain contests are even designed for particular singers to acquire new protégés. In 2010, "a contest to find new disciples for Wang [Xiangrong]" was sponsored by a media company, an internet company, and a clothing company in Xi'an (Gibbs 2013, 81–82).

By forming ties with senior artists, junior singers can boost their statuses in the overall hierarchy. Becoming a famous singer's disciple improves the junior artist's brand and is used in self-promotion and to negotiate higher fees for performances. At the same time, senior singers can increase their presence in the field through relationships with talented, up-and-coming younger singers. Michel Hockx observed a similar dynamic in the literary field in early twentieth-century China: "Advantages of the teacher-student relation included, for the student, having one's writings edited by an experienced writer, being introduced to a publisher, receiving favourable reviews or being defended against bad reviews. The teachers were perceived to benefit from the relation in that it enabled them to build up a 'school' of followers" (1999, 10). Given the importance of such "vertical" relationships, words of praise during singing competitions and promises of master-disciple relations are crucial for individual singers to reposition themselves within the overall field (10).

In recent years, winning singers have sometimes gone on to become future judges—potentially perpetuating the tastes of the judges who chose them and in some cases inviting those senior judges to serve again in future competitions. Abao became a judge on *Starlight Highway* after his success on the show—serving both as a model for and judge of future contestants. Similarly, Li Zhengfei, the "Drinking Song" singer mentioned earlier and one of the "National Top Ten Red Singers" in the *Red Song Contest* of 2007, went on to organize the Shaanxi provincial regionals for the *Red Song Contest* in 2012, where he served as a judge and invited his mentor Wang Xiangrong and others to serve as judges alongside him. This phenomenon of celebrity-singer judges, however, appears to be recent. While singers such as Wang Xiangrong now frequently serve as judges for competitions, Wang noted that folksingers in the past were seldom chosen as judges. Instead, only professionally trained musicians, scholars, and other "experts" were deemed worthy arbiters of taste. Wang also noted that competitions could only improve a singer's status to a certain point. If a singer was too famous, his or her participation as a contestant in certain competitions would be inappropriate. Wang cited one competition he found to be a liminal point in his own career—the 2004 CCTV Western China TV Folksong Competition mentioned earlier. Although the program touted "over three hundred folksong kings," Wang did not participate either as a contestant or judge—too famous to compete as the former and not invited to serve as the latter. Scholars served as judges in that competition— Helen Rees notes that the renowned Chinese music scholar Qiao Jianzhong was a judge on the show—whereas professional folksingers such as Wang were still not honored with such appointments at that point (Rees 2016).

A singer who wins a contest often goes on to join a pool of more established singers in what I call the "grouping of success." Such grouping can have a positive impact on the singer's future employment. For example, after one contest crowned its winning contestants the "Top Ten Northern Shaanxi Song Kings," it became trendy in certain circles to hire all ten singers to perform at one's wedding.[15] Each of the "song kings" became an essential part of the group, thus increasing potential job opportunities. Newly victorious folksinger-contestants are often grouped together with established singers in ways that highlight a common theme or region. When Shi Zhanming, the Shanxi singer I discuss below, won fame in a national contest, he was placed together with three other prominent Shanxi singers (including Abao) in a performance group called "Red

Children" (*hong haizi*) (Wang B. 2010).[16] In another example, Wang Erni, one of the female singers who attempted to emulate Abao's success on *Starlight Highway*, later formed an "all-new northern Shaanxi–style group" (*quanxin Shaanbei fengge zuhe*) with Abao to be on the show "I Want to Be on the Spring Festival Gala" (*Wo yao shang chunwan*) in 2013, which, in turn, led to the two singers winning a spot together on the 2014 CCTV Spring Festival Gala (Wang F. 2014, 58). Each of these examples points to ways in which successful junior artists are joined together with established singers in synergistic groupings that expand the renown of each to broader audiences.

Repositioning Place

Singers' awards in competitions also highlight the places the singers represent. When Abao sought to bring songs from northwest Shanxi, northern Shaanxi, and western Inner Mongolia to the national stage by producing an album of "Chinese Rural Music," he was suggesting that the places represented by the songs ought to be highlighted as representative of China's "rural music" (*nongcun yinyue*) (Wu T. 2006). Abao's televised victories undoubtedly brought national attention to northern Shaanxi and Shanxi—an example of the ability of singer-contestants and singing contests to reposition localities and regions on the national scene.

The "repositioning of place" was evident in Shi Zhanming's success at the 2002 First National Chinese Folksong Competition held in Xianju, Zhejiang Province, a contest of singers from thirty-six ethnic groups around China where Shi was crowned one of the "Ten Greatest Song Kings" (Wang B. 2010). Shi's victory is said to have won honor and respect for the local people and folksongs of his home area, Zuoquan County, Shanxi Province, within the larger national field. Writing of the impact of Shi's achievement, the prominent folksong scholar Qiao Jianzhong placed "Zuoquan folksongs" together with twentieth-century Chinese folksong's "three outstandings" (*san jie*): Mongolian long song, *hua'er*, and Yunnan mountain songs (Qiao 2010, 42). Qiao drew a parallel between how Shi's 2002 contest performance highlighted Zuoquan County on the national stage and how a prominent Zuoquan singer of the earlier generation, Liu Gaiyu, had brought attention to the county during the 1953 Inaugural National Folk Music and Dance Gala Performance, where "the sixteen-year-old female Zuoquan singer ... sang [two typical Zuoquan folksongs] all the way from the provincial capital Taiyuan to the national capital Beijing" (Qiao 2010, 42). Qiao went on to suggest that from the time of Liu Gaiyu's 1953 performance, "Zuoquan songs had their own place in the garden of Chinese folksongs" (2010, 42). In Qiao's analysis, both Liu's and Shi's performances in national events served to insert the locality of Zuoquan into the national map of folksong.

At the same time, various scholars and officials helped Shi Zhanming participate in the 2002 Xianju competition to promote the locality he represented.

When I attended the First National Chinese Folksong Competition in 2002, folksingers of various ethnic and regional groups performed local song traditions in different languages and dialects. Traveling with the singers were scholars and local officials intent on gaining wider audiences for local performance traditions and localities. It was common knowledge that the prominent music scholar Tian Qing, who also served as one of the moderators for the event, was supporting Shi Zhanming's participation in the competition.[17] The case of how Tian Qing came to support Shi Zhanming is an example of how localities form relationships with scholars to promote local traditions.

In mid-September of 2002, a month before the competition in Xianju, Zuoquan County organized a large-scale commemoration for a local Eighth Route Army general. As part of the commemorative activities, the county's Culture and Arts Center held a symposium on the development of two local art forms—*Xiaohuaxi* drama and Zuoquan folksongs (Wang B. 2010). The county invited various cultural luminaries to the symposium, including the vice associate editor of *Music Weekly* (*Yinyue zhoubao*), a professor from the Central Conservatory in Beijing, the associate editor of the People's Music Press (*Renmin yinyue chubanshe*), and Tian Qing, the then-director of the Music Research Institute of the Chinese Arts Research Institute (Wang B. 2010). A performance was put on for the symposium including professional singers and local folksingers, and Shi Zhanming, who had won second place in a local contest back in April 2002, was invited to participate (Xue 2005). After watching the performance, the conservatory professor asked why Shi Zhanming was not participating in the upcoming Xianju competition, and Tian Qing picked up the phone and called the head of the Ministry of Culture's National Folk Literature and Arts Development Center, telling him that Shi Zhanming was precisely the kind of singer the competition was looking for—there was no need for Shi to participate in the preliminary selection process (Wang B. 2010). Tian Qing's phone call is described as a "turning point" in Shi Zhanming's career, opening the way for his success in the Xianju competition and other performance opportunities that followed, including being hired by a military song and dance troupe in Beijing (Wang B. 2010).

Shi Zhanming's victory in Xianju also led to performances and contests that further repositioned Zuoquan folksongs provincially and nationally. In 2004, Shi and Liu Gaiyu were grouped together with two other Shanxi singers—Abao (from Datong) and Xin Lisheng (from Xinzhou)—in a concert of "red children" (*hong haizi*), mentioned earlier, commemorating the sixtieth anniversary of the Second Sino-Japanese War (Wang B. 2010, 6). The grouping of two Zuoquan singers with other Shanxi performers can be seen as a clear attempt to highlight Zuoquan's place within the province—no doubt resulting from Shi Zhanming's and Liu Gaiyu's success on the national stage. Also in 2004, Zuoquan was chosen as the site for the Second National Chinese Folksong Competition (Tian 2004).

During the period when the contest was held, the Zuoquan County government produced a solo album (*zhuanji*) for Shi Zhanming (Wang B. 2010, 6). Thus, I would suggest, not only did Shi Zhanming's performances put Zuoquan on the map and reposition Zuoquan within the nation, but his performances also *brought the nation to Zuoquan.*

The ability of singer-contestants to highlight the places they represent has become one tool for local governments and businesses to advertise localities. The power of singing contests to promote individual singers and regional traditions attracts a variety of patrons with place-based interests. Another *Starlight Highway* participant mentioned earlier, a female folksinger from Zizhou County in northern Shaanxi Province named Cui Miao, received national attention for purportedly spending RMB 1,130,000 (USD 184,591.57) on four rounds of the competition—money borrowed from friends, relatives, and local and regional government offices (Wu Y. 2010). Cui Miao advertised her local region by performing on the nationally televised *Starlight Highway* competition and presenting the show's host with locally made handicrafts onstage. One article contains a photo of Cui Miao handing the host a gift highlighting her region—an elaborate northern Shaanxi-style paper cut (*jianzhi*) featuring a map of China with a flower sprouting out of the region of northern Shaanxi. Atop the flower sit Mao Zedong's head and waving hand, flanked by an iconic Yan'an pagoda (Song 2009, 56). Cui Miao's support from local and regional governments once again points to the ability of singers' televised competition performances to advertise localities on the national stage.

Conclusion

Behind the awards that Qi Fulin laid out on his bed lies a series of liminal spaces—the singing contests—where singers and other individuals have negotiated choices in how to represent a performance tradition. Qi could have sung songs in a different way or performed other songs entirely, and yet the choices he made were validated by judges and audiences. Qi's singing style, repertoire, gestures, and costume—all carefully considered in preparation for each contest—were marked with the stamp of traditionalization. One could argue that the Qi Fulin who stood before us was a composite of his negotiations with scholars, hosts, and judges over the course of his career—negotiations about how *manhandiao* should be performed. While the forces driving a tradition's continuity and change are played out in various arenas by different people, a focal point for that process is found in the image of a singer facing a judge. The singer's performance reflects what the singer and the people advising him or her think about how the performance tradition should proceed and how the singer might distinguish him or herself from other singers. The judge, in turn, offers not only a personal opinion but what he or she believes other insiders of the performance tradition and/or the national mediascape would desire, while at the same time symbolizing popular approval. The exchange between singer and judge focuses on which aspects of the performance tradition should be reconfigured and which should be maintained, as well as how the singer, style, song, locality, and performance genre should be positioned within the national mediascape.

By looking at the stories of individual singers, we see how competitions affect the trajectory of singers' careers. The singers come to symbolize successful or unsuccessful choices in the performance traditions they represent. The focus on these individual case studies also highlights the interrelation of various "mechanisms of traditionalization" explored in this volume. A singer's success in a competition can lead to a CD that canonizes the position of the singer, style, and repertoire in the field (cf. D'Evelyn, chapter 1). A winning performance can also "traditionalize" a new composition or an adaptation of an older song, reconfiguring the popular canon and branding the song as one of the singer's "representative works," sometimes leading to the song's (and singer's) canonization in published anthologies (Bauman 2004; cf. Wilcox, chapter 3; Tuohy, chapter 4). Through these interrelated "mechanisms of traditionalization"—competition, album, representative work, and anthology—individuals and traditions interact and effect mutual transformation.

Dartmouth College
Hanover, New Hampshire

Acknowledgments

An earlier version of this chapter was presented at the American Folklore Society 2013 Annual Meeting. I thank Sue Tuohy for her insightful comments as panel discussant, and I am also grateful to Charlotte D'Evelyn for her feedback on a later version of this chapter. Funding for this research was provided by the US Fulbright Program, the US Department of Education's Jacob K. Javits Fellowship Program, The Ohio State University's Office of International Affairs, College of Arts and Sciences, and East Asian Studies Center, the Society for Asian Music, the CHIME European Foundation for Chinese Music Research, and the Walter and Constance Burke Research Initiation Award for Junior Faculty at Dartmouth College.

Notes

1. To get to Qi's house in southwestern Inner Mongolia requires parking one's car on an elevated highway next to a bridge that crosses the Yellow River and then climbing down

a ladder from the edge of the road. *Manhandiao*, a song genre popular in Jungar Banner in the easternmost part of the Ordos region of Inner Mongolia that is also known as "Mongol-Han tunes" (*Meng-Han diao*) in northern Shaanxi Province, is said to have evolved from Ordos "short-song" (*duandiao*) melodies with fixed Mongolian lyrics into modern-day improvised dialogue songs that use either Chinese lyrics or a mixture of Chinese and Mongolian poetically referred to as "wind mixing with snow" (*feng jiao xue*) (E'erdunchaolu et al. 1992, 1254–77; Yang H. 2006, 70). For more on the *manhandiao* song genre, see Du Rongfang (2005).

2. Qi told me that I was the second foreigner who had made the journey—the first was a German journalist who had come the year before.

3. As singers use success in contests to reposition themselves in the field of singers, their pay grade is affected as well. One article on Wang Erni noted that a string of successes in competitions not only raised her position within the song and dance troupe where she worked to that of its leading performer and "mainstay" (*taizhuzi*) but also increased her salary in terms of the fees she received for invited performances (Wang F. 2014, 57). My fieldwork with professional folksingers in and around Xi'an from 2011 to 2012 made it clear that among the world of professional folksingers in China, there is a clear hierarchy relating one's pay grade to one's relative rank and fame, both nationally and within one's own tradition. During the time of my research, for singers of northern Shaanxi folksongs, this ranged from the lowest rung of the ladder—a university student just starting out his or her career—who earned RMB 100 (USD 16.34) for singing multiple songs at a two-hour rural wedding, to a more established singer who had won some lower-level competitions and earned RMB 2000 (USD 326.72) for performances at an hour-long urban wedding, to a star finale act who could earn RMB 20,000 (USD 3267.15) for singing two or three songs, to a pervasive media sensation such as Abao, who was believed by certain singers with whom I spoke to earn RMB 200,000 (USD 32,671.08) for a concert. While others cited different amounts purportedly earned by Abao, my point here is not to document actual amounts for the upper end of the scale but rather to point to popular ideas about the effects of fame and singer status on income.

4. According to Stephen Jones, "the festivals (*diaoyan, huiyan*) of the 1950s showcasing outstanding folk genres and musicians gave way in the 1980s to contests (*bisai, dasai*)" (2009, 144). For a description of the evolution of folk song contests in one locality in Jiangsu Province from "a harvest celebration" to "a massive government-organized *shan'ge* contest," see Schimmelpenninck 1997, 98–99. According to Anthony Fung, CCTV produced *Dream China* to compete with Hunan Satellite TV's *Super Girl* (Fung 2008, 200).

5. All translations are by the author unless otherwise noted.

6. An example of this type of nexus is Wang Xiangrong, with whom I worked closely (cf. Gibbs 2018). He not only had the cultural cachet of himself being an artist, but by the time of my fieldwork (2011–2012) had moved into various "elite" spheres, becoming the vice-chairman of the provincial musicians' association, an official representative in the government on cultural matters, a national-level representative transmitter of intangible cultural heritage, and a judge in numerous competitions. Despite his various connections to the worlds of artists and elites, Wang constantly stressed his folk origins and his connection to the common people. In one competition where he served as judge on behalf of the provincial musicians' association, Wang was asked to critique three categories of singers, including Chinese-style professionally trained singers, Western-style bel canto singers, and folksingers. No doubt his unique position, which combines elements of artistic, elite, and

popular identities, allowed him to judge such diverse genres, elevating certain singers in the process, while elevating himself and maintaining his position in the overall hierarchy of singers.

7. Both of Wang's titles have been applied to other singers as well. Miao Meng refers to the National Selection of Rural Amateur Performers as a "national peasant art selection" (*quanguo nongmin yishu diaoyan*) (Miao 2008, 73).

8. One of the earlier scholars to discover Wang Xiangrong was the eminent northern Shaanxi folksong expert Yang Cui.

9. Another example of folksongs bringing attention to a region is the case of composer and folksong collector Wang Luobin's "Xinjiang folk songs," which Rachel Harris suggests "remain ... the most powerful mediations of the region's culture" (Harris 2005, 404).

10. Abao is also known as the "*Xintianyou* Song King" (*xintianyou gewang*).

11. For more on the drive toward "being scientific (*kexuehua*)" in the development of a "homogenized pan-Chinese music style," see Frederick Lau (2008, 27).

12. Cf. "Wang Erni": http://baike.baidu.com/view/1461137.htm (accessed April 8, 2013), and "Cui Miao": http://baike.baidu.com/view/338539.htm (accessed April 8, 2013).

13. For Xiao Shenyang's 2009 performance, see 20:10 in http://www.youtube.com/watch?v=_f7n1LMGjfs (accessed February 3, 2016). For Wen Shilong's performance, see http://v.youku.com/v_show/id_XMzM4MjYwMTg4.html (accessed February 1, 2016).

14. Stephen Jones mentions a "contest for drinking songs (*jiuqu dasai*)" held at the company's liquor factory in 2000 (2009, 212). In addition to Li Zhengfei becoming a spokesman, Li's wife became the head of a local distributor for the company.

15. I became aware of this trend during my fieldwork in Xi'an from 2011 to 2012.

16. The same singer, Shi Zhanming, shortly after winning the national contest, was grouped together with singers from northern Shaanxi, Inner Mongolia, and ethnic Tibetan areas in a concert in Beijing titled *The Sound of the Yellow River* (*Huanghe zhi sheng*) (Xue 2005).

17. Tian Qing went on to serve as director of the National Intangible Cultural Heritage Protection Center in Beijing (Rees 2016, 57).

References

Abrahams, Roger D. 1981. "Shouting Match at the Border: The Folklore of Display Events." In *"And Other Neighborly Names": Social Process and Cultural Image in Texas Folklore*, edited by Richard Bauman and Roger D. Abrahams, 303–22. Austin: University of Texas Press.

Bai Bingquan. 2005. *Minzu gechang fangfa yanjiu* [Research on Chinese-style singing techniques]. Rev. ed. Xi'an, China: Shaanxi renmin chubanshe.

Bauman, Richard. 2004. *A World of Others' Words: Cross-Cultural Perspectives on Intertextuality*. Oxford: Blackwell.

Bender, Mark. 2010. Review of *Women Playing Men: Yue Opera and Social Change in Twentieth-Century Shanghai*, by Jiang Jing. *Chinese Historical Review* 17 (1): 120–22.

Blacking, John. 1967. *Venda Children's Songs: A Study in Ethnomusicological Analysis*. Chicago: University of Chicago Press.

Bohlman, Philip Vilas. 2004. *The Music of European Nationalism: Cultural Identity and Modern History*. Santa Barbara, CA: ABC-CLIO.

Bourdieu, Pierre. 1993. *The Field of Cultural Production: Essays on Art and Literature*. New York: Columbia University Press.
Brunt, Shelley D. 2007. "'Changing Japan, Unchanging Japan': Shifting Visions of the Red and White Song Contest." In *A Song for Europe: Popular Music and Politics in the Eurovision Song Contest*, edited by Ivan Raykoff and Robert Deam Tobin, 171–82. Aldershot, UK: Ashgate.
Cai Nan. 2005. "Min'ge wangzi Abao de rensheng" [The life of folksong prince Abao]. *Beifang yinyue* (5): 26.
Chen Jie. 2008. "Nation, Ethnicity, and Cultural Strategies: Three Waves of Minority Representation in Post-1949 China." PhD diss., Rutgers University.
Cui Jian. 2013. "Wang Erni changge huojiang de lianpen" [Wang Erni sings song, wins awards, and receives washbasins]. *Yinyue shenghuo* (2): 38.
Cui Yingjie. 2013. "Zhongguo shaoshu minzu yinyue zai dianshi meiti zhong de chuanbo, fazhan yu bianqian fenxi: yi difang dianshitai, zhongyang dianshitai yuanshengtai yinyue dianshi jiemu de fazhan bianqian wei lie" [An analysis of the broadcast, development, and evolution of Chinese ethnic minority music on televised media: A case study of the development and evolution of original-ecology music television programs on regional television stations and China Central television stations]. MA thesis, Minzu University of China.
de Bruin, Joost, and Koos Zwaan. 2012. "Introduction: Adapting *Idols*." In *Adapting Idols: Authenticity, Identity and Performance in a Global Television Format*, edited by Koos Zwaan and Joost de Bruin, 1–7. Farnham, UK: Ashgate.
Du Rongfang, ed. 2005. *Manhandiao yishu yanjiu* [Research on the art of *manhandiao*]. Hohhot, China: Neimenggu renmin chubanshe.
Edwards, Louise, and Elaine Jeffreys, eds. 2010. *Celebrity in China*. Hong Kong: Hong Kong University Press.
E'erdunchaolu, Wang Shiyi, Da Sangbao, Zhang Shan, and Bao Yulin, eds. 1992. *Zhongguo minjian gequ jicheng: Neimenggu juan* [Grand compendium of Chinese folk songs: Inner Mongolia volume]. 2 vols. Beijing: Renmin yinyue chubanshe.
English, James F. 2005. *The Economy of Prestige: Prizes, Awards, and the Circulation of Cultural Value*. Cambridge, MA: Harvard University Press.
Feng Guangyu. 2004. "Yuantou huoshui tianlai zhi yin: xi kan CCTV xibu min'ge dianshi dasai" [Water flowing from the source, the sounds of nature: Happily watching the CCTV Western China TV Folksong Competition]. *Dangdai dianshi* (3): 28–30.
Foley, John Miles. 1991. *Immanent Art: From Structure to Meaning in Traditional Oral Epic*. Bloomington: Indiana University Press.
———. 1995. *The Singer of Tales in Performance*. Bloomington: Indiana University Press.
Fung, Anthony. 2006. "'Think Globally, Act Locally': China's Rendezvous with MTV." *Global Media and Communication* 2 (1): 71–88.
———. 2008. *Global Capital, Local Culture: Transnational Media Corporations in China*. New York: Peter Lang.
Gibbs, Levi Samuel. 2013. "Song King: Tradition, Social Change, and the Contemporary Art of a Northern Shaanxi Folksinger." PhD diss., The Ohio State University.
———. 2017. "Culture Paves the Way, Economics Comes to Sing the Opera: The Rhetoric of Chinese Folk Duets and Global Joint Ventures." *Asian Ethnology* 76 (1): 43–63.
———. 2018. *Song King: Connecting People, Places, and Past in Contemporary China*. Honolulu: University of Hawai'i Press.

Gorfinkel, Lauren. 2012. "From Transformation to Preservation: Music and Multi-Ethnic Unity on Television in China." In *Music as Intangible Cultural Heritage: Policy, Ideology, and Practice in the Preservation of East Asian Traditions*, edited by Keith Howard, 99–112. Farnham, UK: Ashgate.

Harris, Rachel. 2005. "Wang Luobin: Folk Song King of the Northwest or Song Thief? Copyright, Representation, and Chinese Folk Songs." *Modern China* 31 (3): 381–408.

Hockx, Michel. 1999. "Introduction." In *The Literary Field of Twentieth-Century China*, edited by Michel Hockx, 1–20. Honolulu: University of Hawai'i Press.

Huo Xianggui, ed. 2006. *Shaanbei min'ge daquan* [A complete collection of folk songs from northern Shaanxi]. 2 vols. Xi'an, China: Shaanxi renmin chubanshe.

Hymes, Dell. 1975. "Folklore's Nature and the Sun's Myth." *Journal of American Folklore* 88 (350): 345–69.

Jeffreys, Elaine, and Louise Edwards. 2010. "Celebrity/China." In *Celebrity in China*, edited by Louise Edwards and Elaine Jeffreys, 1–20. Hong Kong: Hong Kong University Press.

Jones, Stephen. 2009. *Ritual and Music of North China, Volume 2: Shaanbei*. Farnham, UK: Ashgate.

Kang Long. 2013. "Yan'an yi jiaoshi yanchang Yingwen ban Shaanbei min'ge shou guanzhu" [Teacher from Yan'an receives attention for performing northern Shaanxi folksongs in English]. *Yan'an ribao* [Yan'an daily], January 21, 2013. Accessed February 1, 2016. http://www.sn.xinhuanet.com/2013-01/21/c_114440609.htm (site discontinued).

Lau, Frederick. 2008. *Music in China: Experiencing Music, Expressing Culture*. New York; Oxford: Oxford University Press.

Liu Xiao and He Zhong, eds. 2012. "Xingguang dadao, Bi Fujian peng hong le duoshao ren?" [How many people have been raised to stardom by *Starlight Highway* and Bi Fujian?]. *Qingdao huabao* (6): 38–43.

Liu, Xin. 2000. *In One's Own Shadow: An Ethnographic Account of the Condition of Post-Reform Rural China*. Berkeley: University of California Press.

Liu Yulin et al. 2010. *Shaanbei min'ge tonglun* [A general survey of northern Shaanxi folksongs]. Xi'an, China: Shaanxi renmin chubanshe.

Lu Weiyang. 2007. "'Nü Abao' Li Yu: shi nian jianshou pu jiu Xingguang dadao" ["Female Abao" Li Yu: Sticking with it for ten years paves the way to *Starlight Highway*]. *Xinwen tiandi* (10): 29–32.

Marshall, P. David. 2006. "The Meanings of the Popular Music Celebrity: The Construction of Distinctive Authenticity." In *The Celebrity Culture Reader*, edited by P. David Marshall, 196–222. New York; London: Routledge.

Meizel, Katherine. 2007. "*Idol* Thoughts: Nationalism in the Pan-Arab Vocal Competition *Superstar*." In *A Song for Europe: Popular Music and Politics in the Eurovision Song Contest*, edited by Ivan Raykoff and Robert Deam Tobin, 159–69. Aldershot, UK: Ashgate.

Miao Meng. 2008. "Huangtu lian'ge—Shaanbei gewang Wang Xiangrong sumiao" [Love song of the yellow earth: A sketch of the northern Shaanxi folksong king Wang Xiangrong]. *Renmin yinyue* (11): 71–73.

Nan Xiangyu. 2003. "Shaanbei gewang Wang Xiangrong" [The king of northern Shaanxi folksongs: Wang Xiangrong]. *Qianjin luntan* (5): 23–24.

Noyes, Dorothy. 2003. "Group." In *Eight Words for the Study of Expressive Culture*, edited by Burt Feintuch, 7–41. Urbana; Chicago: University of Illinois Press.

Qian Wang and Jeroen de Kloet. 2016. "From 'Nothing to My Name' to 'I Am a Singer': Market, Capital, and Politics in the Chinese Music Industry." In *Handbook of Cultural and Creative Industries in China*, edited by Michael Keane, 293–310. Cheltenham, UK; Northampton, MA: Edward Elgar.

Qiao Jianzhong. 2010. "Dashan de qingyun—Shi Zhanming he ta yanchang de Zuoquan min'ge" [The feeling of the mountains: Shi Zhanming and his Zuoquan folksongs]. *Renmin yinyue* (5): 42–43.

Raykoff, Ivan, and Robert Deam Tobin, eds. 2007. *A Song for Europe: Popular Music and Politics in the Eurovision Song Contest*. Aldershot, UK: Ashgate.

Rees, Helen. 2016. "Environmental Crisis, Culture Loss, and a New Musical Aesthetic: China's 'Original Ecology Folksongs' in Theory and Practice." *Ethnomusicology* 60 (1): 53–88.

Rojek, Chris. 2001. *Celebrity*. London: Reaktion Books.

Schechner, Richard. 1985. *Between Theater and Anthropology*. Philadelphia: University of Pennsylvania Press.

Schein, Louisa. 2010. "Flexible Celebrity: A Half-Century of Miao Pop." In *Celebrity in China*, edited by Louise Edwards and Elaine Jeffreys, 145–68. Hong Kong: Hong Kong University Press.

Schimmelpenninck, Antoinet. 1997. *Chinese Folk Songs and Folk Singers: Shan'ge Traditions in Southern Jiangsu*. CHIME Studies in East Asian Music 1. Leiden, Netherlands: CHIME (Chinese Music Europe) Foundation.

Shin, Hyunjoon, and Pil Ho Kim. 2006. "IASPM's 13th Biennial Conference: A Review from the Periphery; 'Making Music, Making Meaning,' Rome, 25–30 July 2005." *Popular Music* 25 (1): 127–30.

Small, Christopher. 1998. *Musicking: The Meanings of Performing and Listening*. Middletown, CT: Wesleyan University Press.

Song Fei. 2009. "Ta cong huangtu gaoyuan zoulai: ji Xingguang dadao 09 niandu di-qi ge yue guanjun Cui Miao" [She came from Loess Plateau: On the seventh monthly champion of the 2009 season of *Starlight Highway*, Cui Miao]. *Shidai renwu* (10): 54–56.

Stillman, Amy Kuʻuleialoha. 1996. "Hawaiian Hula Competitions: Event, Repertoire, Performance, Tradition." *Journal of American Folklore* 109 (434): 357–80.

Tan, Shzr Ee. 2005. "Manufacturing and Consuming Culture: Fakesong in Singapore." *Ethnomusicology Forum* 14 (1): 83–106.

Thurston, Timothy. 2013. "'Careful Village's Grassland Dispute': An A mdo Dialect Tibetan Crosstalk Performance by Sman bla skyabs." *CHINOPERL: Journal of Chinese Oral and Performing Literature* 32 (2): 156–81.

Tian Qing. 2004. "Min'ge yu minzu changfa: zai Shanxi Zuoquan di er jie nanbei min'ge leitaisai xueshu yantaohui shang de fayan" [Folksongs and "national singing style": A speech given at the scholarly conference of the Second National Chinese Folksong Competition held in Zuoquan, Shanxi]. *Yishu pinglun* (10): 8–13.

Tuohy, Sue. 1999. "The Social Life of Genre: The Dynamics of Folksong in China." *Asian Music* 30 (2): 39–86.

Turner, Graeme. 2004. *Understanding Celebrity*. London: SAGE.

Wang Bin. 2010. "Zhanming de lu you duochang" [How long has Zhanming's journey been?]. *Guangbo gexuan* (5): 4–6.

Wang Facai. 2014. "Wang Erni: yaodongli feichu de xiaoxiao niao rongdeng yangshi chunwan" [Wang Erni: Tiny bird that flew out of a cave dwelling gloriously ascends to the China Central Television Spring Festival Gala]. *Yinyue shenghuo* (4): 55–58.

Wong, Isabel K. F. 1984. "*Geming Gequ*: Songs for the Education of the Masses." In *Popular Chinese Literature and Performing Arts: The People's Republic of China, 1949–1979*, edited by Bonnie S. McDougall, 112–43. Berkeley; Los Angeles: University of California Press.
Wu Tong. 2006. "Abao: Cong fangyangwa zou shang Xingguang dadao" [Abao: From shepherd boy to *Starlight Highway*]. *Wenhua yuekan* (2): 30–33.
Wu Yue. 2005. "Shandandan kaihua hongyanyan: xintianyou gewang Abao de gushi" [Wild lilies bloom a brilliant red: The story of the king of *Xintianyou* songs, Abao]. *Minsu wenxue* (1): 4–10.
———. 2010. "Chaozai de xintianyou: Shaanbei min'geshou 113 wan shang Xingguang dadao zhangdan diaocha" [*Xintianyou* overload: An investigation into the 1,130,000 RMB bill for going on *Starlight Highway*]. *Yinyue shenghuo* (8): 9–13.
Xiao, Hui. 2006. "Narrating a Happy China through a Crying Game: A Case Study of Post-Mao Reality Shows." *China Media Research* 2 (3): 59–67.
Xiong Xiaoyu and Li Qin. 2011. "Hongge, honggeshou yu hongge jingshen—zai dangdai shehui yiyi xia dui Zhongguo Honggehui chenggong de sikao" [Red songs, red singers, and red song spirit: Reflections on the success of China's *Red Song Contest* from the perspective of contemporary social meaning]. *Huanghe zhi sheng* (12): 96–97.
Xue Ming. 2005. "Gesheng fei 'yang': yangguan gewang Shi Zhanming de gushi" [A voice that flies "like sheep": The story of the Shepherd King of Songs, Shi Zhanming]. *Minsu wenxue* (1): 11–14.
Yang Hong. 2006. *Dangdai shehui bianqian zhong de errentai yanjiu: Hequ minjian xiban yu diyu wenhua zhi hudong guanxi* [Research on *errentai* in the midst of contemporary social change: The mutual relationship between Hequ folk theatrical troupes and regional culture]. Beijing: Zhongyang yinyue xueyuan chubanshe.
Yang Xin. 2011. *From Beauty Fear to Beauty Fever: A Critical Study of Contemporary Chinese Female Writers*. New York: Peter Lang.
Zhang Shengliang. 2008. "Lun 'Zhongguo Honggehui' de xingqi" [On the rise of China's *Red Song Contest*]. *Zuojia zazhi* (1): 256–57.
Zhao Le. 2010. "Huangtuqi shi Shaanbei min'ge de hun" [Emanations from the yellow earth are the soul of northern Shaanxi folksongs]. *Guangbo gexuan* 334: 4–6.
ZSSX (Zhonggong Shaanxi shengwei xuanchuanbu) [Propaganda Department of the Chinese Communist Party Shaanxi Provincial Party Committee], ed. 2009. *Shoujie Shaanbei min'ge yijie quanguo xueshu yantaohui* [Inaugural national academic symposium on the translation and introduction of northern Shaanxi folksongs]. Xi'an, China: Xi'an Conservatory of Music.

LEVI S. GIBBS is Assistant Professor of Chinese Literature and Culture in the Asian Societies, Cultures, and Languages Program at Dartmouth College. His research focuses on the social roles of singers and songs in contemporary China and the cultural politics of regional identity. He is author of *Song King: Connecting People, Places, and Past in Contemporary China*.

3 Dynamic Inheritance

Representative Works and the Authoring of Tradition in Chinese Dance

Emily E. Wilcox

Thinking through the relationship between artists and traditions in contemporary China requires considering the ways in which socialist modernity—a force that shaped China for much of the twentieth century—fostered new notions of heritage and culture. In his oft-cited "Talks at the Yan'an Forum on Literature and Art" in 1942, Mao Zedong famously called on China's socialist writers and artists to make art serve politics. He also proposed a new approach to creating art; by studying the everyday lives of the common people, Mao proclaimed, artists would create new artistic works that not only promoted new political ideals but also drew heavily on folk culture.

The expectation that revolutionary artists would study, adapt, and promote folk forms was a central tenet of Chinese socialist culture. In his 1942 talks, Mao referred to folk forms as "the rich, lively language of the masses," and he believed that folk forms could most effectively communicate new political ideas to the common people (Mao 1996, 461). This idea of combining new political ideals with folk forms was expressed in the phrase "socialist in content and national in form." First articulated by Joseph Stalin in 1925, and adopted by Mao in the late 1930s, this was the key structure of Chinese revolutionary culture during the period between 1937 and 1965.[1] Although the imperative to employ national forms was challenged during the last decade of Maoist rule from 1966 to 1976—reflected through the dominance of ballet over national dance forms during this period—the emphasis on national forms reemerged in the post-1976 era and continues today. The process of constructing Chinese dance as a "national form" (*minzu xingshi*), which was first popularized during the socialist period, still shapes the creation of Chinese dance in the People's Republic of China (PRC) today.

The term "Chinese dance" refers to a form of modern concert dance developed in the twentieth century that claims to have a basis in performance forms indigenous to the geographical regions included in modern-day China. Examples of indigenous performance forms that have inspired Chinese dance include religious rituals, social dance, local opera theater, martial arts, and historical court dance. Most styles of Chinese dance have undergone a three-part evolution: First, professional dancers conducted field research with folk artists and adapted elements of the folk forms they learned and observed into modern stage productions. Second, movements from successful stage productions were integrated into conservatory training curricula, where they became the basic techniques used to train new generations of professional dancers. Third, the popularization of these stage productions and training curricula led to their imitation by amateurs, spawning often simpler versions practiced in parks, primary schools, and community centers. This chapter is concerned primarily with the first part of this evolution: the process through which folk forms, which are embedded in community life and vary incredibly across space and time, are transformed into professionalized Chinese dance styles that are standardized across the country and performed in modern stage contexts. It thus seeks to understand how the relatively unified form of Chinese dance evolves, in an ongoing process, out of a seemingly endless variety of diverse folk forms.

To discuss Chinese dance, it is necessary to have a grasp of some basic vocabulary. One of the most confusing terms in this context is "folk dance" (*minjian wu*), because it can mean both indigenous folk performance—especially social dances performed by rural communities—and the professionalized styles of Chinese concert dance created from folk forms. Among Chinese dancers and dance scholars, there have been many attempts to clarify this language, for example by using the term "nationalized folk dance" (*minzu minjian wu*) or "academy folk dance" (*xueyuanpai minjian wu*) to refer to professionalized Chinese dance styles and "original-environment folk dance" (*yuanshengtai wudao*) to refer to indigenous folk performance. The problem is complex because the term "folk" has multiple different meanings in the context of Chinese dance: it can mean popular as opposed to elite, amateur as opposed to professional, or unofficial as opposed to official. Depending on which meaning is being used, the term "folk dance" may have a different connotation in each different context (Xu R. 2010; Jin 2012).

When the modern concept of "Chinese dance" (*Zhongguo wudao*) first emerged, it was defined mainly in opposition to Western dance styles, specifically ballet and Euro-American modern dance. Since the early 1950s, Chinese dance has included three main categories: (1) "Han folk dance" (*Hanzu minjian wu*) refers to regional dances of the majority Han ethnicity, such as Northeast yangge (*Dongbei yangge*), Anhui flower drum lamp (*Anhui huagudeng*), and

Yunnan flower lamp (*Yunnan huadeng*); (2) "minority dance" (*shaoshu minzu wudao*), first conceived of in the late 1940s as "frontier dance" (*bianjiang wu*), refers to regional dances of non-Han ethnic communities, such as Uyghur dance (*Weiwu'erzu wu*), Mongol dance (*Menggu wu*), and Tibetan dance (*Zangzu wu*); and (3) "Chinese classical dance" (*Zhongguo gudian wu*) originally referred to dances derived from Chinese indigenous theater (*xiqu*) forms, especially Peking opera (*Jingju*) and Kun opera (*Kunqu*). Today, Chinese classical dance also includes newer schools of technique developed from research on historical court performance and religious artifacts. Two of the most prominent of these are the Han-Tang and Dunhuang schools.

Other types of professional concert dance have also developed in China during the twentieth century that are not typically included in the category of Chinese dance. These include "new dance" (*xinxing wudao*), "Oriental dance" (*Dongfang wu*), "Chinese ballet" (*Zhongguo balei*), "modern dance" (*xiandai wu*), "dancesport" (*guobiao wu*), and "hip hop/street dance" (*jie wu*). The main reason these dance forms are not included in the category of Chinese dance is that they are believed to derive their primary movement vocabularies from nonnative performance practices. The core feature that has historically defined Chinese dance in contrast to these other dance styles is its presumed basis in movement vocabularies and techniques derived from performance practices native to the geographic regions of contemporary China.

Chinese dance presents a conceptual challenge to many common ways that scholars and laypeople in Western Europe and North America think about dance. This is because Chinese dance confounds the common Euro-American idea that dance forms that encourage the continuation of indigenous practices are "traditional," while dances that encourage individual innovation are "modern." This modern/traditional dichotomy is virtually useless in the Chinese dance context because Chinese dance pursues both of these things simultaneously. In other words, Chinese dance is a recent invention that aims to express new experiences and ideas while also placing great value on studying and learning from dance practices of the past. The first widely recognized examples of Chinese dance choreography date to the late 1930s and early 1940s, making Chinese dance as an artistic phenomenon slightly younger than Euro-American modern dance. Furthermore, Chinese dance practitioners have always placed a high value on the importance of individual interpretation as an essential component of cultural continuity. For these reasons, a new vocabulary is necessary for moving beyond the traditional/modern dyad when thinking about creative practices in Chinese dance.

Dynamic inheritance, the idea put forth in this chapter, offers one way of avoiding some of the traps of the traditional/modern dichotomy when thinking about relationships between past and present and between individual innovations and shared cultural legacies in contemporary dance making. Inspired by the work of Chinese dance scholars, this concept seeks to translate and theorize basic assumptions about dance creation and criticism that undergird much of the current scholarship produced by dance scholars working in China. Because the work of Chinese scholars is not often read by scholars working in North America and Western Europe, there exists a disconnect in the way the two groups envision and discuss ideas of culture, identity, and innovation in dance. This chapter seeks to close this gap and to generate possibilities for more exchange of ideas between these different groups.

Apart from questions pertaining to dance, this chapter also addresses broader ideas about relationships between individual invention and cultural inheritance across the arts. In the conceptual framework of dynamic inheritance, individual artists play an important role in the production of Chinese culture, and their contributions are understood as simultaneously innovative and preservationist. Thus dynamic inheritance, as a way of thinking about and doing art, makes it possible to see individual creativity as necessary to the continuation of cultural heritage rather than opposed to it. For artists who wish to draw on existing cultural traditions and at the same time develop their own independent creative voice, dynamic inheritance can provide a method of articulating and carrying out such work that offers a fresh perspective on existing categories.

Dynamic Inheritance: Early Articulations

It is difficult to locate a precise historical moment when dynamic inheritance emerged as the dominant paradigm for artistic creation in China. Many identify 1937–1938 as the time when the idea of "national forms" came to the fore in Yan'an (Holm 1991; McDougall and Louie 1997; H. Wang 2011). Others, however, note earlier interest in the collection and modernization of folk forms, beginning as early as the turn of the twentieth century (Hung 1985; C. Liu 2010; L. Liu 2012; S. Liu 2013). Regardless of how the formation of this paradigm is dated, it is clear that by the 1940s, it had become compulsory for artists and intellectuals affiliated with the Chinese Communist Party to study and adapt folk culture in their work. As Brian DeMare argues, the use of folk forms—what he calls "concessions to local cultural traditions"—was the only way communist-directed artists and intellectuals, consisting largely of foreign-educated urbanites, could attract and communicate with rural audiences (2015, 8).

Apart from its practical uses as a tool of political education, leftist artists and intellectuals in 1940s China viewed the study and creative adaptation of folk art as necessary for building a modern Chinese national culture. Xiaobing Tang describes this process as part of "the imperative of cultural transformation that was at the core of China's search for modernity" (2015, 19). Thus, in China, as elsewhere, the growth of interest in folk forms was closely tied to modern nationalism. Although China was never fully colonized like other parts of Asia, the combination of Western and Japanese imperialism also led to the formation of a postcolonial sensibility (Wilcox 2018). Soviet models played an important role in this process, since Lenin and Stalin both conceptualized the promotion of national culture as progressive and anti-imperialist (Duara 2004). However, dynamic inheritance, as a way of transforming folk forms into national culture, was not a purely Soviet transplant. It was forged through domestic processes and took on qualities and patterns specific to China's local conditions.

In the field of dance, one of these local conditions included the diverse backgrounds of the individuals who developed China's socialist dance culture. When the People's Republic of China was established in 1949, a significant portion of the artists recruited to participate in the new PRC cultural fields had not been working in Communist-occupied areas during the wartime period of 1937 to 1949 (DeMare 2015). This was also true in the field of dance. Dai Ailian (1916–2006), the first president of the China Dancers Association established in 1949, was born and raised outside China and spent most of the wartime years in Chongqing, Shanghai, and the United States (Glasstone 2007). Similarly, Liang Lun (b. 1921), who headed major PRC dance institutions in the Guangdong area after 1949, spent the wartime years in Kunming, Hong Kong, and Southeast Asia (Liang 2011). Although Dai and Liang had not been directly involved in the Communist cultural movement prior to 1949, their ideas played a key role in shaping the trajectory of Chinese dance in the PRC due to the leadership positions they held in important early PRC dance institutions. In this sense, their work was just as central to the development of Chinese dance as that of figures such as Wu Xiaobang (1906–1995), the first vice president of the China Dancers Association, who had a longer history of Chinese Communist Party affiliation.[2]

One of the first publications that envisioned the creation of Chinese dance on a dynamic inheritance model was Dai Ailian's essay "The First Step in Developing Chinese Dance," published in the Nationalist Party newspaper *Central Daily* in Chongqing in 1946. The essay set out Dai's vision for the construction of a new dance style—what she called both "Chinese dance" (*Zhongguo wudao*) and "Chinese modern dance" (*Zhongguo xiandai wu*)—on the basis of indigenous and folk performance (Dai 1946, 8). According to Dai, China had a rich dance history and a plethora of living indigenous dance traditions, among which she included theatrical dance, religious dance, and popular folk dance. What China lacked, Dai argued, was modern concert dance. Born in Trinidad as a third-generation Chinese and later trained in ballet and modern dance in England, Dai had received most of her own dance training abroad, before she moved to China in 1941. During her time abroad, Dai had seen modernized versions of Indian, Japanese, and Javanese classical and folk dances, and she wondered why she had not seen Chinese dance (Glasstone 2007). In her own words, Dai came to China in order to "learn currently existing Chinese dance" and help contribute to the creation of a new, modern Chinese dance form (Dai 1946, 8).

In her essay, Dai put forth her plan for creating this new dance form. An important part of Dai's plan was rejecting the use of dance techniques she called "foreign" (*waiguo de*). Dai writes:

> For the past three years the Chinese Dance Art Society worked hard to create Chinese dance dramas. The narrative content was Chinese, and the performers were Chinese; yet, we cannot say that this was truly Chinese dance drama. We used foreign technique and footwork to tell the story—like using a foreign language to tell a Chinese tale—and this was quite obvious to the audience. We can say that the work of the past three years took the first step in establishing dance as an independent art [in China]. But, as for creating "Chinese dance," that was a mistaken direction. It was because of a lack of knowledge about Chinese dance customs that we followed this method. (1946, 8)[3]

As this passage suggests, Dai viewed the study and understanding of local dance culture, especially native dance techniques and forms, as a necessary condition for the creation of Chinese dance. The use of Chinese content and performers alone, she argued, was not sufficient if the movement techniques were still foreign. Thus, Dai argued that the only way to create Chinese dance correctly was to first go about conducting research on native performance practices, then to use these practices as the basis for new choreography.

Dai's plan for creating Chinese dance also included ideas about what counted as native performance practices. For her, it was important that Han and non-Han sources be considered equally. "If we want to develop Chinese dance," Dai writes, "as the first step we must collect dance materials from all nationalities around the country, then broadly synthesize them and add development" (1946, 8). The initial result of Dai's vision can be seen in the 1946 performance she staged in Chongqing together with Peng Song (b. 1916), local Tibetan and Xinjiang compatriot associations, and students and teachers at Tao Xingzhi's Chongqing-based Yucai Art School (*Zhongyang ribao* 1946; Dong and Long 2008, 8–11, 579–86; Tong 2012, 73, 87–88). The essay cited above doubled as Dai's welcome speech during this show. Titled *Frontier Music and Dance Meeting* (*Bianjiang yinyue wudao dahui*), the program included dance works inspired by Tibetan, Qiang, Jiarong, Yao, Han, Luoluo (Yi), and Uyghur performance practices. Most Chinese dance historians consider this performance the first production of modern "Chinese dance" featuring both Han and minority styles.

Inherent to Dai's vision of Chinese dance was that indigenous performance practices must undergo change to make them appealing to new audiences. Describing the approach used to create the works in the *Frontier Music and*

Dance Meeting, Dai writes, "Introducing [original folk] dances onto the stage would be too simple, [so] out of consideration for formal organization, some have undergone various levels of revision. A few of the works are performed following the originals, while others have been developed and adapted according to either direct or indirect material" (1946, 8). With this explanation, Dai made it clear to her audience that what they were about to see was not purely "authentic" folk dance, in the sense that it was not a perfect replication of dances as they might have existed in their original contexts. Rather, these were folk dances that had been revised and reinterpreted to suit the specific needs of this event.

The newspaper spread in which Dai's essay appeared contained photos and descriptions from the performance program that also indicated the adaptive and creative processes that separated these works from authentic folk dance. The description of the piece "Mute Carries the Cripple," for example, one of Dai's solo dances, begins: "This dance *takes and adapts* elements from Guangxi-style theater" (*Zhongyang ribao* 1946; emphasis added). The description for another piece performed by Dai states that it was "choreographed *according to*" a popular folk song (*Zhongyang ribao* 1946; emphasis added). In each case, the words "takes and adapts" and "according to" signal processes of revision and change on the part of the adaptor or the performer, in this case Dai. In an ideal world, Dai hoped that all indigenous dances across China could be studied and adapted so that one day they could be performed on modern dance stages. She writes, "Due to economic constraints, dance researchers have limited time to travel extensively and carry out comprehensive research exploring the origins of every type of dance material. In the future, it is hoped that people with an interest in dance work will receive the necessary support to complete a full study of all forms of dance in China and use these materials to establish a new Chinese modern dance for the stage" (1946, 8).

From this description, it is clear that Dai envisioned the making of Chinese dance as an ongoing process that would take the work of teams of dance researchers and significant financial support over a long period of time. Chinese dance, for her, was something that did not inherently exist in Chinese culture but had to be created through the sustained and conscious effort of numerous dance scholars and artists.

Just one year after Dai's publication, Liang Lun outlined a similar project in an essay titled "The Problem of Making Dance Chinese" (1947), which he published in a newsletter of the China Song and Dance Drama Art Society (*Zhongguo gewuju yishe*) while on tour in Southeast Asia. Liang had conducted field research among minority groups in China's southwest and had staged a collaborative production of adapted folk dances in 1946 in Kunming (Tong 2012, 86–87). Liang's essay, like Dai's, places high importance on the use of native dance technique. Specifically, Liang calls for the rejection of "Western" (*Xiyang de*) dance styles in the making of Chinese dance. "Previous dance was just using Western technique to express Chinese content. To unearth the dance of the Chinese folk, to create a dance form possessing a truly Chinese air and style is the correct path of today's Chinese new dance movement," Liang writes (1947, 13). Liang also linked the creation of Chinese dance explicitly to nationalism. "Only when Chinese dance art has become Chinese at base," he writes, "capable of fully expressing the citizen spirit of China, will it have its own status in the world" (1947, 13). Liang's statement offers a direct challenge to those who believed that learning European art was the only way to gain cultural recognition in the global arena. In this sense, although they were working outside Communist-occupied areas, both Liang and Dai closely aligned with Mao Zedong's principle that new Chinese culture should be "national in form."

The performance program notes that accompany Liang's essay show that, like Dai, he had put these principles into action in his own works. The notes describe Liang's "Marco Polo Bridge Call and Answer Dance" as being *"adapted from* the folk image of a herdsman, with much folk local color" (1947, 13; emphasis added). Two other dances, described as narrative dance-dramas, are said to be *"based on* Yunnan flower drum forms," with content set in the past ten years (1947, 13; emphasis added). The notes conclude, "All of these dances take folk dance as their foundation. After researching its spirit and patterns, and doing one's best to preserve its authentic style and originality, they then imbue it with a new theme, re-organize it, and re-create it. Whether this method is correct or not must depend on the feedback of the audience" (1947, 13).

The problem of method to which Liang alludes here became a driving question for China's professional dancers after the founding of the PRC in 1949. How would artists working in the socialist state carry out the process of studying and adapting folk forms? It is this question that led to the construction of dynamic inheritance as a methodology.

Dynamic Inheritance: An Artistic Methodology

After the founding of the PRC in 1949, the prescriptive to develop national forms that could express new socialist ideals, promote a diverse native culture, and appeal to a broad public took on heightened importance (Hung 2011; Wilcox 2016b). To facilitate this process, as part of the institutionalization of art in New China, there emerged an almost scientific methodology for creating Chinese dance based on folk forms. By following a set of steps, cultural workers in the dance field could identify and document folk forms, analyze and organize their findings, and use this knowledge to produce new artistic works.

Based on a survey of dance writings from 1949 to 1966, the following chart (table 3.1) schematizes the methodology of dynamic inheritance that was conceived and put into practice by professional dancers, including Dai, Liang,

Table 3.1. Dynamic Inheritance as a Methodology: Key terms used in Chinese texts describing how to create new works of Chinese dance. These terms reflect parts of the dynamic inheritance methodology.

Activities	*wajue* (to excavate)	*shequ/paoqi* (to absorb/to abandon)	*zhengli* (to organize)	*chuangzao* (to create)
Objects	*sucai* (basic materials)	*fengge/weidao* (style/flavor)	*tese/texing* (distinctive characteristics)	*dianxing/ dianxingxing* (type/typicality)
Goals	*baohu* (to protect)	*fazhan* (to develop)	*jicheng* (to inherit)	*fayang* (to promote)

and others who worked with them in state-sponsored PRC dance institutions, during this time.[4] This methodology was applied in all three subfields of Chinese dance—including Han folk dance, minority dance, and Chinese classical dance—and it continues to inform research, teaching, creation, and criticism in all three subfields of Chinese dance in the PRC today. The dynamic inheritance methodology was designed to ensure three principles: (1) that indigenous performance practices would serve as the foundation upon which new dances were built; (2) that artists would be systematic and thorough in their study of indigenous performance; and (3) that artists would be innovative in their adaptation of indigenous sources to serve the tastes and needs of contemporary audiences. As a method for creating dance, dynamic inheritance placed research at the center while at the same time giving significant interpretative responsibility to dance artists.[5]

As outlined in table 3.1, dynamic inheritance methodology has three major components: activities, objects, and goals. Examining these sections one by one shows the process that dance artists follow to create Chinese dance works. Starting with "activities," the first step in the dynamic inheritance process is "to excavate" (*wajue*). This term borrows an image from archaeology in which the researcher digs into the ground, literally unearthing precious artifacts. In the context of Chinese dance, excavation refers to a process of field research known as "collecting customs" (*caifeng*), in which the artist acts as a kind of ethnographer: the artist visits a community, observes dances in the local context, learns parts of the technique, interviews expert practitioners, all while documenting the entire process.[6] The process of excavation thus includes several subprocesses, including documentation and what is broadly known as "collection" (*shouji*). This can include activities such as taking notes or doing sketches, conducting video or audio recordings, and learning to perform certain movement sequences. In the excavation process, researchers attend not only to movements framed as formal performances but also to everyday activities, such as manual labor, cooking, or interacting with friends. Any of these could be legitimate subjects of study for the dance ethnographer.

After excavation, the next step is "to absorb/to abandon" (*shequ/paoqi*). This is the stage in which dancers make decisions about what to include and what not to include when they document and collect folk forms. In his autobiography, Wu Xiaobang describes this process as follows: "When you go down [to conduct field research] you must observe and listen to everything. Within that, there will be dregs (*zaopo*) and there will be cream (*jinghua*). The dregs and the cream are always mixed together, masquerading like pearls mixed with fish eyes. We must pick out the pearls among the fish eyes" (1982, 98). Here, this process refers to the collection of minority dances in 1952, when Wu was assigned the position as founding head of the cultural work troupe attached to the Central Institute of Nationalities, predecessor to the Central Nationalities Song and Dance Ensemble.

The language of selection and discernment was also applied in the creation of Chinese classical dance. Choe Seung-hui (aka Sai Shōki/Choi Seunghee, 1911–1969), a world-renowned Korean dancer who led the construction of Chinese classical dance in the early PRC, makes the following statement in her article "The Future of Chinese Dance Art," published in the *People's Daily* in 1951: "Regarding the work of organizing Chinese classical dance, it can broadly be divided and carried out in two stages.... Thus, the first stage should be focused on absorbing (*shequ*) the most typical, beautiful, martial, and uniquely representative movements and positions from within classical dance. This work of absorbing should on the one hand strive to preserve its original distinctiveness, and on the other to abandon (*paoqi*) some unnecessary movements" (Cui 1951, 5).

As these two passages show, the absorb/abandon dyad introduces an active and self-conscious process of selection into the dance artist's role in relation to indigenous performance materials. While the precise guidelines for what should be absorbed and what should be abandoned at any given time might be different—depending on changing cultural policies, audience expectations, and professional preferences—the act of deciding what elements to include and what to expel was normalized as a necessary part of the dynamic inheritance process. As a methodology, dynamic inheritance instructs individual artists to preserve only what they see fit from the indigenous performance activities they observe and study.

The third phase of activities is "to organize" (*zhengli*). This is one of the most ubiquitous concepts in the history of modern Chinese dance, and it continues to be used regularly in textbooks, scholarly writing, and everyday language among Chinese dance professionals. Etymologically, the term combines the characters "zheng," meaning wholeness or neatness, with "li," meaning reason or principle. The character "li" occurs frequently in terms related to management, philosophy, and the natural sciences, and it suggests the internal rules or patterns that give something order. In the context of dance, "to organize" thus means to find the internal logic of a set of movements gathered through field research and then to arrange them in an orderly fashion according to this logic, so that they form a comprehensible whole. One of the most common ways to "organize" dance movements is to break them down according to body part: hand movements in one list, arm movements in another, foot movements in another, and so on. Organization has a number of practical uses: it allows different folk forms to be compared and used interchangeably; it allows dancers unfamiliar with the forms to more clearly understand and learn them; and, perhaps most importantly, it helps to transform the folk performances from social and cultural complexes to formalized artistic vocabularies. Regardless of the structuring principle used, "organizing" inevitably introduces changes to the folk forms. The regularization and rationalization that occurs in this process can cause folk forms to lose their idiosyncratic or synthetic character, since components that do not fit into the new structure are often left out or transformed. Although organization is a necessary part of the dynamic inheritance process, dancers are typically warned not to go too far. The Chinese proverb "cutting the foot to fit the shoe" is sometimes used to describe overzealous organization (Li, Gao, and Zhu 2004).

The final component of activities is "to create" (*chuangzao*). This is the stage at which the dance artist's role as innovator is most apparent, since it requires him or her to generate a new, original dance work using the materials acquired from research into folk forms. In this context, "creation" also implies authorship, in the sense that dance artists have usually been listed by name as the choreographers of new works they have devised.[7] The main goal of the creation process is to make folk forms appealing to new audiences. The idea is that because people's ways of life are in flux, and audiences are experiencing dance in new social contexts and conditions, performance practices must constantly adapt to remain current with the times. Reflecting on works presented by the Inner Mongolia Cultural Work Troupe in 1949, Troupe director Bu He explains how his choreographers approached the problem of creation in their work:

> Initially, [our choreographers] took untouched folk dances and placed them on stage. Yet, average people did not like it, because once those dances that were normally performed in squares and on the grassland were put on stage, their form became limited, and they weren't as good as the originals. It is important to point out that Mongol people [in the new society] require things with new content and new forms. The old ones already can no longer satisfy them. Therefore, [our choreographers and musicians] created contemporary song and dance stories, and these have been welcomed by the majority of Mongol people. (Fang M. 1949b, 4)

Here, Bu He notes two main factors driving new creation: (1) changes in the spaces in which dances are presented; and (2) changes in people's preferences for new cultural experiences. By making innovations to existing folk forms, dance artists help these forms adapt to new spaces and new preferences, ensuring that they continue to be appreciated.

Apart from activities, the dynamic inheritance methodology also specifies the objects of study that are to be used in the creation of new Chinese dance works. The first and most important of these are "basic materials" (*sucai/yuansu*), generally thought of as the ingredients of a dance choreography. In theory, each subgenre of Chinese dance has an almost unlimited number of basic materials that could be used to create new dance works. Thus, when going out to conduct fieldwork, the dancer expects and hopes to find new basic materials each time. These might be large, such as a ritual frame, a story, or a rhythmic sequence, or they might be small, such as a prop, a technical trick, or a way of holding a specific body part. Special occasions like weddings and festivals are considered to be the best times to find basic materials for use in dance works; however, many choreographers have also made ingenious use of basic materials drawn from everyday life, such as food preparation, transportation, or children's games. Part of the challenge of "excavation" is being constantly alert to activities or behaviors that could be basic materials for a new dance work, and the limits of what could become basic material for a dance piece are really limited only by the dancer's creativity. New materials are constantly appearing in the world all the time as contemporary communities adopt new technologies, habits, and ways of living. Even in the case of historical dance, the discovery of new archaeological sites and artifacts makes possible the ongoing emergence of new basic materials.

Whereas "basic materials" are concrete and identifiable, "style" and "flavor" (*fengge/weidao*) are more abstract. Often, dancers talk about "style" and "flavor" in relation to regional or ethnic categories of Chinese dance—Shandong Jiaozhou-style yangge or Uyghur Dolan, for example—and they serve as the broader aesthetic qualities that identify works within a group as belonging together. In theory, style and flavor should be shared among works that belong to the same category, while basic materials will differ from one work to the next even in the same category. When the process of creation has led a choreographer too far from authentic folk forms, the phrases "lacking in style" or "weak in flavor" will be applied by critics to express disapproval. This indicates that the piece has not been successful in reinterpreting the original material, because it has lost the identifying characteristics of the indigenous form it is supposed to be inheriting. Style and flavor are considered to be the most difficult aspects of Chinese dance to fully master. Because it is difficult to find the right balance between learning from folk forms and enacting personal innovations, displaying a firm grasp of flavor and style while also being creative is considered the mark of a true expert.

"Distinctive characteristics" (*tese/texing*) and "type/typicality" (*dianxing/dianxingxing*) are also qualities that distinguish categories within Chinese dance.

However, they refer to more specific and identifiable qualities than style and flavor. Furthermore, while style and flavor are considered to be relatively continuous through time, distinctive characteristics and type/typicality have more potential for change. In the process of dynamic inheritance, it is common for the creation of new dance works to expand and at times alter what are considered to be the "distinctive characteristics" and "typical" elements of a given dance style. In the case of Chinese classical dance, the dance dramas *Flowers and Rain on the Silk Road* (*Silu hua yu*), premiered in 1979, and *Dancers of the Tongque Stage* (*Tongque ji*), premiered in 1985, fundamentally changed what was considered "typical" for Chinese classical dance. Their popularity introduced two new schools within Chinese classical dance, the "Dunhuang" school and the "Han-Tang" school, respectively (Zhao 1980; Jin 2012; Wilcox 2012). Similarly, the work *Yellow River* (*Huanghe*), premiered in 1988, challenged what was considered "typical" and "distinctive" for Chinese classical dance across gender lines. Summarizing the impact of this piece, Chinese dance critic Jin Hao writes, "[*Yellow River*] changed the previously existing gendered contrast between soft and hard movement in the movement vocabulary, making the male and female dancers both move more toward a middle gender in the form of their movement language" (Jia 2006, 302). Although they broke with existing practices when they first appeared, the popularity of these works meant that they were ultimately accepted as "distinctive" and "typical." Today, students of Chinese classical dance regularly study these works, and critics consider them canonical examples within the style.

The final part of the dynamic inheritance methodology—labeled "goals" in table 3.1—refers to the broader aims that artists are said to be carrying out. These goals are almost always described in pairs, such as "protect and develop" (*baohu yu fazhan*) or "inherit and promote" (*jicheng yu fayang*). Thus, they indicate the dual nature of dynamic inheritance from a conceptual perspective; protection requires development, and inheritance requires promotion. Thinking about these processes as mutually interdependent is what makes the dynamic inheritance approach rather revolutionary. These dualisms insist that the preservation of tradition is an ongoing process of new iterations, like biological reproduction in living organisms. Just as living things produce offspring that are related to but not exact copies of themselves, so cultural traditions are thought to produce related but new practices that change slightly with each new generation. The metaphor can be expanded as follows: objects (basic materials, style/flavor, special characteristics, typicality, etc.) correspond to genetic material; activities (collection, absorption/abandonment, organization, creation) correspond to genetic recombination; and goals (protect and develop, inherit and promote) correspond to the broader act of generational reproduction. Thinking about cultural inheritance in this way opens up the possibility for viewing artistic innovation not in opposition to the continuity of tradition, but instead as a necessary component of it.

Representative Works: The Authorship of Tradition

The ideas and methodologies of dynamic inheritance were so formative in China's socialist period that they brought about new understandings of tradition that are in many ways different from ideas in the Western world. Conventional understandings of tradition in North America and Europe emphasize continuity and sameness over time as a key quality. In the Western contexts, how long something has existed without change is often a measure of how traditional it is, and individual interpretation that might lead to change is seen as dangerous to the preservation of tradition. By contrast, the idea of tradition that developed out of socialist China's dynamic inheritance approach is one in which change is seen as a necessary feature of tradition. In this view, tradition is understood as the product of the cumulative contributions of individuals over time. Therefore, to ensure that tradition remains vital in the future requires having individuals who continue to make their own interpretations. When individual interpretations get incorporated into the larger body of tradition and shape its form in the future, an "authoring of tradition" occurs.

In the past, scholars based in Europe and North America tended to resist China's socialist culture of dynamic inheritance and its resultant ideas about tradition, arguing that the encouragement of creativity and change damages tradition's authenticity. A historic debate between the two views took place at the 1979 Durham Oriental Music Festival in England, when a group of British and American ethnomusicologists accused the China Central Conservatory National Music Ensemble of misrepresenting Chinese musical tradition. According to firsthand accounts, the Western scholars challenged the historical authenticity of several items on the Ensemble's program. Fang Kun, then the director of the Ensemble, defended the Ensemble's program, generating a useful documentation of his understanding of musical tradition. Accounts of the debate were later published in English and Chinese, and the event became a touchstone for reflections on Chinese music and concepts of tradition in contemporary China (Fang K. 1980, 1981; see also Blum 1991; Harris 2004; Trebinjac 2000).

The primary issue that divided the two groups was whether change fosters or harms the continuation of tradition. Robert Provine, an American ethnomusicologist who participated in the event, summarizes the difference as follows:

> Much of the discussion dwelt on varying understandings of "traditional music" (*chuantong yinyue*). Mr. Fang clearly felt that development and change are inherent and essential to the Chinese musical tradition, while the western scholars put forth authenticity and preservation (or at least the absence of destructive modification) as aspects of a reliable tradition. (Fang K. 1981, 2)

In their published comments on the discussion, a point that stood out in the Western musicologists' arguments was the importance of preserving tradition in its original form. Making an analogy to art, Provine writes, "The existence of new types of bright and appealing paints is not reason to cover over the drab colors of the Mona Lisa, but rather a reason to create new paintings" (Fang K. 1981, 12). Here, Provine makes a distinction between the Mona Lisa, which he considers an example of a tradition that should be preserved, and new paintings, which he considers valuable on their own but not a substitute for tradition.

In his written summary of his position, Fang challenged the ideas of his Western colleagues on two accounts: first, he challenged the idea that age is a defining feature of tradition; and, second, he argued that because tradition is always changing, it is problematic to identify any single example as the original or authentic version of tradition. Addressing the first point about age, Fang explains, "The classification of traditional music cannot be made on the basis of age. What period must music date from before it can be called traditional? 500 years ago? 1,000 years ago? Or even earlier, [say] 2,000 years ago?" (1981, 5–6). For Fang, it is problematic to define a date before which music is traditional and after which music is modern. To him, any such date would necessarily be arbitrary. Instead, he prefers to see the creativity of current musicians as continuing a process of tradition that extends both into the past and the future.

When addressing his second point about the problem of defining an authentic version of tradition, Fang used one of the pieces on his Ensemble's program, the pipa solo "Ambush on All Sides," as an example. He writes, "At least several hundred years passed between the first writing down of this ancient piece and the definition of its score in 1818, and in any number of periods it must have undergone reconstruction by artists among the people, as apprentices often surpassed their teachers and one generation was more prolific than another. So is it the teachers or the pupils who are traditional?" (1981, 6).

Here, Fang makes clear his view that traditions are made up of individuals. The implication of this point is that because individuals have always made slight changes to traditions over time, there is no reason this process should stop in the present. As Provine writes, summarizing Fang's view, "holding a tradition in suspension is tantamount to destroying it" (Fang K. 1981, 11). Therefore, in his final assessment, Fang argues that preservation and development are equally important when considering the continuation of musical traditions in the present. He writes, "This really shows that tradition itself is in [a state of] development. The more excellent it is the more vitality it has, and it is certainly not in the static state that some scholars imagine.... What matters is not any concept about the changing of form, but whether or not we preserve and develop the mood of the original piece. This [in itself] may be regarded as a sort of development! Thus, most of the evidence from East and West testifies that 'tradition does develop'" (1981, 6–7; additions in original).

Concluding his argument, Fang states that the most important factor for artists practicing traditional music is making sure that it continues to be relevant to contemporary audiences. This, Fang argues, can occur through new research, new adaptations, and new compositions that draw inspiration from classical or folk tunes. Such new interpretations and even new creations serve in Fang's view not to replace or destroy traditional music, but, rather, to maintain its vitality and expand its richness for future generations.

In the field of Chinese music studies, views of Western scholars have over time become more sympathetic to Fang's views. Work by Jonathan Stock (1996), for example, and the other chapters in this edited volume show that, increasingly, music scholars are viewing individual creativity as an essential component of the development of traditional music in modern China. As a whole, however, Western-trained scholars approaching Chinese dance have shown less openness to this idea. In his account of a typical encounter between Chinese and non-Chinese scholars approaching Chinese dance in the early 2000s, David Y. H. Wu writes, "The local [Chinese] scholars ... present the emergence of national dance as a triumph of scientific research, ethnological documentation, and conservation of natural cultural traditions.... Foreign or non-Chinese anthropologists, on the other hand, see the national dances as newly invented or reconstructed art forms" (2004, 198). As in the earlier discussions about music, contemporary cross-cultural discussions about Chinese dance often center on problems of authenticity and preservation. As Wu's example implies, it is often difficult to reconcile Chinese scholars' conceptions of an essentially dynamic notion of traditional continuity with foreign scholars' desire for a more absolute distinction between the old and the new.

A similar tension can be found in contemporary scholarship on Chinese dance published by western-trained scholars in the dance studies field. Chen Yaping, a Taiwanese dance scholar who received her PhD in the United States, was one of the first scholars to publish on Chinese dance in English. Chen uses the term "invented tradition" to describe *minzu wudao*, a form of Chinese dance that developed in Taiwan but also out of Dai Ailian's Chongqing experiments. Discussing one of Dai's early Xinjiang-style dances, Chen writes, "It was neither a reproduction nor a reinterpretation of any existing dance in Xinjiang; instead, it was essentially Dai's own choreography based on some dance movements typical of the Uighur tribe in Chinese Turkestan" (2008, 43). Chen's main concern is with the reception of Chinese dance in Taiwan, where it was used as a political tool in Nationalist Party (KMT) nationalism and thus developed along different lines from that in the PRC. However, to make her point, Chen upholds the firm opposition between individual creation and authenticity that has been a hallmark of Western ideas of tradition in the past. Referring to Dai's approach, she writes, "From the very beginning, authenticity in representation had rarely been a serious concern for the advocates of *bianjiang wu*" (2008, 44). In Taiwan, she explains, these dances are "endowed [...] with a presumed 'authenticity,'" even though, in her words, they are "entirely fictional" (2008, 45). Chen is correct in pointing out that Dai's *bianjiang wu* choreography did not all closely reproduce existing dance forms and thus should not be understood as "traditional" in a conventional Western sense. At the same time, the absolute distinction she employs between invention and authenticity leaves little room for other conceptions of tradition, such as that employed by Dai and her contemporaries in early formulations of the dynamic inheritance approach.

The idea of dynamic inheritance attempts to shift the conversation about Chinese dance in Anglophone scholarship away from the issue of whether Chinese dance is authentic or invented and toward questions about how Chinese dance operates in China as both an essentially creative endeavor and a form of research that contributes to the continuation of cultural traditions. In contrast to the formulation of "invented tradition," dynamic inheritance suggests the idea of "authoring tradition." Whereas the former emphasizes a break in continuity and implied lack of authenticity, the latter emphasizes the creative role of individual artists in shaping how cultural traditions develop. In the context of Chinese dance specifically, the idea of authoring tradition helps to recognize and legitimate the contributions of members of groups typically underrepresented in research on modern Chinese culture, namely, women and ethnic minorities. Historically, women and ethnic minorities have made enormous contributions to the development of Chinese dance in the PRC, whether as performers, choreographers, teachers, or scholars. A dynamic inheritance approach focused on the authoring of tradition helps to understand and value these contributions as impactful work that has meaningfully shaped the trajectory of contemporary Chinese culture. At the same time, it engages local ideas about the nature of artistic traditions, rather than imposing external definitions and expectations of them.

A key medium through which individual artists author tradition in Chinese dance is the "representative work" (*daibiaozuo*). A representative work is a dance piece that starts out as the original creation of an individual artist, and, due to its popularity and influence, achieves the status of "traditional" among later generations. All of the major styles of Chinese dance that exist today were developed through the accumulation of such representative works. In Uyghur dance, for example, works by past Uyghur dance artists such as Kangba'erhan[8] (1914[9]–1994) and Ayitula (b. 1940) are now seen as "traditional," and works by younger Uyghur dancers such as Yumiti (b. 1987) may soon take on this status (Wilcox 2011). In Chinese classical dance, the examples given above of *Flowers and Rain on the Silk Road*, *Dancers of the Tongque Stage*, and *Yellow River* are also representative works. In each case, the term "representative" has two meanings: on the one hand, the work represents the individual artist or group of artists who created it and whose names remain attached to it in records of Chinese dance history; on the other hand, the work represents the broader cultural tradition with which it comes to be associated, and of which it may be regarded as an embodiment independent of its individual creators.

To understand the processes through which an ordinary dance work becomes a representative work, it is helpful to review a case study. A good example for this purpose is "Cup and Bowl Dance" (*Zhong wan wu*), a Mongol dance solo officially premiered by the Inner Mongolia Song and Dance Ensemble in 1961 (see fig. 3.1).[10] "Cup and Bowl Dance" first appeared at a regional performance festival held in Hohhot, the capital of Inner Mongolia. After receiving "unanimous praise" at the festival, it was reviewed in *Wudao*, China's national dance journal, and was featured in a color photo on the journal's front page (Xu E. 1962, 7, cover). According to the *Wudao* reporter, "Cup and Bowl Dance" was one of one hundred twenty new music and dance works presented at the festival, which apparently fell into two types, both based on the dynamic inheritance methodology: "In some, the authors used basic materials (*sucai*) of folk dance to express new life and new characters ... others were folk dances created on the basis of collection (*shouji*) and putting in order (*zhengli*), with a relatively large amount of additional development (*fazhan*)" (Xu E. 1962, 6).

The author placed "Cup and Bowl Dance" in the latter category, meaning that it was relatively innovative compared to other works in the festival. At the same time, the author praised it and other works for their capacity to represent the local culture of the region: "These works, while diverse in theme and form, show a pronounced national style (*fengge*) and the special character (*tese*) of the region" (Xu E. 1962, 6). This report indicates that "Cup and Bowl Dance" achieved a quality common to all representative works; it struck a perfect balance between old and new. On the one hand, "Cup and Bowl Dance" was eminently recognizable as an authentic reflection of local culture; on the other hand, it stood out and was appealing because of its exceptional innovation.

The individual most responsible for the creation of "Cup and Bowl Dance" was Siqintariha (b. 1932), a woman of Khorchin Mongol descent who joined the Inner Mongolia Song and Dance Ensemble (then the Inner Mongolia Cultural Work Team) in 1948. Originally from an aristocratic family in what is today eastern Inner Mongolia, Siqintariha was an active participant in the construction of Chinese dance during the early Maoist period. She was one of the first minority dancers to perform at the 1949 Chinese People's Political Consultative Congress in Beiping (later Beijing), and she had the distinction of representing China abroad twice at the semiannual World Festivals of Youth and Students, first in Budapest in 1949, and then in Warsaw in 1955 (Neimenggu 1986; Wulanjie 2008). Although Siqintariha had no professional dance training when she entered the Ensemble, she later studied at the top professional dance programs in the PRC:

Fig. 3.1. "Cup and Bowl Dance," premiered in 1961 by the Inner Mongolia Song and Dance Ensemble. Performed here by Siqintariha. Photo courtesy of Siqintariha.

in 1951–1952, she participated in the national Chinese dance research program taught by Choe Seung-hui at the Central Academy of Drama in Beijing; then, in 1954–1956, she was in the inaugural class of the Beijing Dance School (later Beijing Dance Academy) (Wulanjie 2008). The *Wudao* issue that featured "Cup and Bowl Dance" on its cover in 1962 also included an article on the Inner Mongolia Song and Dance Ensemble Dance Team coauthored by Siqintariha, who by that time had been appointed the Ensemble's Vice Director in charge of dance (Siqintariha and Baoyinbatu 1962; Neimenggu 1986). All of these experiences gave Siqintariha familiarity with the dynamic inheritance methodology. At the same time, they gave her the necessary status and influence to have an impact on how Mongol dance was practiced in China.

The creative process Siqintariha followed in the making of "Cup and Bowl Dance" is recounted in detail in her autobiographical essay "From 'Lamp Dance' to 'Cup and Bowl' Solo Dance" (Siqintariha 2008) and in personal interviews with the author (Siqintariha 2012–2015). Below is a condensed version of her accounts:[11]

> In early 1961, the Inner Mongolia Song and Dance Troupe split into groups and went to the countryside to perform. The program included "Lamp Dance," a solo dance choreographed by Jia Zuoguang and performed by the young performer Modegema (b. 1941). When the performances ended, we invited local audiences to give feedback. They had several critiques of "Lamp Dance": the lighting was too dark; the stage mood was depressing and gloomy; and the environment resembled an ancient imperial temple, rather than modern life. In the work, the dancer balanced a lamp on her head, and the tongue of the flame moved as she danced, flickering and floating. This created an eerie feeling, and some felt that she resembled a female spirit or a ghost, rather than a real person. At the end of the tour, we returned to the Troupe headquarters and had a long discussion about the audience feedback. Finally, I was assigned the job of revising the piece. I worked with Modegema, rehearsing rigorously every day. At last, I made the following revisions: the lamp on the dancer's head was replaced with a stack of three porcelain bowls, and in her hands she now held pairs of porcelain drink cups. Instead of starting kneeling on stage, she now emerged from the right side, and the lights were made strong and bright. The idea to replace the lamps with cups and bowls came from my research on the folk dances of Ordos, an area in Western Inner Mongolia. There is a type of dance in which folk artists balance a bowl on their heads and fill it with alcohol, like a drinking game—whoever spills has to take a drink. In the adapted piece, Modegema balanced a whole stack of bowls, and the drinking game component was removed. Replacing the lamp with the bowls changed the visual image of the dance, but it allowed the piece to still inherit some aspects of traditional folk dance. The basic movement vocabulary of "Cup and Bowl Dance" also comes from the Ordos drink bowl dance—the posture and the use of the arms and hands especially—and I added some new ones too. For example, the rapid "*cuibu*" step used at the beginning of the piece

comes from Chinese classical dance. In addition to increasing the technical difficulty of the piece, this gives the work a faster tempo and adds an elegant and upright quality to the female dancer's image. As a whole, we can say that these revisions maintained the original work's structures, while they incorporated elements from folk dance and made its visual impact and mood more suitable to the tastes of new audiences.

Siqintariha's account makes clear that the creation of "Cup and Bowl Dance" involved several layers of source materials: the "Lamp Dance" solo choreographed by Jia Zuoguang; the suggestions from the rural audiences; the techniques learned from Ordos folk artists; and, finally, Siqintariha's own innovations. In Siqintariha's collected essay volume, a photograph of Siqintariha studying with a male folk dancer identified as Nashunhutu shows her learning a posture with drink cups that looks identical to those employed in "Cup and Bowl Dance" (fig. 3.2) (Wulanjie 2008, 390; *Caidie fenfei* 1963). In our interviews, Siqintariha explained that this was the very technique that inspired her to use the drink cups in this work. One of the motivations in adapting this piece, according to Siqintariha, was to create an elegant image of Mongol women, in contrast to the coyer or more playful images found in other dance works of the time. When discussing "Cup and Bowl Dance," Siqintariha repeatedly used the word "*duanzhuang*," or "dignified," to describe the female image it depicted. It is interesting to consider the path she took to generate this image: adapting elements of a drinking game; learning from a male folk artist; introducing steps from Chinese classical dance; and changing the tone from somber and spiritual to upbeat and bright. It is these subtle choices of blending, selection, and adaptation that constitute Siqintariha's authorship and creativity. Such decisions mark the presence of her individual artistic interpretation.

The success of Siqintariha's innovations and Modegema's performances made the work highly popular. Soon after its debut in Hohhot, "Cup and Bowl Dance" was selected to represent China abroad at the World Festival of Youth and Students, held in Helsinki in July 1962, where it took the Gold Prize. Modegema was promoted to a national-level ensemble in Beijing, raising her to the status of China's premier performer of Mongol dance (Feng et al. 2006, 376). Film further expanded the impact of "Cup and Bowl Dance" in 1963, when it was included in *Butterflies Fluttering About* (*Caidie fenfei*), a dance film shown around the country and exported internationally (Z. Wang 2014; *Renmin ribao* 1964). In 1964, it appeared in a modified form in *The East Is Red*, a major production that was also made into a widely circulated film the following year (*Dongfang hong* 1965; Feng et al. 2006, 376). Although "Cup and Bowl Dance," like other works of Chinese dance, was condemned during the Cultural Revolution (1966–1976), it was revived immediately afterward. In 1978, Modegema performed "Cup and Bowl Dance" on a major tour in the United States (Wilcox 2016a). By the early twenty-first

Fig. 3.2. Siqintariha learning a drink cup dance from folk artist Nashunhutu in Hohhot, early 1960s. Photo courtesy of Siqintariha.

century, Chinese dance scholars were counting "Cup and Bowl Dance" as one of the most important and influential works of Chinese dance ever produced (Jia 2006). Scholar of Mongol dance Wang Jingzhi called it "the origin of a varied series of cup and bowl dance works that have canonical and trademark significance" (2009, 416). Indeed, adaptations of this piece are ubiquitous in female Mongol dance productions in China. Recently, the Opening Ceremonies of the Fourth National Minorities Arts and Culture Festival held in Beijing in 2012 included a large Mongolian group dance section titled *Cup-Bowl-Chopstick* that was clearly an extension of this earlier work (*Shengshi* 2012; *Di si jie* 2012).[12]

Fig. 3.3. Siqintariha teaching bowl dance technique to a new generation of students at the Dedema Art School in Inner Mongolia, early 2000s. Photo courtesy of Siqintariha.

What is most significant about "Cup and Bowl Dance" in relation to the idea of tradition has been its impact on dance training. In China, to be a professional in the field of Chinese dance means to have undergone training in a dance conservatory, where each subcategory of Chinese dance has its own distinct curriculum (Wilcox 2011). It is at the level of training that traditions get defined and formalized, since this is the process through which dancers learn to recognize, differentiate, and, most importantly, perform a variety of different dance styles. In the case of female-style Mongol dance, the props employed in "Cup and Bowl Dance"—stacks of porcelain bowls and pairs of small drink cups—have been incorporated as basic elements of the curriculum of Mongol dance. This means that learning Mongol dance in China today requires embodying the movements and techniques used in "Cup and Bowl Dance." At the Inner Mongolia University Art College, the premier school for studying Mongolian dance in China, female students of all levels learn to manipulate cups and bowls, and the movements they learn correspond directly to those found in the "Cup and Bowl Dance" choreography.[13] This technique is also included in a widely used Mongolian dance DVD training series coauthored by Siqintariha (Siqintariha and Zhao 2007). By serving directly as a teacher and mentor to new generations of dancers, Siqintariha has thus ensured the continued "representativeness" of "Cup and Bowl Dance" over the years (fig. 3.3).

Conclusion: Faces of Tradition

The metaphor of inheritance is key to understanding the relationships between present and past, individual and group, and innovation and tradition in Chinese dance. Creators of Chinese dance are said to "inherit" Chinese tradition through their works, and the stuff that constitutes tradition is often given physiological metaphors such as "blood," "marrow," or "essence." While this discourse can encourage troubling forms of cultural essentialism, it also enables flexibility and change in the interpretation of what constitutes Chinese culture over time. Because Chinese tradition is viewed as an inheritance, each new generation has the obligation to embody this tradition in its own way. With each new representative, like a new phenotype from a shared gene pool, a new line of inheritance develops, which shapes the possibilities for the future generations.

In China, this idea that cultural traditions should be continuously reinterpreted, and that individual artists play pivotal roles in this process, is a legacy of the socialist era. As David Holm (1991) argues, even at its most divided, one of the few points that united the Yan'an "national forms" movement was that folk culture, in order to become national culture, would have to undergo change. Thus, in his 1942 "Talks," Mao Zedong compared existing folk forms to the seeds and sprouts of national forms, calling them "literature and art in a budding state" (Holm 1991, 94). In the field of dance, this idea that national culture was "budding" but not yet fully formed afforded tremendous space for dance artists to leverage their own creativity in the development of new Chinese dance works. Over time, works that were successful became incorporated into Chinese dance tradition.

Future research may consider to what extent the dynamic inheritance concept and artistic methodology is specific to socialist China, or whether it also pertains to dance practices in other parts of the world. The comparative work of US-based dance scholar Anthony Shay (2002) has demonstrated similar processes in the creation of national folk dance in the Soviet Union, Mexico, Croatia, Egypt, Greece, and Turkey. Shay demonstrates that in all of these cases, dances that came to represent the shared culture of a nation or ethnic group were artistic products of creative and innovative individuals. As has been the case in Chinese dance, the national dance companies Shay discusses also offer "the representation of the nation ... produced through a single, unique artistic vision" (2002, 39). Thus, the authoring of tradition seems to have happened similarly in these cases.

What may make the Chinese context somewhat different is that individual artists continue to be associated with Chinese dance works even after those works become "representative." That is, in the case of "Cup and Bowl Dance," the work is still dated to 1962, and Siqintariha is still seen as a primary creative force in its adaptation, at least among Chinese dance scholars. Similarly, with the Han-Tang work, *Dancers of the Tongque Stage*, Sun Ying is still recognized as the individual who created this piece and the larger Han-Tang school, even though this school is now also regarded as part of the Chinese classical dance tradition. Shay suggests that in the cases he analyzes, at least among lay audiences, the role of the individual creator is not as widely recognized: "Because the dances purportedly originate with "the people," the characters of the founder-artistic directors and choreographers are often more muted. Many individuals among the public largely believe the fiction that the choreographies they view on stage reflect actual dances as they would be experienced in a traditional field setting" (2002, 39).

It would require a great deal more fieldwork among Chinese audiences and lay practitioners to determine whether Chinese dance is or ever has been widely regarded among the general public as something that would be experienced in a traditional field setting. When the National Folk Dance Ensemble of the Soviet Union, one of the groups Shay analyzes, visited China in the 1950s, the role of the Ensemble's lead choreographer Igor Moiseyev was far from muted. Chinese programs featured a large portrait of Moiseyev on the first page, followed by a biographical statement and essays about Moiseyev's "creative principles" for making folk dance works (*Sulian*, n.d.). Does this mean that Chinese audiences viewed these dances more as Moiseyev's choreography than as representations of Soviet dance traditions? One contribution of the dynamic inheritance approach is the suggestion that this may be a false opposition with which to begin.

As I have argued here, professionals and scholars of Chinese dance in the PRC have historically regarded Chinese dance as the cumulative product of individuals, who conduct research on existing folk dances or cultural artifacts and then create new works from them, often interpreting them in new ways. The phrase "to inherit and develop," often used to describe this larger process, expresses the idea behind this method and approach, which I call dynamic inheritance. Among the many new creations, only some get incorporated into Chinese dance tradition. These are those that become "representative works." By conceptualizing tradition as inherently in flux, this understanding of dance creation challenges the conventional Western dichotomy between tradition and innovation. It expresses an approach to the construction of national culture developed in China's early socialist period that remains in use today.

University of Michigan
Ann Arbor

Acknowledgments

This chapter benefited from generous comments from colleagues when earlier versions were presented in the following venues: American Folklore Society, Association for Asian Studies, China Central University of Nationalities, College of William and Mary, East Chinese Normal University, McMaster University, Mongolian Cultural Center in Washington, DC, Shanghai Academy of Social Sciences, The Ohio State University, and University of Michigan. Funding for this research was provided by the US Fulbright Program, the Shanghai Theatre Academy, the American Council of Learned Societies, and the University of Michigan's Institute for Research on Women and Gender, Center for World Performance Studies, and Lieberthal-Rogel Center for Chinese Studies. This chapter also benefited from helpful feedback from two anonymous reviewers and the editorial staff at *JFR*.

Notes

1. For an account of this concept in the Soviet context, see George Luckyj (1990).
2. A longer discussion of this, including ample documentation, appears in Wilcox 2019.
3. This and all translations in this chapter are by the author of this chapter unless otherwise noted.
4. Primary print sources reviewed include articles about dance published in major newspapers and periodicals, such as *People's Daily* (*Renmin ribao*), *Guangming Daily* (*Guangming ribao*), and *China Pictorial* (*Renmin huabao*), as well as articles published in specialized dance publications including *Dance Study Materials* (*Wudao xuexi ziliao*), *Dance News* (*Wudao tongxun*), and *Dance* (*Wudao*). In addition, I consulted memoirs and biographies and conducted personal interviews with dozens of the leading figures of Chinese dance during this period.
5. Throughout this chapter, I use the English term "dance artist" to describe professional dancers who work in PRC state-sponsored dance institutions. The term "dance art" (*wudao yishu*) has been a standard term for concert dance in Maoist and post-Maoist China. Thus, the term "dance artist" encapsulates the Maoist terms "dance worker" and "dance art worker" (*wudao yishu gongzuozhe*), as well as the post-Maoist terms "dancer" (*wuzhe*) and "dance artist" (*wudaojia*).
6. This concept has a long history that dates back to the folksong collection practices of early China. For a discussion of changes in this practice over time, see Lydia Liu (2012).
7. For example, in 1949, when the Huabei University Dance Team performed dances from Dai Ailian's repertoire at the All-China Literature and Arts Worker Representative Congress, newspapers described these works as "Madame Dai Ailian's dances" (Fang M. 1949a).
8. Names of ethnic minority dancers are transcribed in Pinyin to reflect their spellings in Chinese print sources.
9. Kangba'erhan's birthdate is disputed. The official date is 1922, but recent scholarship suggests the actual date is 1914.
10. A video of this work can be viewed here: https://www.youtube.com/watch?v=2TT_eIDYE04.
11. The following is a condensed summary based on the contents of Siqintariha's essay (2008) and several interviews I conducted with her (2012–2015). It is not a direct quotation but is drawn from her accounts.

12. I observed the original live performance of this work at the Olympic Stadium in Beijing on June 12, 2012.

13. This is based on my observations of the final exams in Mongol dance held at this school in 2012 and 2014. While studying at the Beijing Dance Academy in 2008–2009, I also observed students learning these techniques as part of their Mongol dance courses.

References

Blum, Stephen. 1991. *Ethnomusicology and Modern Music History*. Urbana: University of Illinois Press.

Caidie fenfei [Butterflies fluttering about]. 1963. Beijing: Beijing Film Studio. VCD.

Chen, Ya-Ping. 2008. "Dancing Chinese Nationalism and Anticommunism: The *Minzu Wudao* Movement in 1950s Taiwan." In *Dance, Human Rights, and Social Justice: Dignity in Motion*, edited by Naomi M. Jackson and Toni Samantha Phim, 34–50. Lanham, MD: Scarecrow.

Cui Chengxi [Choe Seunghui]. 1951. "Zhongguo wudao yishu de jianglai" [The future of Chinese dance art]. *Renmin ribao* [People's daily], February 18, 1951, 5.

Dai Ailian. 1946. "Fazhan Zhongguo wudao di yi bu" [The first step in developing Chinese dance]. *Zhongyang ribao* [Central daily], April 10, 1946, 8.

DeMare, Brian James. 2015. *Mao's Cultural Army: Drama Troupes in China's Rural Revolution*. Cambridge: Cambridge University Press.

Di si jie quanguo shaoshu minzu wenyi huiyan [Fourth Minority Art Festival of China]. 2012. Opening Ceremonies souvenir program, Beijing. June 12, 2012.

Dong Xijiu and Long Yinpei, eds. 2008. *Xin Zhongguo wudao de dianjishi* [Cornerstone of Chinese dance]. Hong Kong: Tianma chubanshe.

Dongfang hong [The East is red]. 1965. Joint production of the Beijing Film Studio, August 1st Film Studio, and the Central News and Documentary Film Studio. DVD.

Duara, Prasenjit. 2004. *Decolonization: Perspectives from Now and Then*. London: Routledge.

Fang Kun. 1980. "Guanyu Zhongguo minzu yinyue chuantong de yi ci taolun" [A discussion of Chinese national music tradition]. *Renmin yinyue* [People's music] 1: 38–40.

———. 1981. "A Discussion on Chinese National Musical Traditions." Translated by Keith Pratt, with introduction by Robert C. Provine and response by Alan Thrasher. *Asian Music* 12 (2): 1–16.

Fang Ming. 1949a. "Zuihou jingcai jiemu" [The last exciting act]. *Guangming ribao* [Guangming daily], July 15, 1949, 1.

———. 1949b. "Wei baiwan renmin fuwu de Neimenggu wengongtuan" [Inner Mongolia cultural work troupe that serves a million people]. *Guangming ribao* [Guangming daily], July 16, 1949, 4.

Feng Shuangbai et al. 2006. *Zhongguo wudaojia da cidian* [Comprehensive dictionary of Chinese dance artists]. Beijing: Zhongguo wenlian chubanshe.

Glasstone, Richard. 2007. *The Story of Dai Ailian: Icon of Chinese Folk Dance, Pioneer of Chinese Ballet*. Alton, Hampshire, UK: Dance Books.

Harris, Rachel. 2004. *Singing the Village: Music, Memory, and Ritual among the Sibe of Xinjiang*. Oxford: Oxford University Press for the British Academy.

Holm, David. 1991. *Art and Ideology in Revolutionary China*. Oxford: Clarendon.

Hung, Chang-tai. 1985. *Going to the People: Chinese Intellectuals and Folk Literature, 1918–1937*. Cambridge, MA: Council on East Asian Studies, Harvard University.

———. 2011. *Mao's New World: Political Culture in the Early People's Republic*. Ithaca, NY: Cornell University Press.

Jia Anlin. 2006. *Zhongguo minzu minjian wu zuopin shangxin* [Appreciation of Chinese national folk dance works]. Shanghai: Shanghai yinyue chubanshe.

Jin Hao. 2012. *Xin shiji Zhongguo gudianwu fazhan shi nian guan* [Ten-year perspective on Chinese classical dance development in the new century]. Shanghai: Shanghai yinyue chubanshe.

Li Zhengyi, Gao Dakun, and Zhu Qingyuan. 2004. *Zhongguo gudianwu jiaoxue tixi chuangjian fazhanshi* [History of the creation and development of the Chinese classical dance pedagogy system]. Shanghai: Shanghai yinyue chubanshe.

Liang Lun. 1947. "Wudao de Zhongguohua wenti" [The problem of making dance Chinese]. *Zhong yi* [China art]: 13.

———. 2011. *Wo de yishu shengya* [My artistic career]. Guangzhou, China: Lingnan meishu chubanshe.

Liu, Ching-chih. 2010. *A Critical History of New Music in China*. Translated by Caroline Mason. Hong Kong: The Chinese University Press.

Liu, Lydia. 2012. "Translingual Folklore and Folklorics in China." In *A Companion to Folklore*, edited by Regina Bendix and Galit Hasan-Rokem, 190–210. Malden, MA: Wiley-Blackwell.

Liu, Siyuan. 2013. *Performing Hybridity in Colonial-Modern China*. New York: Palgrave Macmillan.

Luckyj, George S. N. 1990. *Literary Politics in the Soviet Ukraine, 1917–1934*. Durham, NC: Duke University Press.

Mao, Zedong. 1996. "Talks at the Yan'an Forum on Literature and Art." In *Modern Chinese Literary Thought: Writings on Literature, 1893–1945*, edited by Kirk A. Denton, 458–84. Stanford, CA: Stanford University Press. Originally published 1975. In *Selected Works of Mao Tse-Tung*, vol. 3. Beijing: Foreign Languages Press.

McDougall, Bonnie S., and Kam Louie. 1997. *The Literature of China in the Twentieth Century*. London: Hurst.

Neimenggu gewutuan [Inner Mongolia song and dance ensemble]. 1986. *Jiantuan sishi zhounian jiniance* [Memorial album of the fortieth anniversary of the troupe's founding]. Hohhot, China: Neimenggu gewutuan yishu dang'an ziliaoshi.

Renmin ribao [People's daily]. 1964. "Qingzhu Zhonghua renmin gongheguo chengli shiwu zhounian wo zhu Bolan, Nuowei he Jiana shi jie fenbie jüxing dianying zhaodaihui" [Chinese ambassadors in Poland, Norway, and Ghana hold film receptions to celebrate the fifteenth anniversary of the People's Republic of China]. October 10, 1964, 3.

Shay, Anthony. 2002. *Choreographic Politics: State Folk Dance Companies, Representation, and Power*. Middletown, CT: Wesleyan University Press.

Shengshi Zhonghua [Flourishing China]. 2012. Fourth Minority Art Festival of China Opening Ceremonies. Live performance held at the Olympic Stadium in Beijing. June 12, 2012.

Siqintariha. 2008. "'Deng wu' dao 'zhong wan' duwu" [From 'Lamp Dance' to 'Cup and Bowl' solo dance]. In *Siqintariha Menggu wu wenji* [Siqintariha's Collected Works on Mongolian Dance], edited by Siqintariha, 113–16. Hohhot, China: Neimenggu renmin chubanshe.

Siqintariha. 2012–2015. Series of personal communications. Hohhot, China.

Siqintariha and Baoyinbatu. 1962. "Neimeng ren yi gewutuan wudaodui de chengzhang" [The growth of the Inner Mongolia song and dance ensemble dance team]. *Wudao* [Dance] (2): 3, 6–7.

Siqintariha and Zhao Linping. 2007. *Mengguzu wudao jingpin ke jiaocheng* [Curriculum of Mongol nationality dance canonical works class]. DVD series. Hohhot, China: Neimenggu wenhua yinxiang chubanshe.

Stock, Jonathan P. J. 1996. *Musical Creativity in Twentieth-Century China: Abing, His Music, and Its Changing Meanings*. Rochester, NY: University of Rochester Press.

"Sulian guoli minjian wudaotuan" [Soviet national folk dance ensemble]. [1950s]. Performance program printed in Chinese. University of Michigan Asia Library Chinese Dance Special Collection, Chi Dance Bk.148.

Tang, Xiaobing. 2015. *Visual Culture in Contemporary China: Paradigms and Shifts*. Cambridge, UK: Cambridge University Press.

Tong Yan. 2012. *1912–1949 Minguo shiqi wudao yanjiu* [1912–1949 Republican era dance research]. Beijing: Zhongyang minzu daxue chubanshe.

Trebinjac, Sabine. 2000. *Le pouvoir en chantant, tome 1: L'art de fabriquer une musique chinoise* [Singing power, vol. 1: The art of creating a Chinese music]. Paris: Société d'éthnologie.

Wang, Hui. 2011. "Local Forms, Vernacular Dialects, and the War of Resistance against Japan: The 'National Forms' Debate." Translated by Chris Berry. In *The Politics of Imagining Asia*, edited by Theodore Huters, 95–135. Cambridge, MA: Harvard University Press.

Wang Jingzhi. 2009. *Zhongguo Mengguzu wudao yishu lun* [Study of Chinese Mongolian nationality dance art]. Hohhot, China: Neimenggu daxue chubanshe.

Wang, Zheng. 2014. Personal communication. Ann Arbor, Michigan.

Wilcox, Emily E. 2011. "The Dialectics of Virtuosity: Dance in the People's Republic of China, 1949–2009." PhD diss., University of California, Berkeley.

———. 2012. "Han-Tang *Zhongguo Gudianwu* and the Problem of Chineseness in Contemporary Chinese Dance: Sixty Years of Controversy." *Asian Theater Journal* 29 (1): 206–32.

———. 2016a. "Foreword: A Manifesto for Demarginalization." In *Chinese Dance: In the Vast Land and Beyond*, edited by Shih-Ming Li Chang and Lynn Frederiksen, ix–xxiv. Middletown, CT: Wesleyan University Press.

———. 2016b. "Beyond Internal Orientalism: Dance and Nationality Discourse in the Early People's Republic of China, 1949–1954." *Journal of Asian Studies* 75 (2): 363–86.

———. 2018. "The Postcolonial Blind Spot: Chinese Dance in the Era of Third Worldism, 1949–1965." *positions: asia critique* 26 (4): 781–815.

———. 2019. *Revolutionary Bodies: Chinese Dance and the Socialist Legacy*. Berkeley: University of California Press.

Wu, David Y. H. 2004. "Chinese National Dance and the Discourse of Nativization in Chinese Anthropology." In *The Making of Anthropology in East and Southeast Asia*, edited by Shinji Yamashita, Joseph Bosco, and Jeremy Seymour Eades, 198–207. New York; Oxford: Berghahn Books.

Wu Xiaobang. 1982. *Wo de wudao yishu shengya* [My dance art career]. Beijing: Zhongguo xiju chubanshe.

Wulanjie. 2008. "*Xianhua—lazhu—qiaoliang: Siqintariha zhuanlue*" ["Fresh flowers, candle, bridge: Biographical sketch of Siqintariha]. In *Siqintariha Menggu wu wenji*

[Siqintariha's collected works on Mongolian dance], edited by Siqintariha, 367–402. Hohhot, China: Neimenggu renmin chubanshe.

Xu Erchong. 1962. *Sai gong chun lai zao, hua kai bian caoyuan: ji Neimeng zizhiqu duchang, duzou, duwu yanchuhui* [Spring comes early, flowers open on the grassland: Notes on the Inner Mongolia Autonomous Region's solo song, solo instrumental, and solo dance performance meeting]. *Wudao* [Dance] (2): 6–8.

Xu Rui. 2010. "Dangdai Zhongguo minzu minjian wudao de renshi yanbian yu gainian chanshi" [The conceptual explanation and transformation in meaning of contemporary Chinese national folk dance]. *Beijing wudao xueyuan xuebao* [Journal of the Beijing dance academy] (1): 4–10.

Zhao Xian. 1980. "*Silu hua yu* de wudao yuyan" [Dance language in *Flowers and Rain on the Silk Road*]. *Wenyi yanjiu* [Literature and arts research] (2): 98–102.

Zhongyang ribao [Central daily]. 1946. "Dai Ailian lingdao biaoyan bianjiang wudao" [Dai Ailian leads a performance of border dance]. April 10, 1946, 8.

EMILY E. WILCOX is Associate Professor of Modern Chinese Studies in the Department of Asian Languages and Cultures at the University of Michigan–Ann Arbor. She is a specialist in Chinese dance and performance culture, with broader interests in twentieth-century global history, transnationalism, gender, and social movements, and is author of *Revolutionary Bodies: Chinese Dance and the Socialist Legacy*.

4 Collecting Flowers, Defining a Genre
Zhang Yaxiong and the Anthology of Hua'er Folksongs

Sue Tuohy

IN EARLY 1984, I made my first trip to northwest China to begin dissertation research on the relations between folklore, music, and cultural policies, particularly after the ravages of the Cultural Revolution (1966–1976). By the mid-1980s, traditional arts that had been previously banned were being revived, and the discipline of folklore was undergoing a renaissance after having been dismantled. Folklorists, including those imprisoned or exiled from their posts in previous decades, were "rehabilitated" (*pingfan*) and resumed their activities with renewed enthusiasm.[1] Among them were scholars who conducted research on *hua'er*,[2] a genre of folksong popular within northwest China. During my first meeting with scholars in Lanzhou, the capital of Gansu Province, musicologist Gao Jingye began to discuss hua'er songs. During my next meeting, folklorist Ke Yang (1935–2017) exclaimed, "You must do research on hua'er! An understanding of culture in Gansu and the Northwest is inextricably linked to hua'er." And the next day, I met Zhang Yaxiong (1909–1989), who was introduced to me—with a tone of reverence—as the father of the field of hua'er studies and author of one of the earliest anthologies of hua'er songs. Then in his late seventies, Zhang also encouraged me to conduct research on hua'er, to help promote the continuation of the hua'er tradition, and to bring hua'er to the attention of the world. Thus, after only a few days, it became clear scholars in Gansu thought hua'er songs were an important genre of folklore, one deserving attention. Three decades later, I have developed a better understanding of hua'er, the significance of hua'er studies, and the dedication of the many people who have worked collectively to record and promote the genre. I also have developed an appreciation of the central position of Zhang Yaxiong within this process as a pioneer—as he is so often called—who collected hua'er songs and published the influential *Anthology of Hua'er Folksongs* (*Hua'er ji*; hereafter, *Anthology*).

In this chapter I focus on Zhang and his *Anthology* as a case study to explore the collector-editor and the anthology as faces of tradition and as mechanisms through which folkloric materials are defined and promoted as traditions. I begin with this anecdote about my introduction to hua'er songs and researchers, aware of my own role as an individual participating in collective processes of their representation, particularly while writing to many readers who never have heard of hua'er or Zhang. Just as I feel acutely aware of the communal and intertextual nature of this chapter's construction, I want to direct attention to the intertextual and communal nature of both collector-editors and the anthologies they produce as they participate in the creative processes of drawing upon resources around them, past and present, and shape future practices and values.

In the late 1920s and 1930s, encouraged by local activists and his mentors in the interconnected Beijing Folksong Research Society (*Geyao yanjiuhui*), Chinese Folk Literature Movement, and May Fourth movement, Zhang began collecting hua'er songs in northwest China, and he published the first nationally-circulated print anthology of hua'er songs in 1940.[3] Nearly one hundred years later, hua'er has now come to occupy much attention in northwest China, where people sing and listen to the songs, talk and write about them, and research and publish them. While hua'er has not become a "popular" form in China and is but one of many regional genres collectors have anthologized, the genre consistently has been included in national folklore anthologies and music textbooks since the early 1950s and, in 2009, hua'er was put on UNESCO's Representative List of the Intangible Cultural Heritage of Humanity.[4]

Hua'er may seem an unlikely choice for such persistent national, and now international, attention. Hua'er songs are sung in local dialects that people outside the region cannot understand and often include lyrics that many consider obscene or risqué. In the past, hua'er songs were called "wild" songs (*yequ*) and compared to wild weeds (*yecao*) that should be eradicated. Many Chinese writers scorned hua'er songs, Islamic clerics criticized them, and local political leaders opposed them. By custom, singers were not allowed to sing hua'er in their own villages or in front of their parents. Moreover, hua'er has been associated with northwest China, a region often considered peripheral to Chinese culture. After the 1940s, however, Zhang Yaxiong's work played a central role in the process of "elevating" the status of hua'er and contributed to today's public celebration of hua'er. And Zhang did so within a broader context in which intellectuals were calling upon people to study local artistic forms in other parts of China, many of which also are celebrated today as elements of intangible cultural heritage.

One of the primary meanings of the word "hua'er" is "flower"; thus, *Anthology of Hua'er Folksongs* also could be translated as "a collection of flowers," a parallel to the Greek word "anthologia," a gathering of flowers, a bouquet. With a range of terms available to him, Zhang's choice to call the songs "flowers," instead of "wild tunes" or "wild weeds," was an important move in the public redefinition of the genre.[5] By labeling the sounds "music" and the lyrics "folk literature" and "poetry"—and by describing hua'er as a "tradition," a genre of folksong, and an element of Chinese cultural heritage—Zhang discursively placed hua'er within the categories of art, folklore, traditional culture, and heritage. He thereby connected hua'er to the values associated with those categories, a perspectival shift intent on both describing and realizing the place of hua'er. As it describes hua'er, this discourse also seeks to accomplish the process of transforming their meaning. Rather than pulling them up as weeds, people collect the songs as flowers.

Zhang not only collected "flowers" but also worked to define the genre and to forge a path for future hua'er collectors and for the promotion of the idea of hua'er as a folk tradition and as a part of a larger Chinese artistic tradition. But he did not do this work alone. He drew upon the work of local collectors and became part of a community of people involved in a movement to promote the collection and appreciation of China's folk traditions. In his discussion of early twentieth-century scholars involved in research and advocacy work on hua'er in the 1920s and 1940s, Ma Wenhui illustrated this idea of a community of individuals cooperatively engaged in work on hua'er: "They were active and engaged, comparing notes with and encouraging each other in person and discussing their ideas through letters and publications" (1987, 109). And he characterized Zhang Yaxiong as "a pioneer ... [and] the epitome of the great and comprehensive synthesizer (*jida chengzhe*)" (109).[6]

The *Anthology* is a comprehensive work that contextualizes hua'er and itself in relation to a history of Chinese folksongs and publication and to contemporary academic research and sociopolitical situations within China and beyond. In addition to documenting lyrics of over six hundred hua'er song verses, it discusses topics such as the contexts and motivations for Zhang's research, the regional and national significance of hua'er, and Zhang's (and others') theories about hua'er styles, performance, and contexts, as well as the labeling of the genre "hua'er." The *Anthology* is also a highly reflexive and intertextual work. Zhang prints and comments on hua'er song texts sung by others, quotes from his prior writing, and includes the writing and speech of others before him and his contemporary colleagues. He builds upon prior textual practices, including a long "tradition" (*chuantong*) of anthologizing folksongs, and he comments on his colleagues in the early twentieth century who also advocated for using folksong as an educational tool to unite Chinese citizens. The *Anthology* illustrates Zhang's sense of responsibility to these traditions, to hua'er, and to raising awareness of the values of folk materials to the Chinese people and nation.

I will argue that Zhang's work contributed to the continuity of hua'er singing in northwest China and its broader recognition, and it provided materials for later recycling by future writers. Later scholars also discursively framed Zhang as an early representative of a tradition of scholarship on hua'er and as a scholar who toiled to advocate for the values of folksongs in China. The hua'er studies literature contains countless references to the *Anthology* as a "blueprint" for hua'er research, as a "representative work" (*daibiaozuo*) of the first period of hua'er research, and as a work that "followed the past and heralded the future" (*chengxian qihou*). Zhang's work helped cement the idea of hua'er as a genre of China, of the Northwest, of three provinces, and of the multiple ethnic groups with which it is associated, as well as an artistic expression said to reflect the nature of those places and people. Thus, Zhang and the *Anthology* functioned both as mechanisms for constructing a tradition and as faces of that tradition on multiple fronts.

Hua'er Songs and the Genre of Hua'er

Here I will briefly describe hua'er songs to provide background information, but also because I believe that the nature of the songs shaped Zhang's construction of the *Anthology* and that the publication of the *Anthology* was pivotal in constructing hua'er as a genre. Defining hua'er, however, is not easy, in part because the types of songs today included within the genre vary significantly in terms of lyrics, places of performance, and musical styles. As did Zhang, people usually classify hua'er as a regional form of "mountain song" (*shan'ge*), a subgenre of folksong, a classification that links hua'er to other mountain-song genres sung throughout the country. Unlike some genres, however, hua'er is spread throughout a large region encompassing three provinces (and a prefecture in Xinjiang) and is sung by members of different ethnic groups living there—Han, Hui, Dongxiang, Salar, Bao'an, Tibetan, Tu/Monguor, Yugu/Yugur, and Mongolian. Moreover, as always when writing about hua'er, my mind is filled with memories of conversations—and sometimes heated arguments at symposia—about the ways hua'er is defined and about the power of particular publications in shaping public understandings of the genre.

Based on my research, the most convincing argument is that some people in the Northwest, including poets as early as the Ming dynasty (1368–1644), used the term "hua'er" in a more limited sense to refer to songs sung in particular localities within the region. Using "hua'er" as a generic term to refer to different forms of mountain songs sung throughout the region, however, is a rather recent practice, one that gained impetus only after the 1940s. For instance, many scholars argue some songs previously called "*shaonian*" later began to be called "hua'er" after the name spread in the 1940s and 50s,[7] particularly after the publication of Zhang Yaxiong's book (Zhang J. 2011, 63).[8] Since then, a definition of the hua'er genre became solidified and today is recognizable as the one most commonly invoked. I argue hua'er, as it is currently understood, constitutes a "supergenre" that encompasses a range of diverse song styles. In an attempt to bring some type of order to the musical and lyrical diversity within this hua'er supergenre, Zhang and later researchers have devised systems to classify the songs into subgenres, usually associated with named places in the region.[9]

Hua'er songs are sung by men and women, usually in local dialects of Chinese, which vary within the region. Until the 1940s, they usually were sung outside, including outside villages, while working in fields and mountains and at a set of festivals. Today they also are performed on concert stages and television and in schools, and hua'er singing continues as part of everyday life for many people, although many singers still will not sing hua'er in their own homes or villages. Soloists and small groups sing hua'er songs, usually in the form of an antiphonal dialogue or competitive exchange. The songs combine two equally important aspects of music and language.

Hua'er often is classified as a type of love song (*qingge*). Although lyrics often are about love—and quite frequently about sex—they also may focus on scenery, events, people, and lifestyles in the region. Lyrics are usually at least partially improvised, as singers respond to the moment of performance and issues on their minds, and they are sung to one of a set of stock tunes (today called *ling*) chosen by the singer. These are topical songs, usually without fixed texts. Beginning in the early twentieth century, compilers of hua'er anthologies such as Zhang Yaxiong began to represent these improvisatory and ephemeral texts as poems or songs.

Most hua'er songs are lyric songs. Lyrics may contain phrases from stories, but they seldom narrate an event using linear temporality or develop dramatic action. Instead, singers construct lyrics through the juxtaposition of images, textual fragments from previous songs or well-known historical stories, rhyme schemes, metaphors, and formulaic phrase in a series of verses, often alternating between singers in a dialogic style. A characteristic feature of the genre consists of referring or, more often, alluding to other texts without direct reference. Fragments within one verse and verses within one performance of a song dialogue are linked through intertextual processes I call "linking mechanisms" (examples of verbal linking mechanisms within two song texts are discussed below, within the section "The *Anthology of Hua'er Folksongs*"). These provide the means for connecting the present verse to prior texts and for connecting this particular song to discourse and contexts outside the songs. With multiple linking mechanisms and potential referents, the intertextual relations are seldom simple and direct. Moreover, the goal is not simply to articulate relations between texts but to link the ideas expressed within them to other contexts, particularly the performance context. The methods of linking texts may be reinforced through music, as textual fragments within one verse are sung to the same melodic formulae of those in the next verse and in hua'er songs in other performances. Each linking mechanism brings with it possibilities for creating meaning, and each brings with it possibilities for ambiguous meanings. Such techniques contribute to the ambiguity characteristic of hua'er lyrics. Textual and musical artistry rests, at least in part, on the ability to evoke indirect connections while maintaining an equivocal stance needed for the singer to change the direction of a song to suit the singer's needs. The techniques of metaphor, analogy, and free-ranging juxtaposition of images join forces through both the intertextual relations forged within a song and the intertextuality of the genre and a longer tradition of Chinese mountain songs.

Even this brief description illustrates broader practices at work, including the definition and classification of artistic forms, people, and places, and of music and textual structures. People discuss hua'er using resources available to them, including classificatory systems, artistic theories, and value systems (Tuohy 1999). And just as hua'er singers construct intertextual relations between texts, recycle preexisting materials, and follow common musical and lyrical structures, collector-editors similarly draw upon practices used by other anthologizers to construct their anthologies. In other words, I view anthologies and the individuals who have produced them as participants in creative communicative processes similar to those used by folksong singers, who draw upon and recycle previous content and forms while expressing their individual creativity and shaping their expressions for the contexts in which they are situated.

Traditions, Anthologies, and Collector-Editors

I invoke the word "tradition" to reference several different concepts and phenomena. As Ray Cashman, Tom Mould, and Pravina Shukla point out in their introduction to *The Individual and Tradition*, tradition may be characterized as both a process and a resource: "If tradition is a process not unlike recycling, tradition as a resource comprises those things available for recycling" (2011, 3). The individual, a *bricoleur* (4), creates using materials available, the "accessible raw materials, the handed-down knowledge and ways of knowing" and, I will add, ways of doing. This is an individual with agency and an individual formed and performed within social interactions, an "on-going assemblage of performances, an intertextual work-in-progress" (5). These concepts contribute to my emphasis on the communal nature of collector-editors and of anthologies and the ways both are constructed through social interactions within particular contexts as they draw from resources of the past while negotiating the needs of the present. As collector-editors such as Zhang Yaxiong participate in a process of constructing traditions, they compile and transform the materials accessible to them—such as hua'er songs sung by singers and others' collections of folksongs—and they recycle prior methods of editing and printing those materials. In turn, they produce materials and ways of knowing and doing to be used by those after them.

Another common sense of "tradition" is the idea of a collective body of works and practices that extends through time, an idea commonly expressed through such phrases as "the Chinese literary tradition," "the tradition of collecting folksongs," and "the hua'er song tradition." Rather than subscribing to this superorganic notion of tradition, however, I conceptualize it as an "imagined tradition," a concept that refers to the fluid and creative processes by which people imagine "a tradition" and represent their imaginations to others through discourse, performance, and practice (Tuohy 1988).[10] Tradition is not an ordered set of materials with an independent existence stretching through time. Instead, individuals construct a tradition in particular contexts; they select and interpret resources as representatives of that tradition, resources that fit their imagination of the basis of that tradition and its value in relation to the present, while appealing to the past.

Thus, although there was a historical practice of collecting and publishing folksongs in China, writers such as Zhang elevated that practice to the status of a tradition and discursively fit their own work into this socially constructed tradition of collecting and publishing folksongs. And, although people sang songs in the mountains in northwest China, I argue it was only in the twentieth century that these songs became represented as a genre of folksong named "hua'er" and became elevated to the status of a regional and national folksong tradition. Zhang Yaxiong's decisions to collect songs, to imagine them as part of a genre of "hua'er folksongs," and to give tangible, public form to the "tradition" of hua'er through the publication of the *Anthology* were individual decisions to be sure. But they were decisions shaped by his experiences growing up in Gansu Province and his interactions with local scholars interested in hua'er and scholars in other parts of China working within the folksong collection movement, a movement that was represented simultaneously as "new" and as part of a long "tradition" (*chuantong*) of collection, and a movement connected to nationalism and nation building in early twentieth-century China.

It takes a lot of work to construct a genre and a tradition, and anthologies—and the collector-editors who produce them—are mechanisms in this process. David Stern considers the anthology as a literary genre, the mechanics of its production, and its functions, including how it has been "used to authorize and canonize different ideological and political visions" and "has served as a stimulus for the creation of community" (1999, 85). He points to the "constancy with which the anthological genre has served as a primary instrument for the transmission of tradition in Judaism" (1999, 85). In a similar vein, in an early twentieth-century article on changing goals and practices in Welsh folksong collections, Alfred Perceval Graves and J. Lloyd Williams discuss folksong collections as a form of collective pedagogy through which diverse members of a group come to learn about each other, and they quote "Sir Harry Reichel's fine appeal": "Our Empire is tending more and more to become a Confederation of Sister Nations.... Such cohesion can only exist, provided the different parts understand and appreciate each other. Through what medium can they better get to know each other's true spirit and ideals than through their folksongs" (1910, 213). As will be discussed next, Zhang Yaxiong had similar aims for his *Anthology*, albeit contextualized with China as a nation and as a people.

Anthologies are inherently intertextual and communal forms. They are collections of works of those other than their editors, often framed as a community that editors hope to represent, and written for a community of readers imagined by the editors. Editors, in turn, are influenced by the contexts in which they work, including real or imagined critics and institutional goals of their publishers, and in relation to political, social, pedagogical, and/or commercial aims (Di Leo 2004; Lockard and Sandell 2008). Barbara Benedict argues that, "because of their cooperative means of production and multiple authorship, anthologies are material expressions of a kind of community, and their format also directs readers to understand them as vessels of a common enterprise" (2003, 242). While not always explicitly stated, one function of anthologizing is to create a common tradition through the dissemination of shared collective resources, thereby contributing to the creation of a community to be united by the anthologized works and their values.

Anthologies are a form with longevity and spread throughout the world, and their construction is guided by a basic logic and organization. They function as what Bourdieu refers to as "structuring structures, as principles which generate and organize practices and representations that can be objectively adapted to their outcomes without presupposing a conscious aiming at ends or an express mastery of the operations necessary in order to attain them." These structuring structures become internalized, producing actions that "reproduce the structure" (Bourdieu [1980] 1990, 53). By collecting diverse works together, anthologies provide an interpretive frame based on a logic of connectedness of that which is contained within them. Their prefaces explain their goals, and annotations, texts, and images further serve to interpret the works and their significance. Prior anthologizers provide models for future anthologizers, as illustrated in Jack Zipes's work on the Grimms' *Kinder- und Hausmärchen* (Children- and Household-Tales; 2014). And anthologies provide structures, resources accessible to and internalized by editors, to follow, modify, and/or challenge.[11] Thus, when Zhang began to compile the *Anthology*, he did so with such structures and expectations already in mind.

The connections between anthologies and the national state, particularly in relation to nineteenth-century Romantic nationalism in Europe, have been discussed by scholars who have demonstrated the ways national anthologies contribute to (or at least intend to contribute to) the mobilization and constitution of national identity (Burke 1992, 295).[12] As Galit Hasan-Roken states, "Collecting oral folk creativity, writing it down, and publishing it in anthologies is one of the most noted components in the formation of national identity in modern times" (1999, 71). Moreover, in many parts of the world, including China, the connections between folklore anthologies and nationalism also were linked to the development of folklore studies (Hasan-Roken 1999, 81; Baycroft and Hopkin 2012). These processes had important implications for the structuring structures of anthologies. National anthologies, named after particular nations, proliferated. And within the nation, folk literature and arts became an important realm for anthologizing within nationalist movements, some of which posited themselves as revolutionary and worked to overturn older canons by creating new anthologies intended to reflect "new" ideologies for the nation's people.

Folklore anthologies are produced for a public that extends beyond the face-to-face interaction order often associated with folklore, as Richard Bauman argues in his analysis of an anthology compiled by Henry Row Schoolcraft. Bauman illustrates the ways "folklore is transformed as it is decontextualized and recontextualized ... to the national and international cultural spheres [and] ... to the ways in which particular texts are indexically linked to the circumstances of their production and to other discourses" (1993, 248). And he illustrates how, similar to the telling of a tale, these instances that extend beyond contexts of copresence follow similar processes and are "communicatively constituted, built upon situated communicated practice" (1993, 249). His analysis of Schoolcraft's practices opens up a "place of folklore not only in the immediate lifeworld of face-to-face storytellers and audiences but in the larger-order processes of the modern world" (1993, 267), thus reformulating ideas of anthologies and their collector-editors.

I draw the term "collector-editor" from Valdimar Hafstein, whose article on the genealogy of representations of creative agency and the "dynamic tension between tradition and creativity" (2014, 10) seems to build upon Bauman's work. Hafstein discusses "normative understandings of creativity that control the circulation of culture" (37), particularly in relation to historically layered concepts of "author, folk, editor, tradition, creation, originality" (37, 11). He proposes that the "collector-editor ... is a more helpful figure for ... understanding creativity and the circulation of culture" (9). Hafstein works to suggest "alternative ways of conceiving creative agency beyond the figures of the author and the folk, ... to help imagine creative agency differently, and to think in other terms about creative processes that are collaborative, incremental, and distributed in space and time" (36–37). This idea of the collector-editor as a central figure in collaborative and incremental processes of creative agency is useful in conceptualizing Zhang's work particularly and Chinese folksong collections more generally, within which Zhang contextualizes his work.

Contexts of Anthologies and Traditions of Anthologizing in China

There is a long history of anthologizing what today are called "folksongs," a history many contemporary scholars call a "tradition" (*chuantong*).[13] Ethnomusicologist Xiao Mei reflects on the history of recording and compiling of folk customs and songs (*caiji fengyao*) (2007, 17). Like many others, Xiao traces this history to the Zhou dynasty (1046–256 BCE) and members of the ruling elite who compiled collections of folksong lyrics and, less frequently, music (2007, 17). And like many others, including Zhang Yaxiong, she points to the *Book of Songs* (*Shijing*)[14]—and more particularly to a section within it titled the "Airs of the States" (*Guofeng*)—which she argues later scholars followed implicitly and explicitly through time as a foundational work in the anthologizing of folksongs (2007, 22).

Earlier called "The Three Hundred Poems"—a phrase used by Zhang Yaxiong in the *Anthology*—the *Book of Songs* became one of the "Five Classics" that, since the Han dynasty (206 BCE–220 CE), were a core part of the Confucian canon studied by scholar-officials and literati. The "Airs of the States" contains what are considered to be folksongs compiled by officials in the Zhou dynasty court who were sent out to collect songs within the Zhou's territory to learn about local affairs, sentiments, and customs. Most poems focus on topics of love and related emotions of longing and absence; perhaps originally sung by young men and women as a form of courtship, some have more risqué themes, albeit expressed metaphorically through comparisons and imagery. Others address topics such as political satire, war, customs, and everyday life. The officials edited the texts for stylistic consistency, added titles, grouped verses into thematically related sets, and changed lyrics to conform to their poetic conventions (such as regular four-syllable phrases). These basic methods of editing and printing folksongs have been followed by later anthologizers.

While twentieth-century folklorists sometimes invoked the *Book of Songs* to discuss the "corruption" of folksongs in print anthologies, they viewed it as part of a Chinese historical tradition. Historian and literature specialist Guo Moruo (1892–1978) claimed the "Airs of the States ... was more valuable and lasting than other portions [of the *Book of Songs* that were] written by aristocrats and religious and palace writers" ([1950] 1980a, 15), and he thought it "illustrated the vitality and endurance of indigenous folk materials" ([1958] 1980b, 19). Twentieth-century folksong anthologies, including Zhang's *Anthology*, often reference the *Book of Songs*, and later researchers compared the songs in this collection to more contemporary folksongs. For instance, hua'er researchers have claimed,

"It is not an overstatement to call hua'er the *Shijing* of the Northwest" (Wang and Xue 1983, 141).

In the early twentieth century, following the end of the Chinese empire and the founding of the Republic of China, song anthologies proliferated, with some produced for the newly instituted public school system and mass movements, including the Anti-Japanese (Resistance) and Save the Nation movements (Wong 1984; Li C. 2007; Liu [1991] 2015). Collections of folk literature were produced in a heady context in which intellectuals were developing the "modern" discipline of folklore and vigorously calling upon others to collect and value the artistic work of the "people."[15] Particularly influential was the Folksong Collection Office at Peking University (*Beijing daxue geyao zhengjichu*), which began publishing the periodical serial *Folksong Weekly* (*Geyao zhoukan*) in 1918. As noted ethnomusicologist Qiao Jianzhong wrote, "the folksong movement ... was the largest-scale folk collection activity since the *Book of Songs* and had a huge influence" (2004, 26). Editors of folksong anthologies looked back to several millennia of Chinese anthologies that remained accessible to them through a textual tradition of printing, copying, and commenting on prior writing; they also were influenced by European folklorists living in China at the time, publications by foreign scholars, and European anthologies of folksongs.[16]

Articles encouraged people to recognize that, rather than being low class or vulgar, folksongs were a valuable artistic tradition worthy of study as well as the potential basis for a Chinese national poetry. While simultaneously promoting ideas that the "common people" had a rich culture, they also advocated that folksong, as the "voice of the people," could be used to enhance a Chinese national spirit. This effort to change values and minds took work. Prefaces to folksong anthologies in the 1920s and 1930s often lamented that, in the past, people looked down upon the artistic work of the folk/people (*minjian*). As the well-known historian and folklorist Gu Jiegang (1893–1980) wrote about folksong lyrics, prior to the 1920s, "it never occurred to me that such verses were meritorious enough to put into print" (Ku [1926] 1931, 67). Similar statements have been made about the lack of attention to and records of hua'er historically.[17]

After 1949, another upsurge in collections of songs from the folk and working classes was connected to policies of the government and ideologies of the Chinese Communist Party (CCP). Prefaces often explained these people had been left out historically, and their inclusion in anthologies reflected a goal elevating the folk/working classes as the dominant class in China. Leading intellectuals advocated writing a new "Airs of the States" to express the artistry of the New China, and anthologies of "revolutionary" folksongs were published (Li Y. [1960] 1980). A massive folksong collection project, sponsored by the central government, began in 1961 (*Zhongguo minjian gequ jicheng*) but was abandoned during the Cultural Revolution and then resumed in 1979 as part of the Chinese

Nationalities Folk Music Collection series (*Zhongguo minzu minjian yinyue jicheng*; see Jones 2003).

Zhang Yaxiong's Life through Hua'er

Most writings about Zhang's life, whether autobiographical or biographical, focus on his work on hua'er. Indeed, I have found no publications on Zhang other than those that relate his life to hua'er. Biographical publications primarily began in the late 1980s and increased substantially in the early twenty-first century. Most introduce Zhang's role as the "first" compiler of a nationally circulated anthology, while others provide more in-depth discussions of Zhang in relation to the development of hua'er studies and/or folksong studies more generally (Teng 2012; Wei 2005; Liu [1991] 2015; Zhang J. 2004, 2011; Zhao [2016] 2017), his interactions with other hua'er collectors (Guo and Jidazhaizhu 2005; Guo Z. [2012] 2013), and the contexts of his life and the *Anthology* (Ma 1987; Qiao 2004; Zhang L. 2005, 2006). Publications mention he grew up in Yuzhong County in Gansu Province, then point to Yuzhong as an area of hua'er singing. Many mention he was a reporter, then discuss his columns on hua'er. And many publications after the 1990s mention he was a member of the Nationalist Party (*Guomindang*), was sent to prison, and his reputation began to be restored in the early 1980s, again connecting the restoration of his reputation to his public reappearance in hua'er studies circles and to the public reappearance of the earlier editions of the *Anthology* and its republication in 1986. Even Zhang's autobiographical writing is limited primarily to his experiences with hua'er. These publications construct and give coherence to Zhang's life through hua'er. Thus, this intertextual body of work is a prime example of the processes through which the individual's life is constructed discursively and iteratively over time and in different contexts in relation to a folkloric tradition (Cashman 2011). Here I will contribute to this process, highlighting the events most often mentioned by Zhang and others.

In 1929, while a teenager and "filled with heroic dreams" (Zhang L. 2006, n.p.), Zhang went to study journalism in a special school designed to educate "civilians" or the "common people" (*pingmin xuexiao*) in Beijing, where members of the folksong movement were concentrated.[18] There he met movement participants, among them CCP members from the Gansu-Qinghai region. They stressed the study of local musical forms, and because, in the Gansu-Qinghai area, hua'er was one of most important, they encouraged Zhang, a Northwesterner, to work on hua'er. Most publications credit Zhang Yiwu (1895–1951) as one of the first people to spark Zhang Yaxiong's interest in hua'er (Wei 1991, 2005; Zhang L. 2006; Xiao 2007, 47); Zhang Yaxiong referred to himself as a student of Zhang Yiwu. Also a native of Yuzhong County, Zhang Yiwu was an active participant in the Beijing Folksong Research Society; he later became an organizer in the Gansu branch of the CCP underground and helped Zhang Yaxiong to move along "the revolutionary path" (Lanzhoushi Yuzhongxian zhengfu 2012, n.p.). Zhang's first piece on hua'er, "Hua'er: A Preface" (*Hua'er xu*), was published in a national newspaper in 1931, with the encouragement and support of editor Xu Lingxiao (1882–1961) and Yuan Fuli.[19] Zhang described it as a "brazen and daring experiment" (1986, 50).

After graduating in 1931, Zhang returned to Gansu to concentrate on hua'er songs, although he considered himself to be an "outsider" to folklore and music studies (Zhang 1986, 10–11). He worked as an editor for the *Northwest Daily News* (*Xibei ribao*). Illustrating the influence of Beijing nationalists and local CCP members, Zhang published articles advocating antifeudalism and free marriage and a newspaper column supplement called "Freedom's Hua'er/Flower" (*Ziyou zhi hua'er*), which drew criticism from conservatives and those opposed to printing hua'er lyrics, which they considered low class, in a newspaper (Zhang L. 2006, n.p.). He then moved to the *Gansu Republican Daily News* (*Gansu minguo ribao*), where he served as a reporter and editor-in-chief of the newspaper's literary supplement. He began a column titled "one day, one flower" (or, a hua'er song a day; *yiri yiduo hua'er*), where he published song lyrics and articles on hua'er. In 1936, he published "Hua'er Afterword" (*Hua'er houxu*), an article copied and discussed multiple times within the *Anthology*. He considered it to have "broader appeal, one that attracted boundless interest among the readership" of the newspaper (Zhang 1986, 50). He called upon others to participate in collecting the songs and to send materials for his column. Over three hundred people, including local collectors, contributed hua'er song texts, information on historical and dialect issues, and letters encouraging Zhang. Zhang used much of this material in the *Anthology*.

For instance, Ya Hanzhang (1916–1989), a Gansu native and ethnologist who worked in the Gansu CCP underground, corresponded with Zhang. Already a hua'er enthusiast who had collected hua'er songs during his youth, Ya submitted many song lyrics and articles, which Zhang published in the newspaper column and within the *Anthology*.[20] Zhang also scoured through historical documents, including local gazetteers (*difangzhi*), searching for earlier references and records of regional mountain songs. Again, he included in the *Anthology* descriptions of the records he found, including "Ten Poems on My Good Recollections of Lintao" (*Wo yi Lintao hao*) written by Wu Zhen (1721–1797), a Qing dynasty poet and official from Lintao in Gansu Province.

After losing his job, Zhang took up shorter-term positions at other newspapers and traveled to cities such as Wuhan, where former classmate and CCP member Du Zhusheng encouraged him to more broadly disseminate knowledge about hua'er. He moved to Chongqing in Sichuan Province, where he published the *Anthology* in 1940, before returning to the "native place" of hua'er songs.

After he began working at a newspaper in Qinghai Province in 1944, he did firsthand research in Qinghai and at hua'er festivals in nearby Gansu and added this material to the 1948 revised edition. He returned to Gansu in 1947 and worked as the head of the Wartime Gansu News Inspection Department (*Zhanshi Gansu xinwen jianchachu shangxiao chuzhang*), run by the ruling Nationalist Party of Republican China. While Zhang may have considered these positions and relationships with Nationalist Party government leaders to be useful at the time, they became a source of problems he faced later.

In 1950, as he was preparing a third revision of the *Anthology*, he was labeled a counterrevolutionary because of his participation in the Nationalist Party (rather than because of his writings on hua'er) and spent seven years in a "reform through labor" (*laodong gaizao*) prison. After 1957 he worked in a limestone factory and similar jobs "wearing the hat" of a counterrevolutionary and "bad element" (Zhang L. 2006, n.p.). During the Cultural Revolution, Red Guards burned his manuscripts and whatever copies of the *Anthology* they could find, calling them "bullshit and yellow" (obscene) (Zhang L. 2006). Qiao Jianzhong writes, "Because of the author's many complicated misfortunes after 1949, the book was buried for more than thirty years and it was not until the 1980s that the reputation of the book and its author was restored" (2004, 19). As Zhang Lin recounts, Zhang Yaxiong was invited to the Second Gansu Provincial Arts and Literature Conference in 1980. Many hua'er researchers had "directly and indirectly been nourished by Zhang and the *Anthology*," and he was called to the stage. According to Zhang Lin, Zhang had wanted to return to his work on the third edition of the *Anthology*, but "he did not even have one copy of his book." A farmer stepped on stage and gave him his copy of the *Anthology*, saying he had saved it during the book burning; Zhang Yaxiong broke down in tears of grief and joy (Zhang L. 2006).

The *Anthology of Hua'er Folksongs*

In this section I will briefly describe the construction, contents, and characteristics of the *Anthology*. Writing a brief description of the *Anthology* is a difficult task, however, for at least three reasons. First, there are three different editions of it published within China; each succeeding edition comments on and quotes from previous editions; and all editions comment on and quote from Zhang's columns in newspapers, creating one form of intertextuality and reflexivity. Secondly, it is a highly intertextual work that comments on and includes quotes, often loosely cited, from a wide range of works written by others: the *Book of Songs*; earlier and contemporary writings about hua'er; publications about folklore, dialect studies, the folksong movement, the education of the masses, and so on from the early twentieth century through the 1940s; others' comments on and prefaces to previous editions; and the writings of others who quote Zhang's writings. And thirdly, all three editions are wide ranging in their coverage of topics and are loosely organized, in the sense that Zhang moves back and forth between topics throughout different sections of the book, a characteristic that stems in part from the first two points. Although I will mention aspects of the first two editions, I primarily will discuss and cite from the most recent edition (1986) because it is the most "complete," in that it contains most of what was included in the earlier editions, and it best represents the ways Zhang contextualized his work within an intertextual community.

The *Anthology* was first published in 1940 in Chongqing, the provisional capital of the Republic of China during much of the Japanese war. It began with the title page—Research on Northwest Folksongs: Hua'er Anthology (*Xibei minjian geyao yanjiu zhi yi: Hua'er ji*)—followed by a dedication by He Yaozu, a Guomindang Republican government official. In the "Foreword," Zhang explained that, after he had prepared the book for printing, the press suggested revisions; for instance, it "wanted me to include a discussion of feudalism and issues of folklore in other countries" in the first chapter, which he added.

The second edition was published in 1948 by the United Publishing House (*Lianhe chubanshe*), distributed by the New Life Bookstore (*Xinsheng shudian*) in Lanzhou, Gansu, and the Cultural Service Society (*Wenhua fuwushe*) in Xining, Qinghai, and printed by the Northwest Cultural Society (*Xibei wenhua xiehui*). The preface to the second edition began by commenting that the *Anthology* is "a strange book.... You say the folk (people; *minjian*) don't have art? This is folk art. You say the folk don't have literature? This is literature of the folk. You say the folk don't have poetry? This is poetry of the folk.... It is based on twenty years of experience collecting, compiling, and publishing hua'er.... Just remember that 365 people [contributed to this work and it] ... relied on help of friends to get it republished" (1986, 143).

The second edition retained and expanded on the structure of the first edition, with more detailed discussions of the significance of folksong research (Zhang Y. 1986, 12–13), materials Zhang collected during his years in Qinghai, corrections to the first edition, and so on. The second edition also included a long quote from a prepublication review published in 1947 that quoted extensively from the manuscript and listed additions the reviewer thought particularly important, such as the glossary of dialect and special vocabulary commonly used in hua'er singing and musical notations, and a more detailed discussion of the chapter on "The Native Place of Hua'er" (*Hua'er de jiaxiang*), and of issues related to music, performance venues, and particular song cycles. The reviewer also was pleased the second edition would be published in the Northwest, saying the publication of the first edition was too limited, and many Northwesterners were unable to purchase the book (quoted in Zhang Y. 1986, 143–45).

The third edition was revised and published in 1986 by the Chinese Federation of Literature and Art Circles. Glad the revised edition would finally be published, the editor, Yang Hui, briefly summed up the revisions: "To preserve the original style, revisions were minor except in a few sections when the wording expressed inappropriate or old-fashioned viewpoints" (Zhang Y. 1986, 218). The third edition included the prefaces and sections from both earlier editions as well as a few of Zhang's later comments on the earlier publications and his ongoing reflections of his processes of research. And, rather than being printed right to left and top to bottom, the third edition was printed horizontally, left to right, following the preferred format of books published in the People's Republic of China (PRC) after 1949.

All three editions were divided into two parts. The first part—titled "A Discussion of Narratives and Theories about the Northwest Mountain-Song Hua'er Collection" (*Xibei shan'ge "hua'er" ji xulun*) in the 1940 and 1948 editions and "The Process of Conducting Research on Hua'er" (*"Hua'er" de yanjiu guocheng*) in the 1986 edition—was the longest section. It contained chapters introducing hua'er, Zhang's reasons for doing this work, the literary implications of hua'er (*hua'er de wenxue yiwei*), styles and musical-textual structures of hua'er songs, information on historical records and performance practices, local dialect and distinctive features of hua'er, and so on. This first section was arranged within ten (in 1986, twelve) loosely structured chapters, including a final chapter titled "Miscellaneous Writing on Hua'er" (*Zahua "hua'er"*). Hua'er song verses were interspersed throughout as examples of theoretical points or as examples that Zhang interpreted.

The second part—titled "A Selection of 'Hua'er'" (*"Hua'er" xuan*) in the 1940 and 1948 versions and "A Choice Selection of 'Hua'er'" (*"Hua'er" jingxuan*, which also could be translated as "carefully chosen," "handpicked" hua'er, or "the best of the bunch of flowers") in the 1986 version—constituted the "anthology" proper. Unlike part one, hua'er verses were printed without Zhang's (or another person's) interpretation, although Zhang sometimes added short annotations. Based on the third edition, the work contained the lyrics to 627 numbered songs—or more precisely verses from songs—163 verses in part one and 464 in part two. These included hua'er songs collected by Zhang and others—including those on anti-Japanese themes supposedly composed by the "people" and a few composed by scholars and activists—as well as verses of a few songs that were not hua'er songs.

Contexts of and Zhang's Motivations for Publishing the Anthology

In all three versions, Zhang wrote reflexively about his motivations for doing this work, his feelings, and the contexts in which he collected and published the *Anthology*. For instance, in the preface, he explained that progressive scholars and activists in Beijing, such as Zhang Yiwu, along with the May Fourth and folksong collection movements, provided him with inspiration and guidance (1986, 25–26). He also acknowledged he "used his experience as a journalist to his advantage to collect valuable materials" (11–12). Zhang particularly emphasized the impact of the Japanese War on his work. For instance, he "was in the midst of the work, had collected over three thousand songs and had begun to interpret and annotate them when the Japanese war broke out" and he left his native place to "participate in that 'holy war' (*shengzhan*)" (1986, 10). Recounting the war period and his travels to Chongqing, he wrote that he "very carefully kept these things so painstakingly collected, to which [I] held such a sentimental attachment, close to my body so they wouldn't be lost, protecting them throughout my journey" (1986, 10). He then finished editing them, and they were published on January 22, 1940, in Chongqing, and "it was not until autumn of 1948 that there was a chance to undertake a republication and add additional materials" (1986, 10).

In the "Author's Preface" (*zixu*) to the 1948 and 1986 editions, Zhang emphasized that the process of collecting and compiling the work—from records of local customs to decisions about annotations of words and methods for printing local dialect—was done with "careful deliberation" and was "actually a collective endeavor." It relied on collaborative work with 365 people, those who submitted texts and articles to him and those he interviewed, sometimes with and sometimes without attribution. He explained that, at the time, he had recorded their names but "unfortunately, during the frequent air raids on Chongqing, the list of names was lost. Today I remember that there were 365 people who provided materials, including young shepherds, porters, young laborers, cart drivers, farmers, students, workmates, scholars and friends of all social classes who empathized with the work I was doing" (1986, 11).

Publishing this work in what Zhang called the "unusual period" of the Japanese war that resulted in "unprecedented migrations of people and culture throughout the country," Zhang believed in studying hua'er songs as a vehicle to learn about local artistry, to spread new ideas to local people, and to encourage people to learn and care about people in other parts of the nation. To emphasize these themes of promoting a "national" consciousness, he quoted extensively from an advertisement for his book in the *Central Daily News* (*Zhongyang ribao*), including the following section:

> We should use these [songs] to replace and revise the typical decadent music.... Our compatriots of the Great Northwest will inevitably smash [the enemy] to bits with the sharp sword and gunfire in the midst of these high songs. But we cannot be self-contented; we must strengthen the burgeoning national consciousness [and] raise the struggling national spirit. Compatriots! Citizens (cultured people, *wenhua renmin*)! Now in a time when the blood of all China's nationalities and the culture of all regions are intermingling, this collection must be read by the people of all nationalities and classes in the east, west, south, and north of our country. (Quoted in Zhang Y. 1986, 141–42)

Zhang did not want this use of folksong as propaganda to remain emotionally moving only on the surface. We "should not consider it to be a temporary instigation of the arousal of emotions; we ought to look at it as a fundamental form of education inspiring learning" (1986, 23).

In the 1948 edition, he added a section further explaining the importance of studying hua'er/folksongs in relation to five general principles: (1) collect folk literature as materials for social history; (2) conduct research on customs; (3) study local dialects as a means of popularizing literature and art; (4) collect materials that "reflect local conditions and are suited to local needs" to be utilized in educating the masses; and (5) understand the "vocabulary of the broad masses" to provide a local nature for propaganda. The first two principles were motivations for collecting folksongs generally, while the last three were "motives for publishing folksongs during this unusual period" (1986, 12). Moreover, these three principles had one "simple conclusion: First learn from the masses (*dazhong*), then disseminate back to the masses.... In other words, let the masses educate us before we work to educate the masses. The collection of folksongs constitutes a textbook given to us by the masses" (1986, 12–13).

Zhang emphasized the important role played by "the ear," arguing folksongs were particularly useful for spreading ideas to illiterate people (1986, 25–27): "The peasant masses' most important sensory organ is intuition [and their] most developed organ of reception is the ear. The function of the ear is to listen.... [To] propagandize among the peasant masses, we must stress methods which stimulate the sense of hearing" (1986, 24). He considered the songs to be appropriate vehicles of propaganda because they were short, passed around quickly, and possessed local flavor (26). And he compared this method to other media based on "looking and listening" that activists were using throughout the country to spread ideas (23, 25–27).[21] More specifically, Zhang was interested in tactics to ensure the War of Resistance against Japan would be carried to a successful end, tactics that depended on working with the peasants. "Time does not allow for the people to first learn to read before [we] can propagandize among them. [W]e must find the most appropriate propaganda methods to use among the peasant masses," who, although illiterate, "could still understand the meaning and significance of the war" (23). He advocated for the composition of "war of resistance" hua'er songs, claiming "the people have an interest in learning these songs" (30–33, 90–91).

Organizational and Editing Practices

The genre of folksong anthologies in early twentieth-century China had its own structuring structures and expectations of certain types of coherence. Anthologies usually presented the songs as products and reflections of periods, groups, or events within China. They were organized around a place (such as a region or province), group (such as the masses, *qunzhong*, or a particular nationality), and/or genre (such as folksong, *min'ge*, or mountain song), and many followed common criteria for selection as well as uniformity in the printing and spacing of texts, the language(s) used, and styles of annotation. These principles were practical solutions as well as part of the aesthetic guiding anthologies more generally. While much English-language writing on anthologies focuses on questions related to the canonization of works (Goody 1998, 2004), these were less of an issue in relation to the *Anthology*. Zhang was not intent on canonizing particular songs or in teaching people to sing hua'er songs. Instead, he worked to make the genre of hua'er recognized as a valuable Chinese artistic tradition.

Zhang did not consider hua'er "songs" as songs per se (in the sense of fixed texts with fixed melodies and titles), but instead as improvisatory and variable lyrics. He presented verses from longer texts and often included multiple versions of verses with lyrics on one topic. This type of anthology favored "complete" verses that were printed as poems, with their boundaries marked with spatial formatting and numbers. The ideal of complete verses within the *Anthology* differed from hua'er performance practices, since not only was the music left out but only parts of the performed texts made it into the printed text. For instance, a large portion of hua'er performance is spent singing sounds without explicit meaning, such as vocables, formulaic phrases, and short textual-melodic phrases such as "ah, Lianhua Mountain" and "ah, song-group leader (*chuanbashi*) listen, ah." Although he discussed them, Zhang did not print these padding words and formulaic phrases, and he often omitted entire series of verses.

As a "regional" folksong collection, the *Anthology* framed the Northwest as a region within the nation of China. Thus, it constituted hua'er songs and the people as "national." The book introduced "national" points to people in the region using local language and songs. And, with a goal of introducing the rest of China to hua'er, the work required "translation" and annotation of terms to make these oral texts legible to readers unfamiliar with hua'er, local dialect, and customs in northwest China. Thus, Zhang added to the printed text more words, in the form of annotations explaining the meanings of local terms, references, and allusions, for instance. He discussed the difficulty of capturing through written transcription the expressive emotion of hua'er songs as sung, but "what other choice do we have? At least we're able with paper and ink to capture and preserve a little bit of the silken threads" (1986, 52). He explained difficulties he had deciding how to transcribe dialect terms (135). He sometimes chose homophonous characters to indicate pronunciations, rather than using other means, such as a phonetic system for Chinese invented by Zhang Taiyan (1869–1936) that Zhang Yaxiong originally thought might be useful but then reconsidered, questioning whether anyone had the time to learn and use it (1986, 136). Zhang also had to define "hua'er," a word most readers would have understood as "flowers."

Defining and Naming Hua'er, Its Region of Circulation, and Its Artistry

In the opening chapter of the two earlier editions (1940 and 1948; a section was added to the 1986 version before this chapter), titled "What Is Hua'er?," Zhang explained that "hua'er falls within the mountain-song class of folksong." He then explained he wrote three older accounts describing hua'er in some detail and he would use those as a "blueprint" for his discussion in this volume. The first of these older accounts was his "Hua'er: A Preface" (*Hua'er xu*), published in 1931 when he was in Beijing, which defines hua'er as "a type of mountain song that circulates in the Gansu-Qinghai-Ningxia regions; it also often is called shaonian. 'Hua'er' refers to a woman one is fond of; 'Shaonian' is a label men use to refer to themselves" (1986, 33). While a simple definition, it served to classify hua'er as mountain songs, a type of music with which Chinese readers from different areas would be familiar; to specify the region with which hua'er is associated; and to introduce two terms that often were used to label songs in the region. This basic definition of hua'er has been quoted repeatedly in later publications.

He pointed out that some hua'er song lyrics themselves also help to characterize the genre and reflexively comment on what singing means and expresses. As one of many examples in a section titled "Using Mountain Songs to Explain Mountain Sounds" (*Yi shan'ge jie shan'ge*), he included the following verse that uses the word "hua'er":

> Premium cotton from Liangzhou in Gansu
> A weaver uses to make a handkerchief.
> You sing a hua'er and I'll respond;
> Let's find a road on which to walk together.
> (Zhang Y. 1986, 132, song text #160)

> Gansu Liangzhou de hao mianhua
> Fangxianzhe yaozhi ge shoupa
> Ni man "hua'er" wo dahua
> Xun shang ge dalu zou ba

In another section, he again described the area of circulation of hua'er, this time phrasing it in relation to watersheds of the Datong, Xia, and Tao rivers, and the effect of hua'er singing in the region: "Between the mountains and rivers, dialogue singing creates an electric network of emotional silken threads (*qingsihua zuo dianwang*) that embraces the singers and listeners and the mountains, rivers, grasses, trees, flowers, and birds within it." He then contrasted "house songs" (*jiage*) with mountain songs such as hua'er: "House songs are preexisting tunes recited and repeated from memory" (1986, 52, 97). Hua'er songs are about "scenery, lives, and emotions, sung freely as one wishes, singing and responding, questions and answers" (1986, 52). Later in the work, he also distinguished the two genres based on traditional customs related to performance venues, saying house songs are sung within the home and village buildings and must "keep within the bounds of unnecessary and elaborate formalities" (1986, 97).

Zhang repeatedly represented hua'er songs sung among the people as the "clear and frank spirit of the Northwest," and he tied the songs to the now often-stated nature of the people of the Northwest as "brave, resolute, straightforward and freedom seeking," an idea he believed was reflected in the structures and performance practices characteristic of the genre. He contrasted hua'er songs with the poetry of the literati and ruling classes and lamented that Confucian values had stifled this clear voice of the folk. He countered dominant conceptions of poetry and art and previous "tampering" of folksong by ruling classes:

> Some consider Greece to be the native place of philosophy; now we can confidently state that the folk (people; *minjian*) are the native place of poetry. Among the folk, poetry becomes tune and song. When it spreads [to the literati, they] ... apply rouge and powder, dressing up the songs to be pretty, and there remains no way to recover a daughter's natural beauty. Folksong has been considered a pretty daughter in a humble family that has survived through the lips of shepherds and peasants, then was concealed by Chinese Confucianism and decayed under unrealistic arguments and control of Confucian society; the scholar-official class usually avoids mentioning the taboo words of sex.... Therefore the more straightforward words about sex are more frequently found among the folk. (1986, 34–35)

He described instances in which his work changed the minds of local people. For instance, he wrote that when he was collecting hua'er songs, a person said to him: "I haven't paid attention to hua'er in a long time; reading the 'Hua'er Afterword' made me regret that so much. One mid-autumn festival when I was excited, I sang a hua'er song and a person called me uncivilized. When someone sings songs like 'Misty Rain' and 'Taohua River' [*Maomaoyu* and *Taohuajiang*, popular songs in the 1930s and 40s], others consider him to be civilized. Now because of the gentleman's [Zhang's] work, ... I now impolitely represent the ... peasant masses and thank you!" (1986, 103).

Part of Zhang's work involved describing the artistry of hua'er lyrics. When composing lyrics, singers usually make use of various forms of metaphor, comparison, and figurative language. Zhang discussed such characteristics in the first two editions of the *Anthology*, for instance, in relation to a set of texts. In the 1986 edition, he added a section with the subtitle "Metaphor (resemblance, *bi*), Description (direct exposition, *fu*), Implied Comparison (evocative, *xing*)," thereby invoking terms used in historical commentaries about these three types of creative methods that characterize songs in the *Book of Songs*. Zhang commented on commonalities of methods used within hua'er lyrics and "ancient mountain songs" in the "Three-Hundred Songs" (an alternate reference to the *Book of Songs*; 1986, 57).

As Zhang explained, hua'er songs often rely upon a metaphorical strategy called *bixing*; initiating metaphors (*biyu*) are used within the first one or two lines of each verse to introduce the main topic (*xing*; also called *benti*) of the verse put forth in the next few lines of the song, one of the types of linking mechanisms discussed above. Because initiating metaphors often consist of textual fragments from other texts and contexts, they allude to references spatially and temporally removed from the context of performance and from the main topic they serve to introduce. The initiating metaphor may be a metaphor, analogy, image, or figure of speech that usually has some implicit or explicit connection to the primary topic of the remainder of the verse (and, presumably, the point of the entire verse), but the relationship between the initiating metaphor and the main topic often is not directly transparent.

For instance, Zhang included the following verse, phrased in a male voice, that begins with an initiating metaphor of an unexpected military coup that led to the closing of the city gates of Lanzhou (the capital of Gansu Province). It then moves to describe another unexpected change, perhaps unfaithfulness, and the closing of a lover's heart. The connection is made more explicit through the repetition of the term "transformed" (*bianle*), which is the sixth character in line one (within the word "mutinied") and line three, both indicating a change in attitude or "heart," as well as through the analogy of locked gates and a locked heart of the singer's "little sister," a term commonly used in songs to refer to a lover/potential lover:

Lanzhou City's troops have mutinied;	*Lanzhou chengli bing bianle*
The four gates are locked up tightly.	*Si xiaomen shangle suole*
As [I] watch, little sister's heart changes;	*Yankan gamei xin bianle*
[Her] big eyes now won't look at me.	*Dayanjing bukan ge wole*
(Zhang Y. 1986, 149, song text #194)	

Published within the second part of the *Anthology*, which contains hua'er song lyrics without extensive interpretation, Zhang did not annotate this verse, since the meaning of the lyrics would be clear to readers. By that point in the book, Zhang already had explained the use of metaphors and the *bixing* structure of song lyrics, the meaning and use of the term "little sister" (*gamei*), and the regional dialect term "ga," meaning "little."

References to Other Texts and People

One of the most striking characteristics of the *Anthology* is the sheer number of references to other works and people. Many of these are unattributed other than using phrases such as "ancient documents" and so on. Zhang did not include singers' names, perhaps because he lost the list of names during the chaos of wartime Chongqing as well as because others from whom he collected texts did not include their names; more generally, attribution of singers was not the norm in publications of anthologies from the early 1900s through the early 1980s. In many instances, however, he did refer to particular collectors, including those from whom he liberally quoted and paraphrased, sometimes without attribution.

For instance, he acknowledged the work of collector Ya Hanzhang and Ya's contributions to his own thinking on the divisions of hua'er styles and lyrical and musical structures. Zhang explained that, in 1936 while working as a newspaper editor, he received letters from Ya. He quotes from one letter and explains, because the letter contained such valuable material, he published it in the newspaper under the title "Hua'er: A Second Preface" (*Hua'er zaixu*) (Zhang Y. 1986, 74–75) and again in the *Anthology*, with his own modifications. According to Guo Zhengqing, Ya wrote the "Second Preface" article to supplement and extend Zhang's own article, "Hua'er: A Preface" (*Hua'er xu*), published in the newspaper earlier in 1936. Ya also provided Zhang with "tips on annotations" of song lyrics, place names, and historical information (Guo Z. [2012] 2013, n.p.). In another section of the *Anthology*, Zhang again discussed Ya Hanzhang (using the pseudonym Jidazhaizhu). He wrote that Ya recorded over one hundred Hezhou hua'er song texts and praised Ya's work, writing that Ya "sympathetically devoted his efforts to the work of researching folk customs, 'wild tunes' [a term often used to refer to hua'er prior to the 1950s], and local dialect. Therefore, the materials he copied were extremely useful in terms of preserving the true nature of hua'er" (Zhang Y. 1986, 119). Zhang included a large number of song lyrics recorded, and often annotated and interpreted, by Ya. And he extensively quoted (or perhaps paraphrased) Ya's description of singing styles and song texts. For instance, he quoted from Ya's extensive discussion of the "Five Watches" tune (*Wugengqu*)—a discussion spanning topics such as the long history of the song type; quotations from "ancient documents" about the five watches and their significance; and song lyrics from the Song Dynasty (960–1279) and later printed poetry collections, children's songs, and other genres—while quoting lyrics from each form, followed by a set of hua'er song lyrics on the theme of the five watches and interpretations of their meanings (1986, 103–9, 120–21). In addition to the "Five Watches," other themes of narrative hua'er (*xushi hua'er*) addressed by Zhang—also supplied and discussed by Ya Hanzhang—were the "Heroes of the Yang Family" (*Yangjiajiang*) (Zhang Y. 1986, 103–5, 191–93), the "Romance of the Three Kingdoms" (*Sanguo yanyi*), and songs about the twelve-month cycle (*Shi'er yue*), all of which are common themes of song in many parts of China.[22]

It often is difficult to decipher which sections and ideas are Zhang's and which are from others. Guo Zhengqing argues the *Anthology* is a mansion of Zhang Yaxiong's construction, but it is one that contains Ya Hanzhang's plans and construction materials. Moreover, I have come to doubt the *Anthology* became a "model" for future anthologies, in part because the bulk of the work is less an anthology than a loosely structured set of intertextual materials that introduce the genre of hua'er through a synthesis of practices, texts, and ideologies circulating over time. I am convinced, however, this work was central in the dissemination of the idea that hua'er was a genre and a tradition to be valued and promoted.

The Afterlives of Zhang and His *Anthology*

After the publications of the first two editions of the *Anthology*, Zhang was imprisoned and exiled from public circles, but others published anthologies of and works about hua'er. Particularly after the founding of the PRC in 1949, a spate of hua'er publications and recordings were published by presses through the 1950s, including at least at two hua'er anthologies and an introduction to hua'er written by hua'er singer Zhu Zhonglu in 1950, 1953, and 1954.[23] By the late 1950s, publications increasingly emphasized "new hua'er," many of which focused on political themes such as "bitter songs about the Old Society" and "New Socialist praise songs." In 1966 the last collection of hua'er songs until after the Cultural Revolution was published by the Gansu Nationalities Press (*Gansu minzu chubanshe*).

Returning to the early 1980s, the period where this chapter began, hua'er scholarship and publications resumed, and many began to write about Zhang Yaxiong and the *Anthology*. Hua'er scholars emphasized that the topics raised by Zhang have been among the key questions in what are called "hua'er circles" over the last seventy years, and they pointed to the importance of the *Anthology* in articulating these questions (Ma 1987; Wei 2005; Zhang L. 2006). Some, such as Qiao Jianzhong, invoked the trope of the toiling folksong collector and characterized Zhang's "love for spreading knowledge about the folk arts of his native place, a kind of love that led him to be unafraid of the rugged route [he traveled], in spite of being bombarded by aggressors, and a kind of love that made him unafraid of the time-consuming effort of sifting through one hua'er verse after another; this kind of love made him resolved to collect in one book the best lyrics of hua'er, the most important historical material, and the most representative of activities and offer them to a large-scale readership" (2004, 25).

Zhang is an individual who left his mark on and enacted tradition (Cashman, Mould, and Shukla 2011, 1–2), a face and mechanism of tradition, "understood as a process of cultural construction ... created by individuals out of experience" (Glassie 2003, 179–80). He participated in a number of communities linked through networks, discourse, and textual traditions. And he included the work of many others to create an anthology, itself an intertextual form that relied on the creativity of others, as Zhang recontextualized song lyrics, texts, annotation practices, interpretations, and theories of others that he acknowledged explicitly and implicitly in the densely intertextual *Anthology* he produced. As Bauman writes, "reentextualizations carry direct evidence of their history along with them; the published texts tell us where they've been" (1993, 249). The *Anthology* was a cultural production shaped by historical and contemporary practices, themselves part of broader imperial, national, and international contexts and practices.

Among the consistent tropes in writing about hua'er since the 1940s is the idea that hua'er songs and their singers had historically been reviled and worse. Zhang's use of the term "hua'er/flower" in the title of the *Anthology* helped to discursively transform the songs from a "wild weed" (*yequ*) to "beautiful flowers" in the "Garden of One Hundred Flowers" (*baihuayuan*), leading the way to hua'er's designation as a part of the "Intangible Cultural Heritage of Humanity." Today, people continue to sing hua'er in the mountains of northwest China, while others do so in nationally televised folksong competitions and in local bars catering to a younger people enamored by China's "urban folk music." Hua'er is promoted as a "local product" and cultural heritage of the Northwest, and young scholars continue to write dissertations on hua'er songs, citing the work of Zhang Yaxiong. Zhang's promotion of hua'er and hua'er studies' promotion of Zhang mutually and multiply intersected through ongoing discourse over the course of the last seven decades, illustrating the importance of collector-editors and their anthologies in the social construction of tradition and in the dissemination of values.

Indiana University
Bloomington

Acknowledgments

I express my gratitude to the many scholars, singers, and hua'er lovers (*aihaozhe*) who, over the last three decades, have patiently shared with me their ideas about hua'er. I also thank Wei Quanming and Zhao Zongfu who have more recently contributed their ideas about hua'er historiography and Zhang Yaxiong as well as the reviewers of this chapter.

Notes

1. In this context, *pingfan* refers to reevaluating and restoring the reputations and/or positions of people wrongfully denounced, imprisoned, or otherwise harmed during prior political campaigns from the 1950s through the 1970s. All translations of Chinese-language texts are by the author.

2. The Chinese term "hua'er" can refer to one song, many songs, and the song genre. In English, I use the singular form to refer to the genre and add the term "song(s)" to refer to a hua'er song or hua'er songs. The most common meaning of "hua'er" is "flower" but in song lyrics it may have other meanings; therefore, I use the term "hua'er" rather than "flower songs."

3. Publications on hua'er studies historiography often use the phrases "nationally circulated" or "specialized book" to emphasize that, prior to Zhang, others had written about hua'er in poetry, short articles, and unpublished collections (Li F. 1983, 160–61; Teng 2012). Zhang mentions many of these writers within the *Anthology*. The question of who was the "first" hua'er collector and researcher has been a topic of debate in recent years. See, for instance, Wang Pei (2014).

4. The video submitted with the nomination file to UNESCO provides a basic introduction to hua'er and examples of hua'er singing and festivals (UNESCO, ICH, n.d.).

5. As will be discussed below, for several centuries, some people in the region had used "hua'er" in their writings to refer to songs sung in parts of the region; and the term also circulated locally during the time of Zhang's work. But "hua'er" was only one of several terms used to label the songs.

6. Ma's use of *jida chengzhe* is a historical allusion to a quote by the philosopher Mencius who characterized Confucius as the epitome of the great and comprehensive synthesizer.

7. "Shaonian" is another local term used to refer to hua'er songs, particularly within Qinghai. Like "hua'er," it has multiple meanings but most often refers to a young male. Thus, the title of the song "Hua'er yu shaonian" can be translated "Flower and Youth," "Female and Male," and/or "Hua'er Songs."

8. A Christian missionary in Xining at the time, Josef Trippner, refers to Zhang as "a man from the newspaper" (1952, 264) and writes that, in Qinghai, the name "hua'er" was barely known by the people in the 1940s and Qinghai's shaonian are different from the songs Zhang collected (1952, 264–66). Noted hua'er scholar Xi Huimin (1931–2000), however, argues, "the name hua'er was historically derived; it definitely was not the construct of Zhang Yaxiong and did not start to become popular only with the publication of the *Anthology*. It is unrealistic to believe that anything not built on the base of the people, that relies on the dissemination and promotion of one person or one book . . . could become accepted and popular among the people in a short time" (1983, 10). Gao Jingye claimed that, once hua'er gained national attention, people in different areas began calling their mountain songs "hua'er" (interview, 1984).

9. The number and names of these subgenres or styles (*liupai*) have been the topic of heated debate among hua'er scholars for the last several decades; for a detailed discussion, see Sue Tuohy (2003; 1988, 141–68, 306–10).

10. I developed this concept of imagined traditions after reading Benedict Anderson's theory of "imagined communities" (1983). My primary research question was how and why hua'er songs became defined as a regional genre and a "tradition," the processes by which the genre became included in a reconfigured Chinese national artistic tradition, and the bases on which that national tradition was imagined, expressed, and enacted (Tuohy 1988).

11. See Joe Lockard's and Jillian Sandell's succinct discussion of a series of anthologies that simultaneously build upon prior anthologies (and models of anthologies) while challenging them (2008, 228).

12. See also Philip Bohlman (2004), Lockard and Sandell (2008), Theodore Mason (1998), and John Street (2000).

13. Literary anthologies proliferated after the third century, particularly in relation to classical texts and elite poetry; see, for instance, Xiaorong Li (2009), Zhongling Wang ([1993] 1996), and Pauline Yu (1990).

14. Also called the *Book of Poetry* or *Book of Odes*, the *Shijing* is traditionally dated to the Western Zhou, 1046–771 BCE. For discussions of Music Bureau (*Yuefu*) anthologies,

including their intertextuality and relations between orality and print, see Joseph Allen (1992), Alexander Beecroft (2009), and Charles Egan (2000).

15. Most scholars date the beginning of "modern" folklore studies to this period. See, for instance, a recent article by noted folklorist and hua'er scholar Zhao Zongfu ([2016] 2017, n.p.); see also Weipang Chao (1942, 1943), Chang-tai Hung (1985), Laurence Schneider (1971), and Tuohy (1988, 84–103).

16. For a discussion of the influence of European, American, and Japanese folklorists on Chinese folklore studies, see Chang-tai Hung (1985); see Dechao Li (2014) on the influence of the Grimms' publications in China.

17. Such tropes have a long history. In the preface to a Qing Dynasty poetry collection, the anthologizer Wang Duanshu attempts to counter potential criticism that the anthology contains low-class work: "Even though some poems are vulgar, lewd, and ridiculous, I still collect them. Is my collection promiscuous? I would say no. When Confucius compiled the *Book of Songs*, he did not exclude the music of Zheng and Wei [erotic songs]" (X. Li 2009, 105).

18. Some sources list the school as the Beiping (Beijing) City Private University for the Common People (*Beipingshi sili pingmin daxue*), while others specifically say it was a school established in 1918 under the leadership of Cai Yuanpei, president of Peking University and an early advocate of the Chinese folksong movement.

19. Yuan (1893–1987) published in the *Folksong Weekly* (vol. 82) a short article on hua'er in 1925 but, rather than using the character for "flower," Yuan used the homophonous character for speech.

20. Guo Zhengqing characterizes Ya Hanzhang as "a pioneer in theoretical research on hua'er" and discusses in detail Ya's work and his relationship with Zhang Yaxiong, arguing, "the communications about hua'er between Ya Hanzhang and Zhang Yaxiong are . . . both an important event in research on hua'er in the 1930s and 1940s and a magnificent chapter in the history of Chinese hua'er research" ([2012] 2013, n.p.).

21. These ideas of folk literature as educational and spiritual tools were common among a group of scholars who continued to carry out research on folklore during the war period (Liu [1991] 2015, n.p.).

22. Another example of explicit attribution can be seen within a section on dialogue singing that is titled "Li Dexian's Study of Hua'er" (*Li Dexian du "hua'er"*; Zhang Y. 1986, 110–11).

23. Zhu Zhonglu (1922–2007), the "king of hua'er" (*hua'er wang*), learned to sing from his father and other older hua'er singers. But he also attended middle school, where he learned to read and write. He is known also for publications and was the head of the Qinghai Hua'er Society in the early 2000s; see Tuohy (1988) and Zhang Junren (2011).

References

Allen, Joseph. 1992. *In the Voice of Others: Chinese Music Bureau Poetry*. Ann Arbor: Center for Chinese Studies, University of Michigan.
Anderson, Benedict. 1983. *Imagined Communities: Reflections on the Origin and Spread of Nationalism*. New York: Verso.
Bauman, Richard. 1993. "The Nationalization and Internationalization of Folklore: The Case of Schoolcraft's 'Gitshee Gauzinee'." *Western Folklore* 52 (2/4): 247–69.

Baycroft, Timothy, and David Hopkin, eds. 2012. *Folklore and Nationalism in Europe during the Long Nineteenth Century.* Leiden, Netherlands: Brill.

Beecroft, Alexander. 2009. "Oral Formula and Intertextuality in the Chinese 'Folk' Tradition (Yuefu)." *Early Medieval China* 1 (1): 23–47.

Benedict, Barbara M. 2003. "The Paradox of the Anthology: Collecting and Difference in Eighteenth-Century Britain." *New Literary History* 34 (2): 231–56.

Bohlman, Philip V. 2004. *The Music of European Nationalism: Cultural Identity and Modern History.* Santa Barbara: ABC-CLIO.

Bourdieu, Pierre. (1980) 1990. *The Logic of Practice.* Translated by Richard Nice. Stanford, CA: Stanford University Press.

Burke, Peter. 1992. "We, the People: Popular Culture and Popular Identity in Modern Europe." In *Modernity and Identity*, edited by Scott Lash and Jonathan Friedman, 293–308. Cambridge, MA: Blackwell.

Cashman, Ray. 2011. "The Role of Tradition in the Individual: At Work in Donegal with Packy Jim McGrath." In *The Individual and Tradition: Folkloristic Perspectives*, edited by Ray Cashman, Tom Mould, and Pravina Shukla, 303–22. Bloomington; Indianapolis: Indiana University Press.

Cashman, Ray, Tom Mould, and Pravina Shukla. 2011. "Introduction: The Individual and Tradition." In *The Individual and Tradition: Folkloristic Perspectives*, edited by Ray Cashman, Tom Mould, and Pravina Shukla, 1–26. Bloomington; Indianapolis: Indiana University Press.

Chao, Weipang. 1942. "Modern Chinese Folklore Investigation, Part I: The Peking National University." *Folklore Studies* 1: 55–76.

———. 1943. "Modern Chinese Folklore Investigation, Part II: The National Sun Yat-Sen University." *Folklore Studies* 2: 79–88.

Di Leo, Jeffrey R., ed. 2004. *On Anthologies: Politics and Pedagogy.* Lincoln: University of Nebraska Press.

Egan, Charles H. 2000. "Were Yüeh-fu Ever Folk Songs? Reconsidering the Relevance of Oral Theory and Balladry Analogies." *Chinese Literature: Essays, Articles, Reviews (CLEAR)* 22: 31–66.

Glassie, Henry. 2003. "Tradition." In *Eight Words for the Study of Expressive Culture*, edited by Burt Feintuch, 176–97. Urbana: University of Illinois Press.

Goody, Jack. 1998. "Canonization in Oral and Literate Cultures." In *Canonization and Decanonization: Papers Presented to the International Conference of the Leiden Institute for the Study of Religions*, edited by A. van der Kooij and K. van der Toorn, 3–16. Leiden, Netherlands: Brill.

———. 2004. "The Transcription of Oral Heritage." *Museum International* 56 (1/2): 91–96.

Graves, Alfred Perceval, and J. Lloyd Williams. 1910. "Welsh Folk-Song Collections." *The Celtic Review* 6 (23): 207–13.

Guo Moruo. (1950) 1980a. "Women yanjiu minjian wenyi de mudi" [Our purpose in conducting research on folk literature and art]. *Minjian wenyi jikan* [A collection of articles on folk literature and art]. Reprinted in Zhongguo minjian wenyi yanjiuhui, Shanghai fenhui, vol. 1, 14–18.

———. (1958) 1980b. "Guanyu daguimo shouji min'ge wenti" [Concerning the extensive collection of folksongs]. *Minjian wenxue* [Folk literature] 5. Reprinted in Zhongguo minjian wenyi yanjiuhui, Shanghai fenhui, vol. 1, 19–27.

Guo Zhengqing. (2012) 2013. "Ya Hanzhang yu Zhang Yaxiong de hua'er zhi jiao" [Exchanges on hua'er between Ya Hanzhang and Zhang Yaxiong]. *Gansu wenyi* [Gansu literature]. Reprinted in *Xibei wenxuewang* [Northwest literature web], January 9, 2013. http://www.gszj.net/Html/2013010999020.html (site unavailable at time of publication).

Guo Zhengqing, ed., and Jidazhaizhu [Ya Hanzhang]. 2005. "Ya Hanzhang hua'er zhushu jiaogao: Hua'er zaizu" [Ya Hanzhang's annotated and corrected manuscript, Hua'er: A second preface]. *Gansu minzu yanjiu* [Research on Gansu nationalities] 3: 63–85.

Hafstein, Valdimar Tr. 2014. "The Constant Muse: Copyright and Creative Agency." *Narrative Culture* 1 (1): 9–47.

Hasan-Roken, Galit. 1999. "Textualizing the Tales of the People of the Book: Folk Narrative Anthologies and National Identity in Modern Israel." *Prooftexts* 19 (1): 71–82.

Hung, Chang-tai. 1985. *Going to the People: Chinese Intellectuals and Folk Literature, 1918–1937*. Cambridge, MA: Council on East Asian Studies; Harvard University Press.

Jones, Stephen. 2003. "Reading between the Lines: Reflections on the Massive 'Anthology of Folk Music of the Chinese Peoples.'" *Ethnomusicology* 47 (3): 287–337.

Ku, Chieh-kang [Gu Jiegang]. (1926) 1931. *The Autobiography of a Chinese Historian: Being the Preface to A Symposium on Ancient Chinese History*. Translated by Arthur W. Hummel. Leiden, Netherlands: Brill.

Lanzhoushi Yuzhongxian zhengfu, xianwei dangshi ban [County committee on the history of the Party, Yuzhong County, Lanzhou City, ed.]. 2012. "Gansu wuchan jieji geming de xianquzhe" [Zhang Yiwu: Pioneer of the proletarian revolution in Gansu]. *Gansu, Yuzhong* government website, August 23, 2012. http://yzx.lanzhou.gov.cn/art/2016/12/27/art_1758_91822.html.

Li Chuanxin. 2007. "Yitao Kangzhan gequ xuanji" [A series of Anti-Japanese War song anthologies]. *Chuban shiliao* [History of published materials] 2: 56–57.

Li, Dechao. 2014. "The Influence of the Grimms' Fairy Tales on the Folk Literature Movement in China (1918–1943)." In *Grimms' Tales around the Globe: The Dynamics of Their International Reception*, edited by Vanessa Joosen and Gillian Lathey, 119–34. Detroit: Wayne State University Press.

Li Fu. 1983. "Shitan hua'er de gelü wenti" [A brief discussion of questions about the rules and form of hua'er]. In Zhongguo minjian wenyi yanjiuhui, Gansu fenhui, vol. 2, 158–65.

Li, Xiaorong. 2009. "Gender and Textual Politics during the Qing Dynasty: The Case of the *Zhengshi ji*." *Harvard Journal of Asiatic Studies* 26 (1): 75–107.

Li Yang. (1960) 1980. "Shehui zhuyi xinshidai de xin Guofeng: Du *Hongqi geyao* sanbaishou" [The new Guofeng of the socialist period: Upon reading the three hundred songs in the *Songs of the Red Flag*]. *Wenxue pinglun* 1. Reprinted in Zhongguo minjian wenyi yanjiuhui, Shanghai fenhui, vol. 2, 87–99.

Liu Xicheng. (1991) 2015. "Kang-Ri zhanzheng he jiefang zhanzheng shiqi de minjian wenxue yundong: *Zhongguo xin wenyi daxi, minjian wenxue (1937–1949)* daoyan" [The folk literature movement during the Anti-Japanese War and War of Liberation: Introduction to *A compendium of Chinese new literature and arts: A collection of folk literature (1937–1949)*]. Reprinted in Liu Xicheng de boke [Liu Xicheng's blog], August 4, 2015. http://blog.sina.com.cn/s/blog_6312a10e0102w1tm.html.

Lockard, Joe, and Jillian Sandell. 2008. "National Narratives and the Politics of Inclusion: Historicizing American Literature Anthologies." *Pedagogy: Critical Approaches to Teaching Literature, Language, Composition, and Culture* 8 (2): 227–54.

Ma Wenhui. 1987. "Shitan Zhang Yaxiong de *Hua'er ji* zai hua'er souji, zhengli he yanjiushang de diwei" [A discussion of the position of Zhang Yaxiong's *Anthology of Hua'er Folksongs* in hua'er research, compilation, and research]. *Gansu shehui kexue* [Gansu social sciences] 3: 109–12.

Mason, Theodore O., Jr. 1998. "The African-American Anthology: Mapping the Territory, Taking the National Census, Building the Museum." *American Literary History* 10 (1): 185–98.

Qiao Jianzhong. 2004. "Hua'er yanjiu diyi shu: Zhang Yaxiong he ta de *Hua'er ji*" [The first book of hua'er research: Zhang Yaxiong and his *Anthology of hua'er folksongs*]. *Yinyue yanjiu* [Music research] 3 (114): 19–28.

Schneider, Laurence. 1971. *Ku Chieh-kang and China's New History: Nationalism and the Quest for Alternative Traditions*. Berkeley: University of California Press.

Stern, David. 1999. "Afterword." Special issue on the Anthological Imagination in Jewish Literature. *Prooftexts* 19 (1): 83–86.

Street, John. 2000. "Invisible Republics and Secret Histories: A Politics of Music." *Cultural Values* 4 (3): 298–313.

Teng Xiaotian. 2012. "Guanyu 'hua'er' de zaoqi jizai yu yanjiu huodong" [A discussion of the early period of historical records and research activities on hua'er]. *Qunwen tiandi* [Folk art and literature] 5: 4–7.

Trippner, Josef. 1952. "Die 'shao nien': Lieder in Ch'ing-hai" [Shaonian songs in Qinghai]. Supplement, *Folklore Studies* S1: 264–305.

Tuohy, Sue. 1988. "Imagining the Chinese Tradition: The Case of Hua'er Songs, Festivals, and Scholarship." PhD diss., Indiana University, Bloomington.

———. 1999. "The Social Life of Genre: The Dynamics of Folksong in China." *Asian Music* 30 (2): 39–86.

———. 2003. "The Choices and Challenges of Local Distinction: Regional Attachments and Dialect in Chinese Music." In *Global Pop, Local Language*, edited by Harris M. Berger and Michael Thomas Carroll, 153–85. Jackson: University Press of Mississippi.

UNESCO, ICH (United Nations Educational, Scientific and Cultural Organization, Intangible Cultural Heritage). n.d. "Hua'er." http://www.unesco.org/culture/ich/index.php?lg=en&pg=00011&RL=00211.

Wang Dian and Xue Li. 1983. "Lun Taomin hua'er de yishuxing" [On the artistry of Taomin hua'er]. In Zhongguo minjian wenyi yanjiuhui, Gansu fenhui, vol. 1, 141–50.

Wang Pei. 2014. "Hua'er yanjiu diyiren de jilu he chuanchengzhe: Li Fu hua'er chengjiu shuping" [The first collector and transmitter in hua'er research: A discussion of Li Fu's achievements in hua'er research]. *Xi'an yinyue xuebao* [Xi'an music journal] 33 (3): 75–80.

Wang, Zhongling. (1993) 1996. "Anthologies and Annotations as Dynamic Forces in the Movement of Literary History." *Social Sciences in China* 17 (3): 129–38.

Wei Quanming. 1991. *Hua'er xinlun* [New articles on hua'er]. Lanzhou, China: Dunhuang wenyi chubanshe.

———. 2005. *Zhongguo "hua'er"xue shigang* [A history of Chinese hua'er scholarship]. Lanzhou, China: Gansu renmin chubanshe.

Wong, Isabel K. 1984. "Geming Gequ: Songs for the Education of the Masses." In *Popular Chinese Literature and Performing Arts in the People's Republic of China, 1949–1979*, edited by Bonnie S. McDougall, 112–43. Berkeley: University of California Press.

Xi Huimin. 1983. "Linxia hua'er yishuxing de kaocha yanjiu" [Investigative research on the artistry of Linxia hua'er]. In Zhongguo minjian wenyi yanjiuhui, Gansu fenhui, vol. 2, 9–38.

Xiao Mei. 2007. *Zhongguo dalu 1900–1966: Minzu yinyuexue shidi kaocha: Biannian yu ge'an* [Mainland China 1900–1966: A chronicle and case studies of ethnomusicological fieldwork]. Shanghai: Shanghai yinyue xueyuan chubanshe.

Yu, Pauline. 1990. "Poems in Their Place: Collections and Canons in Early Chinese Literature." *Harvard Journal of Asiatic Studies* 50 (1): 163–96.

Zhang Junren. 2004. *Hua'er wang Zhu Zhonglu: Renleixue qingjing zhong de minjian geshou* [Zhu Zhonglu, the king of hua'er: The anthropology of a folksinger]. Lanzhou, China: Dunhuang wenyi chubanshe.

———. 2011. "1949 nian yiqian de hua'er yu hua'er yanjiu: Hua'er xueshushi yanjiu zhi yi" [Hua'er and hua'er research before 1949: Research on the history of hua'er studies, part 1]. *Zhongguo yinyuexue* [Studies in Chinese music] (2): 60–71.

Zhang Lin. 2005. "Zhongguo cai 'hua'er' diyiren Zhang Yaxiong" [The first collector of hua'er, Zhang Yaxiong]. *Yinyue shenghuo* [Musical life] (9): 35–38.

———. 2006. "Wangge xilie: Hua'er yu shaonian" [A series of elegies: Hua'er and shaonian]. A series of thirteen blog posts from July 10 to July 17, 2006. Accessed July 12, 2017. http://zhanglin.blog.ifeng.com (site unavailable at time of publication).

Zhang Yaxiong. 1986. *Hua'er ji* [Anthology of hua'er folksongs]. 3rd rev. ed. Beijing: Zhongguo wenlian chubanshe. First published 1940. Chongqing, China: Qingnian shudian. 2nd rev. ed. published 1948. Lanzhou, China: Lianhe chubanshe.

Zhao Zongfu. (2016) 2017. "Xuelixing chuancheng baohu feiwuzhi wenhua yichan de kexue shijian: Minxian baiming hua'er geshou diaocha shilu" [Scientific practices in the reasoned passing on and safeguarding of intangible cultural heritage: Preface to *Ethnographic research on hua'er singers of Min County*]. *Minsuxue luntan* [Folklore forum], April 29, 2017. http://www.chinesefolklore.org.cn/forum/viewthread.php?tid=42765.

Zhongguo minjian wenyi yanjiuhui, Gansu fenhui [Chinese folk literature and arts research society, Gansu branch], ed. 1983. *Hua'er lunji* [Anthology of articles on hua'er]. 2 vols. Lanzhou, China: Gansu renmin chubanshe.

Zhongguo minjian wenyi yanjiuhui, Shanghai fenhui [Chinese folk literature and art research society, Shanghai branch], ed. 1980. *Zhongguo minjian wenxue lunwen xuan, 1949–1979* [Anthology of theoretical articles on Chinese folk literature, 1949–1979]. 2 vols. Shanghai: Wenyi chubanshe.

Zipes, Jack. 2014. *Grimm Legacies: The Magic Spell of the Grimms' Folk and Fairy Tales*. Princeton: Princeton University Press.

SUE TUOHY is a faculty member in the Department of Folklore and Ethnomusicology and adjunct faculty in the Department of East Asian Languages and Cultures at Indiana University. She has conducted research on and in China for over three decades on music and society in northwest China, cultural heritage programs, music in social movements, and environmentalism.

5 From Field Recordings to Ethnographically Informed CDs
Curating the Sounds of Yunnan for a Niche Foreign Market

Helen Rees

THIS CHAPTER DEPARTS from the largely intra-Chinese focus of the preceding case studies, highlighting instead a notable series of ethnographic CDs of Yunnanese folk music issued since 1995 by small recording companies based in the Netherlands and New Zealand.[1] Despite circulation figures that seldom exceed a few hundred, the series has had a major impact on foreign scholars' knowledge and understanding of the performing arts of this remote southwestern province. It has also helped bring a handful of gifted folk musicians to foreign concert platforms. While the direct impact of the CDs within China has been minor, many of the featured recordings have become significant historical documents, some in ways that could not have been anticipated in the 1980s and 1990s when most of the recordings were made. More broadly, the story of the CDs illuminates the centrality of specific historical, technological, and academic developments in both China and the West to the public dissemination of folk music recordings.

All twelve CDs feature the field recordings of Zhang Xingrong (b. 1941), a music professor based at the Yunnan Art Institute (Yunnan yishu xueyuan) in Kunming (map 5.1); many of the recordings were created in cooperation with his videographer wife and research partner Li Wei'er (aka Li Wei, b. 1945).[2] It was a highly improbable stroke of fate that brought Zhang and Li's pioneering field collection to the attention of the outside world, and a collaborative effort on the part of numerous scholars, translators, recording engineers, and record producers of different nationalities to work with Zhang and Li to curate the resulting CDs.[3] For English speakers, Zhang and Li's readily available and carefully annotated field recordings have made Yunnan by far the best musically documented

Map 5.1. Map of Yunnan. Created by Inne Choi.

of China's southwestern provinces, bringing the sounds of its multifarious ethnic groups to the ears of a niche market of scholars, students, composers, festival organizers, and folk music cognoscenti.

To put this in context, one should remember that even into the early 1990s, few thoroughly annotated recordings of mainland Chinese folk genres were readily available abroad. This was especially true for rural and amateur urban traditions, whose representatives were also seldom chosen to perform overseas. (Such opportunities tended to be reserved for official state troupes and salaried civil servant musicians.) The situation began to change in the last decade of the twentieth century, thanks in particular to European companies such as Pan (Netherlands), Ocora (France), AIMP (Switzerland), and Nimbus (UK); pioneering scholars, including Qiao Jianzhong, Stephen Jones, and François Picard; and the nonprofit European Foundation for Chinese Music Research, founded in 1990, which combines research, archival, and impresario functions. The majority of the recordings thus made available, other than those by Zhang Xingrong and

Li Wei'er, have come from the north, the southeastern coastal areas, and Turkic regions of the far northwest.

Having had the privilege of studying with Zhang while conducting dissertation fieldwork in Yunnan over the 1991–92 academic year, I became involved early on in his audiovisual publication projects. In some cases I participated in the fieldwork, and in all cases other than the earliest CD (*Baishibai* 1995) I was one of the bevy of translators and go-betweens who translated liner notes and facilitated communication between Zhang and Li, who speak only Chinese, and their foreign partners. I draw on my own experience, therefore, along with documents I archived at the time, email communications, and published recollections, to describe from an insider's perspective how these projects came about, the process by which we cooperated in order to turn field recordings into ethnographically informed CDs, and the major curatorial decisions that were made. I then consider the impact and influence of the Dutch and New Zealand CDs in light of the goals and circumstances of the work and the style of curation adopted. Next, I address the long-term importance of Zhang and Li's overall field collection, of which the Dutch and New Zealand CD issues constitute a significant part. Finally, I reflect on the confluence of historical circumstance, market forces, and academic tradition that brought the CD projects to their final form.

The Genesis of the Projects

In 1984, Zhang Xingrong was a middle-aged teacher at the Yunnan Art Institute in Kunming, the provincial capital. Trained at the institute in the 1960s as an *erhu* (two-string fiddle) performer and composer, he had been assigned a permanent job there. By the early 1980s, he was teaching the analysis and composition of traditional instrumental music, but noticed that the published materials largely omitted Yunnan province, in particular its numerous ethnic minority inhabitants.[4] Taking advantage of the fact that in 1982 the Ministry of Culture was engaged in a series of documentation projects on traditional music, Zhang proposed his own project to the Yunnan Art Institute authorities. As he stated later in an interview,

> Because I was a native of Yunnan, I felt I wanted to do something for the region by writing a book about its music. . . . When I approached the School authorities, the Dean's response was very positive, since no one else had had this idea. . . . The Chairman had a good relationship with his superiors, and I was granted Y3,000, the first time any such grant had been made. Everything was in my favour—the time, the place and the resources. I was free to choose my own team, which I kept small. It included my wife, Li Wei, an experienced sound technician [and videographer]. I was able to get an excellent driver, Hong Baoshun, who accompanied us on seven of our trips.[5] (Body 1995, 60)

This initial foray into fieldwork, which began in July 1984, was not without its vicissitudes.[6] The wealth of folk music, local instruments, and traditional performers Zhang and Li found and recorded, however, exceeded their wildest expectations, and in short order their work led to two anthologies of musical transcriptions (Zhang 1986, 1990a), one anthology of folk legends about musical instruments (Zhang 1990b), and two video compilations shown on local television. More importantly, Zhang moved from an initial interest primarily in melodic structure to a more all-encompassing observation of the social functions of different types of music (Body 1995, 63–64). He also found that he had to discard a number of preconceived aesthetic notions:

> Because of my musical education in Han [Chinese] and Western music, when I first started working in the area of [m]inority music, I found some of the music very hard to appreciate. The first reaction was often one of shock and surprise. . . . My preconceptions were challenged, and my curiosity was aroused. . . . On one occasion I was recording a Lisu ensemble of *qiben* [plucked lute], *jiezi* [bowed lute] . . . and *juelie* [transverse flute]. The music sounded very discordant. It seemed that the lutes were not playing at the same pitch as the [flute], and that the instruments had not been tuned properly. I took the instruments from the players, and tuned them to match the [flute]. The ensemble began to play again, but by the end of the first phrase the players were all busy retuning their instruments. When I listened to the recording later I realized my mistake; the "out-of-tuneness" which I had attributed to bad musicianship was actually an intentional layering of different intonations and was an essential part of this music.[7] (Body 1995, 63–64)

Very soon Zhang grew to appreciate the extraordinary skill and artistry of many of the folk musicians he was encountering (Body 1995, 65), and this one initial survey project grew into a lifelong passion. As of the time of writing (2018), Zhang, now in his mid-seventies, is still actively traveling, recording, and working with the musicians he has met, some of whom are now friends of thirty years' standing.

In the 1980s and early 1990s, however, the one thing that was lacking was any outlet through which to disseminate the sound recordings from which Zhang had made the two volumes of published transcriptions.[8] Here, fate intervened: a New Zealand graduate student, Nicholas Wheeler, met Zhang on a visit to Kunming in 1993 and bought a copy of the 1990 volume of transcriptions. On his return to Victoria University, Wellington, he showed it to Jack Body, a prominent composer on the music faculty with a strong interest in Asian music.[9] Fascinated by the varied content, Body himself visited Zhang in Kunming soon afterwards and asked if he would be interested in collaborating to issue the audio recordings in New Zealand. Zhang agreed, and was invited to Body's university as a visiting scholar for two months between November 1994 and January 1995. Assisted by several translators, he and Body spent most of the time selecting and editing examples of ethnic minority instrumental music for release as a four-CD set by Auckland-based Ode Record Company; this eventually came out in 2003 as *South of the Clouds: Instrumental Music of Yunnan* (Zhang 2016, 138–49).

In addition, Body contacted Bernard Kleikamp, proprietor of Leiden-based Pan Records, on Zhang's behalf. Kleikamp agreed to issue a fifth CD, this one composed of ethnic minority folksongs (published in 1995 as *Baishibai*); he also agreed to underwrite the research expenses and provide a high-quality audio recorder for Zhang and Li to investigate polyphonic folksongs in Yunnan (the four CDs that resulted from this undertaking came out as two double-CD sets, *Alili* 2004 and *Nanwoka* 2005) (2016, 138–49). Ultimately, Pan Records issued three further CDs of Zhang's recordings, one focusing on a local ritual genre (*Dongjing Music* 1998) and two documenting ethnic minority operatic genres (*Bai Opera* 2017; *Dai Opera* 2017).

Curating the CDs

Putting together the audio recordings, photographs, and liner notes for each of these CDs and CD sets was a major undertaking; it involved many different people and thoughtful decision-making about how to present the materials for a largely foreign, English-reading audience whose members were likely to have a strong interest in traditional musics of the world and a desire for in-depth documentation of the sounds they would hear.[10] From the outset, Body and Zhang's intention was to create an educational, informative product (Zhang 2016, 138), and fortunately both Ode and Pan were amenable to quite thick, detailed liner-note booklets replete with maps and photographs. For each CD, Zhang provided meticulous liner notes that gave the date of recording; listed the names, ages, and villages of residence of the performers; described any instruments used; gave lyrics when possible; and frequently added biographical and contextual information. Rendering this directly into English, however, was rarely feasible without some extra explanation and editing to assist non-Chinese readers in better understanding the materials. As one of the translators (and in most cases the main or final translator, responsible for finalizing major editing decisions with Zhang and other participants), I became accustomed to lengthy discussions via email and fax to clarify each track's description, check for errors, and amplify contextual information. In some cases, I also had to do considerable additional research myself on the ethnic groups involved in order to make the liner notes as useful as possible to the nonspecialist reader. Below, I describe three examples of this process, each of which gave rise to different foci of discussion and posed different challenges.

Dongjing Music *(Pan 1998)*

In the case of the first CD on which I worked, *Dongjing Music: Where Confucian, Taoist and Buddhist Culture Meet*, I was the sole translator and was closely involved in the discussions as to what to include and how to present it (fig. 5.1).[11] This was because Zhang and I had made many of the recordings together in 1992, when I was conducting fieldwork for my PhD dissertation in Yunnan, and I was extremely familiar with the topic. Dongjing music is a primarily ritual genre widespread throughout ethnically Han, Bai, and Naxi communities in Yunnan, with some presence also in Sichuan province to the north and among Yunnanese Han émigrés in Burma. It is the music of the dongjing associations (*dongjinghui*), amateur musico-ritual societies that celebrate calendrical and life-cycle rituals on a *pro bono* basis in local temples and homes (Zhang 1998; Rees 2000). Each county, or sometimes subcounty region, has its own distinctive repertoire and ritual practices, and we took care to include examples from five different areas: Baoshan and Dali in the west of the province, Chuxiong in the center, and Tonghai and Mengzi in the south (map 5.1). We picked regions that have historically had strong dongjing traditions and in which we had been able to make good quality recordings with plenty of contextual information.

A crucial decision that had to be made was what types of sound to include. The best-known, and most immediately attractive, items of dongjing repertoire are those that involve the full instrumental ensemble of flutes, bowed and plucked strings, and percussion. The ensemble provides heterophonic accompaniment for flowing melodies to which passages of scripture are sung, and it also plays purely instrumental pieces to accompany physical actions such as the making of offerings at the altar. We included several examples of these, but also featured three types of performance that are more obviously utilitarian, though equally crucial to the conduct of the ritual: the impressive drum pattern that opens the day's ritual proceedings (track 1), syllabic chanting (track 12), and the highly stylized reading of a memorial to the gods (track 14). Zhang's liner notes provide detailed information on the history and current practice of the dongjing associations and fully describe each track, and I added a short reading list at the end for anyone wishing to learn more about the topic. The trickiest part of the translation was dealing with passages of quite abstruse Taoist texts; for this, I obtained expert advice from Judith Boltz, a Taoist text specialist at the University of Washington. In assembling the tracks and liner notes, we very much wanted listeners to appreciate the full gamut of the dongjing auditory experience and to grasp how the music fitted into the quite complex ritual process. For the same reason, we selected photographs showing not only the different groups but also different segments of rituals, and created a graphic explaining the layout of altars and seats for a typical temple ceremony.

From Field Recordings to Ethnographically Informed CDs | 131

Fig. 5.1. Album cover, *Dongjing Music* (Pan, 1998).

CDs of this nature typically garner only a handful of reviews, but the major review I have found, by ethnomusicologist Frederick Lau, suggests that our efforts were successful in the eyes of our niche audience: "It is refreshing to find such an informative collection of Chinese religious music. The detailed and clearly written liner notes provide a brief history and succinct description of the music in the recording. The musical genres are explained in easily understandable language. Besides the excellent photos and skillfully mixed recording, the CD also provides a useful map indicating the regions from which the music was gathered and a list of sources for further reference. This recording is a timely contribution to our understanding of recent religious survival in China against a backdrop of unprecedented socio-economic change" (2000, 239).

South of the Clouds *(Ode 2003)*

Infinitely more challenging was the project *South of the Clouds: Instrumental Music of Yunnan* (Ode 2003). This set of four CDs presented field recordings made by Zhang and Li between 1984 and 1994, plus a handful of later additions. I came on board in 2001 as the last of a succession of four translators, and as coeditor with Jack Body of the liner notes. The sheer number of ethnic groups included—over twenty, each with their own language (and in some cases more than one)—was daunting, as was the variety of instruments and genres represented, with many of which I was unfamiliar. In addition, the project had proceeded in fits and starts since the burst of activity over 1994–95 and had already involved three different interpreters and translators. Thus, from 2001 to publication in 2003, Zhang, Li, Body, and I were essentially checking, correcting, streamlining, and amplifying the results of hundreds of hours of effort already sunk into the work.

This final push to complete the CD set got underway in July 2001, in the depths of the New Zealand winter. The four of us converged for a week in the freezing cold of an unheated beach house in the little town of Waihi Beach, working eight hours a day to check the minutiae of all 153 tracks and their metadata against Zhang's original field notes, his transcriptions, his drawings and photos of the different instruments represented, and the English-language typescripts prepared by the earlier translators. One set of English-language typescripts listed the tracks selected over 1994–95 for use on the CDs, while the other listed every example from Zhang's original recordings, along with an impressive amount of extra information from Zhang's detailed field notes about the individual performers, instruments, and contexts of performance. Since Body spoke no Chinese, I interpreted for everyone. Body annotated the first set of typescripts with notes about things to insert or delete, new numbering of tracks, and more contextual information (fig. 5.2).

Over the next fifteen months or so, we further refined the liner notes, using both Zhang's original field notes and extra information from him, from other scholars, and from secondary sources. Body was an unflagging and meticulous editor and producer. He would send me his questions by email, I would translate them into Chinese and send them on to Zhang with some of my own added in, Zhang would respond to me, and I would translate his response into English and forward it to Body for inclusion in the liner notes.[12] I still preserve printouts of our many emails, which record the technical complexities we had to untangle by this point. For example, in an email from September 4, 2002, Body alerted me to an anomaly that had arisen through the last-minute insertion of some extra recordings: "Catastrophes are waiting to ambush us. I've just discovered that the track listings don't match the first CD. Please note that on the disc TK 14 goes to 23, 16 to 24 (as AXI tracks) and that in the notes tracks 19 & 20 need to be

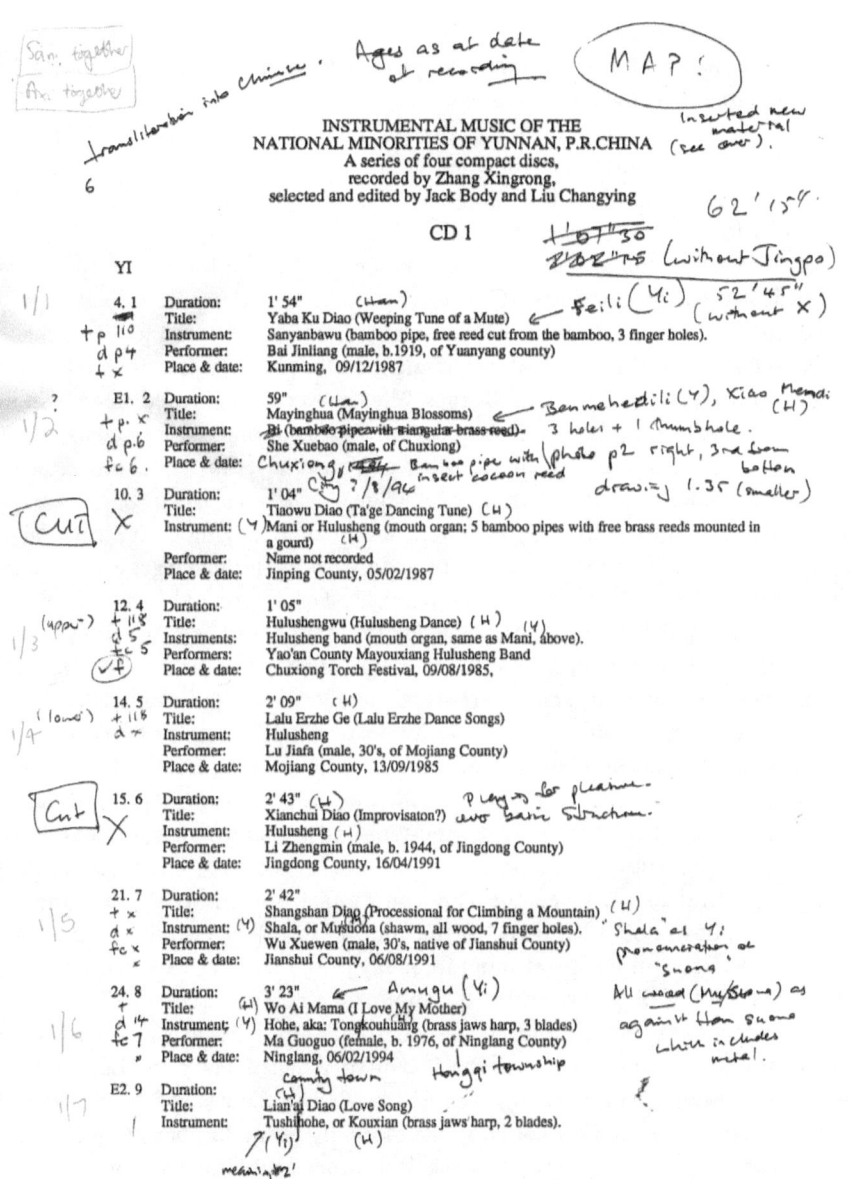

Fig. 5.2. Typescript annotated by Jack Body, 2001.

reversed! New notes attached, but in listening to the CD you need to play . . . 1–13, 15, 17–24, 14, 16, 25–41." We did eventually get everything sorted out, with tracks and metadata correctly married up.

Beyond clarifying the technical details, the major point of curatorial discussion was how to introduce the twenty-plus ethnic groups within the limited space available in the liner-note booklets. Zhang and Body had decided in the mid-1990s to select examples from all twenty-four officially recognized ethnic minorities indigenous to Yunnan, along with examples from three more groups still awaiting official classification. The aim was to give the fullest possible picture of the extraordinary ethnic and musical variety in the province. This made perfect sense, given the lack of any equivalent audio survey at the time, but it did present a number of editorial challenges. The typescripts prepared as a result of the intensive recording lab sessions of the mid-1990s organized the tracks under China's official ethnic group labels. Most of Yunnan's ethnic minorities, however, have little name recognition in the outside world, so clearly it was necessary to provide basic information on each one, rather than leaving each ethnic label unexplained (a problem that would not arise with a similar target audience in China, of course). Before I joined the team, Body had created initial drafts of mini descriptions for each officially labeled group to insert into the liner notes, but given the paucity of information available at the time in English and the eccentricity of some of the sources, most of these left much to be desired.

In particular, as with official ethnic/racial classification systems in most countries, including the United States, the neat labels assigned by the Chinese government do not entirely match up with the situation on the ground, tending to gloss over crucial historical distinctions and contemporary developments. China's official ethnic classification system is well known to be an artifact largely of the 1950s and 1960s, when the new communist government sent teams of researchers out to document and list the country's various ethnic groups, with a view to understanding the ethnographic lay of the land and ensuring proper representation for all groups in the new political structure. Faced with a bewildering variety of over four hundred self-identified minorities, the officials tasked with ethnic classification eventually settled on fifty-five official non-Han categories, in some cases by lumping together several—or, in the case of the Yi, several dozen—groups of people who often spoke mutually unintelligible languages and dialects, sometimes lived nowhere near each other and followed quite distinct customs, usually had different ethnonyms for themselves, and didn't always appreciate being made part of a larger umbrella grouping (Fei 1981; Harrell 1990, 1995; Mullaney 2011). Thus, simply stating that a performer and track belonged to, say, the Yi ethnic group was not particularly helpful. While we decided to retain the umbrella "Yi" label for the twenty-seven tracks on CD 1 whose performers bear this official ethnic designation, we grouped together and flagged items from, respectively, the Nisu, Axi, and Sani "subgroups," in order to make clearer the cultural and stylistic diversity subsumed under the official label. There were a number of other cases where intralabel ethnic distinctions were specially noted.

Further complicating the situation was the fact that many ethnic groups in Yunnan are actually part of broader ethnic conglomerations spread across China's borders into Southeast Asia, and indeed at least a few of the musicians recorded had a history of cross-border migration. Of necessity, the field recordings were confined to the territory of Yunnan province (cross-border fieldwork in the 1980s and 1990s was almost impossible), but I felt that the ethnographic descriptions needed to take into account the broader regional picture and to provide alternative ethnonyms and ethnonymic spellings—otherwise the picture presented could be extremely misleading to our readers.

The first draft's description of the group termed "Kemu" in Chinese, for example, simply noted that they "are not found in the official listing of ethnic minorities—it has yet to be determined ... whether they are a distinct, independent group, or a sub-group of an existing minority." In fact, however, better known by other transliterations, such as Kmhmu, Kammu, Khmu, and Khamu, this is a long-recognized ethnic group several hundred thousand strong, mostly resident in Laos, with a number of publications about them (e.g., Proschan 2001), and a beautiful CD of field recordings from Southeast Asian and US-resident Kmhmu issued by Smithsonian Folkways in 1999 (*Bamboo on the Mountains*). Based on the information available in early 2002, therefore, I rewrote the description as follows:

> KEMU (KMHMU, KAMMU, KHMU or KHAMU)
>
> The Kemu are the largest of the Mon-Khmer groups in northern Laos, where about 400,000 live. There are also 32,000 in Vietnam, several thousand in Thailand, and a small number in the extreme southern tip of Yunnan. The Chinese government has not yet assigned an official ethnic classification to its tiny Kemu population, and data on the group in China is limited. Just over 6,000 inhabitants of Yunnan belong to groups not yet classified, of whom some are Kemu. Most Kemu live in mountainous regions, and their traditional religion is animistic. Bamboo is central to the manufacture of many of their musical instruments, and musical styles vary from region to region. (*South of the Clouds* 2003, vol. 2, 28)

I also included the Smithsonian Folkways CD in a list of recommended extra readings and audiovisual resources appended to the liner notes, in order to afford readers the opportunity to explore more widely and put this CD set in a broader regional context.[13]

Similarly, the first draft's introduction of the group whose Chinese umbrella ethnonym is "Dai" was not completely wrong, but it was quite misleading in parts: "DAI: The 840,000 [Dai] are distributed along the Mekong River and near the Salween and Ruili rivers. Culturally speaking they are Southeast Asian and are quite similar to the Thai of Thailand. The mid-April Water-Splashing Festival ... is celebrated with the belief that disaster and illness can be warded off by splashing one another with water.... Most Dai are Theravada Buddhists, and Buddhism plays a central role in their culture." My final rewrite relied on published secondary sources (e.g., Davis 1999) and emailed advice from experts to refine the description, stressing the differences among different "Dai" communities and adding the Southeast Asian dimension to the demographic and cultural depiction:

> DAI (or TAI)
>
> The Chinese ethnic category Dai (Chinese pronunciation of Tai) includes several Tai-speaking groups, of whom the best known are the Tai-Lue of Xishuangbanna Prefecture in the far southwest corner of Yunnan, and the Tai-Neua of Dehong Prefecture, which lies on the far west border with Burma. Chinese citizens classified as Dai, most of whom live in Yunnan, number just over one million, but there are many millions more Tai over the borders in Burma, Thailand, and Laos, and there is significant cross-border trade and cultural exchange. Most Tai espouse Theravada Buddhism, which has had a huge influence on their culture, and celebrate the southeast Asian Buddhist holiday of Songkran. Known in China as the "Water Splashing Festival," this has become a huge tourist attraction.... The Tai-Lue and Tai-Neua, who speak mutually unintelligible Tai languages and historically had very little contact with each other, have quite different writing systems dating back many centuries, both Pali-derived. (*South of the Clouds* 2003, vol. 2, 9)

A third discussion point in many of the emails Body and I exchanged concerned languages and romanization. Yunnan province is known for its huge linguistic diversity, with dozens of different languages and highly localized dialects awaiting any fieldworker attempting a cultural survey. Many of the local languages and dialects have no commonly used written form, or, if they do, many speakers do not know how to write them. When Zhang and Li set out on their collecting trips from 1984 onwards, some of the musicians they encountered could communicate with them in the local dialect of Chinese, while many could not; much of the time they had to rely on local officials and schoolteachers to interpret. Sometimes they could only obtain a tune title in its Chinese translation, while often they were able to note down the tune titles and instrument names in the local language. One of the conundrums Body and I had to address with the English translation was the method by which this was done: Zhang and Li followed a common field practice of this era of transliterating minority terms and names into Chinese characters rather than using the International Phonetic Alphabet (IPA), a method that produces a less accurate approximation to the original pronunciation than IPA would.[14] While the resulting character transliterations are reasonably readable for a Chinese audience accustomed to this way of representing other languages, when rendered into standard Chinese pinyin romanization for English readers, the result is fairly clumsy and clearly somewhat removed from the minority language original. In addition, for readers with no knowledge of Chinese, it would be impossible to tell which romanized terms were actually Chinese and which came from a minority language.

With Zhang's agreement, Body and I devised a partial solution to the problems. Where we were able to ascertain from reliable sources what a close approximation to the original language pronunciation was, we substituted that for the Chinese character transliteration. Thus, for example, the Dai (Tai) free-reed gourd pipe transliterated into Chinese as *bilangmudao* was replaced by the Latin alphabet romanization *bilamdao* (*South of the Clouds* 2003, vol. 2, 9–10). Throughout, in order to help readers differentiate among the different languages, we marked minority language terms by noting the language of derivation—for example, "*bilamdao* (Dai)." While some might object that leaving the Chinese terms unmarked and only marking the minority language terms could imply a marginalization of the minority languages in a CD set dedicated to the performing arts of Yunnan's non-Han peoples, it was the only practical way to proceed and provide information as efficiently as possible.

Music of the Bai Opera and the Dai Opera in Yunnan Province *(Pan 2017)*

The third CD set discussed here illustrates a different type of curatorial decision taken by Zhang Xingrong, together with a familiar set of practical problems that ended up delaying production. In the late 1990s, following the very successful polyphonic folksong expeditions (which resulted in the release of the Pan CD sets *Alili* in 2004 and *Nanwoka* in 2005), Zhang contracted with Pan's proprietor, Bernard Kleikamp, to make recordings for two CDs of ethnic minority opera in Yunnan (ultimately *Bai Opera: Only the Mountain Echo Responds* and *Dai Opera: A Song Wafts into the Heart*, which came out together in 2017 as a set titled *Music of the Bai Opera and the Dai Opera in Yunnan Province*).[15] The recordings and photography were completed in 1998 and 1999, with Zhang and his Japanese student Ito Satoru working as a team; I was eventually asked to be the main translator for the liner notes. These two CDs are especially significant because no other recordings of these two genres are available outside China.

Zhang's concept here was unusual and very useful for anyone interested in the massive changes China's traditional arts have undergone over the last sixty years or so. He chose to juxtapose performances by artists of the state-supported professional Dali Bai Autonomous Prefecture Bai Opera Troupe (Dali Baizu

Fig. 5.3. Album cover, *Bai Opera* (Pan, 2017).

Zizhizhou Baijutuan) and Dehong Prefecture Dai Opera Troupe (Dehong Zhou Daijutuan) against field recordings of the traditional storytelling and folk theatrical genres from which these modern stage genres were created in the 1960s. Our selection of photographs for the album covers highlighted this choice: the cover for the Bai opera CD shows a modernized performance, while that for the Dai opera CD shows a traditional village performance (figs. 5.3 and 5.4). The fact that we could now embed lengthy explanations of the history of each genre, as well as much more detailed explanations of each track, into the CDs themselves, allowed us to provide far more information to listeners wishing to delve deeper into the subject. Whereas we had previously been constrained by what could be fitted into physical liner-note booklets, here we provided only the basic metadata on the attractive cardboard sleeve, but could give readers embedded essays of over sixty-six hundred words for the Bai CD and almost five thousand words for the Dai CD. In addition, it was now technically easy—and did not eat up scarce space—to provide Chinese characters where appropriate for names of people and

Fig. 5.4. Album cover, *Dai Opera* (Pan, 2017).

places. As a single-package, go-to resource for these two theatrical genres, this two-CD set could offer a far more comprehensive introduction and guide than the CDs of the previous two decades.

The familiar problem that hit us, however, was language and transliteration. With most of the Bai opera being in the local dialect of Chinese, most Bai performers being fluent in Chinese, and a Bai translator having begun the translation into English many years previously, that translation was fairly straightforward, although there were still many email exchanges with Zhang to clarify obscure points. Things were far more complicated with the Dai materials: the Dai opera and traditional arts out of which it developed are all sung in the local Dai (i.e., Tai-Nüa) language, and many of the performers did not speak much Chinese. In the late 1990s, Zhang had followed the common local custom of noting down Dai-language names and terms in Chinese characters that approximated most closely to the Dai pronunciation, which, for all the reasons enumerated above, made the translation into English very difficult. Eventually, I requested that we visit the Dehong opera troupe to clarify the many points that I needed to sort out in order to produce a readable and maximally useful English translation. Three of us, including Zhang and me, made the expedition in April 2014. I had prepared by creating a list of all the Chinese-character names and terms I was having difficulty with, and for part of a morning, I worked with the troupe's very patient translator to reverse engineer the Dai-language originals. He took the list home and during the afternoon typed all fifty items out in the modern Dai script, later reading them aloud for me to record.

I then emailed Zhang's Chinese-language liner notes and the list of names and terms in the modern Dai script to Ito Satoru, who had assisted with the original recordings and had in the interim become a leading scholar and filmmaker specializing in Tai-Nüa language, ritual, and arts. Ito provided two forms of standard romanization used by Tai-Nüa specialists, and we decided to use the simpler one for the liner notes. The explanation of the two types of Dai opera, for example, reads in the embedded liner notes as follows: "Dai opera as found today can be divided into 'old Dai opera' (*tsoeng thaw*) and 'new Dai opera' (*tsoeng maeh*)" (*Dai Opera: A Song Wafts into the Heart*, embedded liner notes, p. 2). For English readers the romanization used for the two Dai terms provides a closer approximation to the Tai-Nüa pronunciation than the Chinese transliterations (*zhengtao* and *zhengmai*) would have done. For this CD, therefore, we were able to privilege the Tai-Nüa language (with any Chinese terms marked specially), stating at the head of the embedded liner notes that "Unless otherwise noted, all italicized terms are in the Tai Nüa language" (ibid., 1). In a few instances, Ito was also able to clarify and better contextualize some Tai-Nüa concepts, terms, and geographical references.

Impact and Influence of the Pan and Ode CDs

Unlike some of the other case studies addressed in this volume, the twelve CDs over which so many of us labored so hard for many years have not themselves had a high-profile impact on the individuals and traditions featured; any influence has often been more indirect, and frequently unanticipated. The recordings included on the first six CDs (*Baishibai*, *Dongjing Music*, and the *South of the Clouds* set) were mostly made between 1984 and 1994, with no thought that they would ever achieve commercial circulation, even within a niche academic/traditional music enthusiast market. The fact that they did obtain this kind of limited circulation was serendipitous.

By contrast, the recordings on the last six CDs (the two-CD sets *Alili* and *Nanwoka* and the Bai and Dai opera set) were underwritten by Pan Records with the positive expectation that they would be released for that market. However, even the recordings for these last six CDs were all made between 1995 and 1999, a few years before China suddenly embraced UNESCO-style intangible cultural heritage ideology and started on a fad for "original ecology folksongs" (*yuanshengtai min'ge*, i.e., those sung in the original dialect and local style by village-born singers who preserve an indigenous aesthetic) (Rees 2012, 2016; Chang 2017). In the 1980s and 1990s, it was inconceivable to most observers interested in actual village music-making that China would ever abandon (or at least modify) its preference for Western art music and Westernized, professionalized, staged versions of the country's own traditions. And even though we were fairly sure there would be an eager niche market in Europe, New Zealand, and other areas Pan and Ode typically reached, we had no intention or expectation of breaking into the commercial world-music scene—unadulterated field recordings are, after all, very much a minority taste there too (Taylor 2012, 178). Thus, when we were all working on these projects, we were doing so primarily to document an extraordinary soundworld not otherwise accessible (especially to people outside China), to preserve and bring to notice the legacy of folk musicians whose artistry might otherwise have died with them, and to increase understanding in the outside world of a little known but musically rich corner of the Chinese hinterland (and quite a large corner at that—the total area of Yunnan province, at 394,000 square kilometers, is slightly bigger than that of Germany and Belgium combined). Our curatorial decisions—determining what to include, and how to present and explain it—were driven by these aspirations, and seem to have hit the mark with at least some of our target audience (Anonymous 1997, 21; Lam 2003/2004, 155).

Consonant with our modest goals and the type of listener we aimed to reach, the size of the pressings for the Pan CDs gives a sense of the limited extent of our customer base:

Baishibai (1995): 1,500 copies (3 runs of 500 each)
Dongjing Music (1998): 1,000 copies (2 runs of 500 each)
Alili (2004): 500 copies
Nanwoka (2005): 500 copies
Bai Opera/Dai Opera (2017): 500 copies

Furthermore, 10 to 15 percent of each initial run was given away as promotional copies to authors, musicians, and the press. At the time of writing (2018), all of the Yunnanese CDs are still in stock, in numbers ranging from fifty or more to several hundred. They have, in fact, largely met our expectations: they have sold quite well at events such as the annual international meetings of the European Foundation for Chinese Music Research, which typically brings together sixty to one hundred or more specialists from Europe, China, and elsewhere, and have become well known within a rather specialist circle that appreciates the "local atmosphere and . . . actual sound of this type of music in the field" (Anonymous

1997, 211). Indeed, Zhang Xingrong, Li Wei'er, Jack Body, Bernard Kleikamp, and I have actively promoted them within this circle via presentations and roundtable discussions at several conferences. However, circulation remains only in the hundreds, as is the case for many CD issues of this type.[16] Given the predictably limited appeal of the recordings, Zhang was fortunate that a record producer was willing to take a chance on the CDs. Kleikamp explained to me that "I was most of all interested in repertoires that other record companies were not covering, and ethnic groups in China was a field I was personally very interested in" (email, February 5, 2018).

Some of the media projects and initiatives analyzed earlier in this volume have played a major role in defining public perceptions of a tradition or a field of study, or in promoting the careers and reputations of particular performing artists; the latter is particularly the case, of course, for singers who have won prizes in televised competitions or achieved "representative transmitter" status. Our cluster of twelve CDs, all conceived of and mostly published before folksingers started making it big on television, and before China had invented the concept of "representative transmitters" (*daibiaoxing chuanchengren*), has made nobody's career, since at the time there was no career of this nature to be made. Some of the village musicians featured in Zhang's recordings, such as the wonderful Lahu multi-instrumentalist Zhang Laowu (1932–c. 1998, *South of the Clouds*, CD 3), were renowned within their own communities and had from time to time come to official notice.[17] For most of them, however, such as Zhang Laowu, participation in Zhang Xingrong's academic recording sessions had no immediate effect on their wider reputations and no material benefit beyond a welcome small participation fee.

At the other end of the age spectrum, two of the Yi tracks on *South of the Clouds* (CD 1) were recorded in 1994 by the superb eighteen-year-old Jew's harpist Ma Guoguo, who has since become a nationally known performer. Nevertheless, these two short tracks were certainly not instrumental in propelling her down the path to fame. This is not to say that folk musicians may not gain local approbation for participating in a scholarly recording—I was present on one occasion in summer 2008 when a couple of groups from villages Zhang had not originally intended to record lined up of their own accord to take their turn after the planned session with another ensemble was over.

In addition, while the Pan and Ode CDs themselves may not have brought much direct benefit to most of the participating musicians, the documentation projects of which they were a part have sometimes had a greater impact. For example, because Zhang was asked on several occasions to put together a troupe of folk artists to travel abroad for festivals—e.g., to Taiwan in 2001 and 2002 and to the Netherlands for the Amsterdam China Festival in 2005—two dozen or more of the musicians he has met through these and other projects have had the opportunity to tour overseas and, thus, to become better known to the worlds of academia and Chinese officialdom (Zhang 2016, 280–97). Since 2007, a handful have achieved national- or provincial-level "representative transmitter" status, with their participation in occasional recordings and tours a contributing factor (Rees 2012, 32). And in at least one case, a previously unknown genre discovered in 1995 in the course of Zhang and Li's fieldwork for Pan's polyphonic folksong project has attracted national attention: the exquisite, complex polyphonic folksongs of the Hani of Honghe County, near the Vietnam border, have become a major focus of local official promotion, and in 2006 they were inscribed in China's first list of national-level intangible cultural heritage (Zhang 1997; Zhou, Wang, and Zhang 2007, vol. 1, 106–107; *Alili* 2004, CD 1). This was truly an unintended consequence of a foreign-funded recording expedition, and one that radically shifted the scholarly, official, and public perception of Hani performing arts.[18]

As far as the researchers were concerned, the kudos of outside attention did help Zhang Xingrong and Li Wei'er get their work taken more seriously in Yunnan itself, especially in the pre-intangible cultural heritage days. As Zhang explained to Jack Body in 1995, "I took [a news bulletin] back to Yunnan to impress them with the fact that my work [had] received recognition and validation in Beijing. It is common for local officials to be uncertain of the value of things. And this project in New Zealand will also strengthen my position. I am glad to have the chance to publish the recordings which have been lying dormant for so many years" (quoted in Body 1995, 61).

One final place in which the *South of the Clouds* recordings had a modest unexpected impact was the world of New Zealand art music composition. Jack Body, who both masterminded this set for Ode Record Company and initiated Zhang's later collaborations with Pan Records, was for several decades until his death in 2015 one of New Zealand's leading composers. It was the unusual auditory features suggested by Zhang's 1990 volume of transcriptions that captured Body's attention in the first place; once he was able to hear the originals, he followed his usual custom of making detailed transcriptions of his own. From these he created a chamber piece titled "From Yunnan," which was performed at the Central Conservatory of Music in Beijing in 2009. He also had his composition students at Victoria University, Wellington, write original pieces inspired by some of the field recordings he and Zhang were working on, ultimately creating a tape of eight compositions in 2004 (Zhang and Rees 2016, 146–48). There is a certain charming irony to this, given the fact that for the first few decades of the People's Republic, a major motivation for recording folk music was less academic enquiry than to supply composers with raw materials (Du 1992, 9; Ben Wu 1998, 36–37). The New Zealand CD set succeeded in doing this, as well as documenting the ethnographic background to the wonderfully varied and unusual music on offer.

What of the Future?

In many ways, Zhang and Li hit the Yunnan folk music scene at a remarkably propitious time. In the mid-1980s, with the Cultural Revolution already over for several years, traditional customs and performing arts were making a comeback, and television, tourism, and the internet were not yet factors in villagers' lives.[19] By the second decade of the twenty-first century, however, all these innovations have made their presence felt, along with mass migration to the cities by rural youth, with the result that many previously flourishing traditional arts are now greatly attenuated. As so often happens, Zhang and Li's field recordings have become a unique historical resource, and the careful attention paid to documentation and ethnographic description is proving invaluable. As one reviewer of *South of the Clouds* noted, "The liner notes do something still rare, by including the names and photographs of individual musicians. This means that some genuinely virtuoso performers, such as Yang Dehong, a [Bai lutenist], or Li Yusheng, a Prmi oboist, emerge from the crowd of the 'folk' and become visible to an international audience" (Davis 2004, 309). In other words, in years to come, people increasingly removed in time from the Yunnanese musical scene of the late twentieth century will have a sense of who was creating the soundscape of that sonically rich era—of the individuals within the traditions.

This matters for the future, because, as numerous well-known examples attest, originating communities increasingly want access to historical recordings of their traditions and ancestors, with repatriation of copies, the establishment of regional and national archives, creative outreach, and selective online availability all possible modes of achieving this (Seeger and Chaudhuri 2004; Nannyonga-Tamusuza and Weintraub 2012; Lobley 2014; Thram 2018). Already, in fact, at least one group of musicians Zhang recorded has used the recordings to help revive their earlier singing style (Zhang Xingrong, personal communication). And while Zhang's ongoing digitization project is aimed at ensuring long-term archival preservation of his unusually well-organized field collection, the many foreign and domestic CDs, videos, and DVDs have certainly helped with medium-term preservation, as well as with disseminating rare materials.

Finally, both the commercial audiovisual products and the entire archived collection of Zhang and Li's field materials should furnish a wealth of possibilities for restudies. Despite encouragement from early ethnomusicological luminary Alan Merriam (1964, 51–52), musical restudies are remarkably thin on the ground; one of the longest-running and most productive is based on the sound recordings, photographs, silent films, and field logs of Dutch scholar Arnold Bake, who crisscrossed India, Ceylon, and Nepal starting in the 1930s and documented dozens of traditions, many still alive in the late twentieth and early twenty-first centuries. Since 1984, Nazir Jairazbhoy and Amy Catlin have retraced Bake's steps in India, video camera in hand, using his original materials and metadata to track down people, places, and genres and explore how musical traditions have endured, changed, and in some cases vanished (Tingey 1989; *Bake Restudy 1984 1991*; Jairazbhoy 1991). In similar fashion, Zhang and Li's pioneering work and thorough documentation will provide a kind of baseline from which future projects can jump off and a reference point for any Yunnanese communities seeking to locate, appreciate, and perhaps in some cases revive musical traditions that were once part of daily life. Zhang himself has recently expressed an interest in conducting such a study based on his and his wife's own earlier work.

The Pan and Ode CDs are only a part of the larger story of Zhang and Li's thirty-plus-year field research odyssey. Nevertheless, their role in facilitating new projects and discoveries, in documenting unique traditions at a time of momentous change, and in bringing international academic attention to the music of a previously obscure Chinese backwater has been significant. Before the first of these CDs emerged, the world of Yunnan's performing arts was largely a closed book to foreign scholars, sinologists, and folk music enthusiasts. In producing CDs of Yunnanese traditional music, it would have been all too easy to fall unconsciously into the exoticizing and shallow trope of colorful ethnic diversity, of minorities who are stereotypically "good at singing and dancing" (*nengge shanwu*)—the image showcased since the mid-1990s by Yunnan's ever-growing tourism industry (Rees 2000, 23–27; Li 2013). The curatorial decisions taken in making, selecting, and contextualizing the recordings, however, were aimed at achieving precisely the opposite effect. To this end, Zhang, Li, and their non-Chinese collaborators strove not only to explain the music and the huge variety of musical instruments but also to provide listeners with multiple avenues to embark on their own exploration of the complex social and human aspects of Yunnan's remarkable soundworld. As one reviewer put it, "Listening to the recorded music pieces in the anthology [*South of the Clouds*], and reading notes about them and their musicians, one gets a clear sense that there is much more to learn about Yunnanese musics and cultures" (Lam 2003/2004, 159).

Concluding Thoughts

By the 1990s, publication of ethnographic recordings by companies based in Western countries had been underway for several decades.[20] Many facets of such recordings had changed over the years, including the ethnic groups presented, the types of technology used, the opportunities for fieldwork, the expectations for explanatory notes, and the financial realities of distribution. It was fortuitous that Yunnan's soundworld opened up in the last two decades of the twentieth century, at precisely the same time that small, independent labels unaffiliated to government institutions found it financially feasible to issue ethnographic CDs from previously obscure places. As Bernard Kleikamp wrote recently of the late 1980s and 1990s, "It was a time of pioneering and experimenting, and literally any CD would sell—there was an insatiable demand from the CD buying public" (Kleikamp 2018, 1).[21] Looking back, the story of the twelve Yunnanese CDs represents a unique temporal intersection between the history of Chinese folk music performance and scholarship on the one hand and the history of Western niche independent labels on the other.

The process of curation, too, represented a particular moment in the Western and Chinese ethnographic—and ethnographic recording—traditions. By the 1990s, there was a general expectation among Western cognoscenti that such recordings would be furnished with far more detailed descriptions and explanations than had been the case with earlier collections, with greater attention paid to individual performers and cultural context. This mirrored a shift that was beginning to happen in Chinese ethnomusicology as well, and one that was well suited to Zhang's meticulous note taking. Given the complexities of the materials presented in the Yunnanese CDs and the difficulties of communications in a largely pre-internet era, it took the combined efforts of an extended network of participants to achieve ethnographic recordings that would satisfy these demands: performers; local officials and arts specialists; local interpreters fluent in Chinese and one or more minority languages; drivers capable of negotiating Yunnan's often dangerous mountain roads; Zhang Xingrong, Li Wei'er, and sometimes other expert "outsider" fieldworkers; several Chinese-English translators; a number of European and New Zealand–based "culture brokers" (Kurin 1997); and two committed, patient independent record labels willing to take a chance on the unknown.

By now, towards the end of the second decade of the twenty-first century, the internet and other digital technologies are facilitating much more direct self-presentation by skilled folk musicians in China, especially younger ones; however, where cross-cultural presentation is the goal, the need to combine local expertise with information geared to the new audience is likely to continue, albeit probably via somewhat less convoluted logistics than those that obtained in the 1990s and the first few years of this century.

University of California, Los Angeles
Los Angeles

Acknowledgments

I wish to thank Zhang Xingrong for agreeing that our CD collaborations would be a suitable topic for this essay, and Bernard Kleikamp for kindly providing crucial information by email and permitting me to use three Pan Records CD covers as illustrations. All of us involved owe a debt of gratitude to the late Jack Body, without whom none of these CDs would have been made. In addition, Amy Catlin-Jairazbhoy, Levi Gibbs, Anthony Seeger, Bell Yung, and two anonymous reviewers provided invaluable suggestions for improvement. Inne Choi created the map.

Notes

1. I use the terms "ethnographic CDs" and "ethnographic recordings" in the sense defined by Anthony Seeger: "often made in natural circumstances in geographically or socially distant places, produced for an audience culturally different from that of the performers, often accompanied by notes presenting the music and its use to the new audience" (1991, 290).

2. Romanization of Chinese names and terms is according to standard *Hanyu pinyin*, and names of Chinese and Japanese citizens are given in East Asian order, i.e., surname first, given name second. Original spellings are retained in direct quotations from published sources. I have chosen to translate Yunnan yishu xueyuan as "Yunnan Art Institute," which was the official English translation used by its journal during the period in the 1990s covered in this chapter. In recent years, the institute has become a university and now uses "Yunnan Arts University" as its English name.

3. A two-video set of Li Wei'er's footage of Yunnanese music, dance, and rituals has been issued abroad by another small media company, Apsara Media for Intercultural Education (*From China's S.W. Borders* 2001). It was handled in a similar cooperative fashion by Zhang, Li, Amy Catlin, Nazir Jairazbhoy, and myself, but space precludes further discussion here.

4. Yunnan's population in 1978 was reported as just over thirty million; by the 2010 census, it had risen to almost forty-six million. Two-thirds of its inhabitants are classified as Han Chinese, China's dominant ethnic group; the remaining one-third is split among over twenty officially recognized ethnic minorities, mostly of Tibeto-Burman, Tai, Miao-Yao, and Mon-Khmer origin (*Yunnan cidian* bianji weiyuanhui 1993, 735; Zhonghua Renmin Gongheguo guojia tongjiju 2012).

5. Y3000 (3000 yuan) was equivalent to about US$1,330 at the official exchange rate prevalent in July 1984 and somewhat less than that on the black market. College teachers at this time usually made less than 100 yuan a month, and private individuals could not buy a car or obtain a driver's license, so travel to most parts of Yunnan was effectively impossible without an official vehicle. Thus, this sponsorship was crucial to Zhang and Li's ability to undertake their project.

6. Zhang sets out the exact schedule of their field trips from 1984 on in his autobiography (2016). More informally, in a 1995 interview he described various challenges they faced (Body 1995, 60–63).

7. The recording that led to this epiphany may be found on track 26, CD 2, of the CD set *South of the Clouds: Instrumental Music of Yunnan* (2003). To contextualize Zhang's recollection of his reaction, it is worth pointing out that in the latter part of the twentieth century, China's educational institutions and media followed a partially Soviet-influenced

aesthetic of preferring Western art music and refined, European-influenced "modern" versions of folk genres to the "coarser" sounds and local tuning systems of much indigenous traditional music. The trend has been modified somewhat since the early twenty-first century as a result of the intangible cultural heritage wave that has engulfed the country (Rees 2009, 2016).

8. At the time, the logistical obstacles to domestic publication were considerable, and there was in any case little public appetite for original field materials (Jones 2003, 299)—problems that several other scholars mentioned to me around this period.

9. Jack Body (1944–2015) was a renowned composer with a passion for world music, which he often transcribed meticulously, and which inspired some of his compositions. He was also a fine gamelan player, with extensive artistic and academic connections in Southeast Asia and China (Shennan, Whitehead, and Askew 2015).

10. For practical reasons, not least because many of the recordings were the results of surveys of large geographic regions, and half were made before commercial release was even a possibility, very few of the musicians participated in the postproduction phase. Thus, unlike some other pioneering fieldwork-based albums (see, for example, the album discussed in Seeger 1991, 296–97), the discussions described here took place almost entirely among the fieldworkers and their foreign colleagues.

11. The tape itself was mastered over two days in September 1995 in Leiden, with Zhang and Li Wei'er working in conjunction with Bernard Kleikamp, recording engineer Jan van Rhenen, and an interpreter (Zhang 2016, 175). Li was also very familiar with dongjing music, having documented it on video during the 1980s.

12. This somewhat cumbersome process was further complicated by the fact that until partway through the process, the email system Zhang was using didn't provide for reading or typing Chinese characters. Instead, we had to use pinyin in our email exchanges. Given the vast number of homophones in Chinese, we occasionally got stuck and had to resort to expensive faxes.

13. I gave a copy of the Smithsonian Folkways CD to Zhang as well, as such CDs were not distributed in China at the time. He was extremely interested in this rare opportunity to compare what he had found among the tiny Kmhmu community in Yunnan with the much wider range of communities and genres sampled in Southeast Asia and among the US diaspora.

14. So common, in fact, was this custom of transliteration into Chinese characters that a whole set of standardized Chinese character equivalents for minority language names and terms arose in the Chinese-language minority studies literature. With less familiar items, however, it can be quite hard to reverse engineer the minority language original. Not entirely to my surprise, an American review of the CD set, while laudatory overall, did fault the use of "nonstandard romanizations of Chinese pronunciations of indigenous names" (Davis 2004, 309).

15. The ethnic group designated "Bai" by the Chinese government numbers approximately 1.6 million and lives primarily in and around Dali in west-central Yunnan. Historically, they were often referred to as "Minkia" (David Y. H. Wu 1990; Bryson 2017). The "Dai" here are the Tai-Nüa (or Tai-Neua) inhabitants of Dehong Prefecture on the Burma/Myanmar border.

16. I am grateful to Bernard Kleikamp for generously supplying this information, and permission to use it, in emails of January 27, 2018, and February 5, 2018. He adds that among

his large stock of ethnographic CDs from Asia, Europe, and elsewhere, the bestselling CD reached sales of five thousand to six thousand copies; in the 1990s, all the CDs Pan released at least broke even, and many made tidy profits. My recollection of a conversation in Auckland in 2001 with the then-proprietor of Ode Record Company was that he stated he would be issuing four hundred copies of the four-CD set *South of the Clouds*.

17. Zhang Laowu, for example, was invited to the Yunnan Art Institute in 1962, where some of his repertoire was recorded and a mimeographed volume of transcriptions of his playing was produced (Yunnan yishu xueyuan yinyue xi 1962). By the time Zhang Xingrong met him again in the 1980s, however, he was living in poverty, with no official recognition of his talents (Body 1995, 65).

18. Zhang and Li's work overall—going way beyond their projects with small foreign media companies—has certainly had an impact on which local genres and folk artists get studied at the university level. Zhang has authored a Beijing-published textbook with a CD of examples whose first run was three thousand copies (Zhang 2006), and his transcriptions have frequently been borrowed by other textbook authors, sometimes without attribution.

19. Just as important, it became possible again for researchers to document the traditional art forms that had been denigrated for so many years. As in Zhang and Li's case, a number of Chinese researchers benefited from small amounts of government funding, newly available audiovisual equipment, and the generally greater freedom of intellectual enquiry. As a result, many new projects were pursued with great energy. An insightful overview of the history of Chinese scholarship on folk and other traditional performing arts after 1949 is offered by Stephen Jones (2003).

20. Notable early examples include the "demonstration collection" of the Berlin Phonogramm-Archiv, which seems to have garnered its first few sales in the 1920s, with a version released in 1963 by Ethnic Folkways Library (Reinhard and List 1963); and the *World Collection of Recorded Folk Music*, edited by Romanian scholar Constantin Brailoiu and issued in the 1950s with the support of the International Music Council of UNESCO (Touma 1985).

21. The window of opportunity was quite brief: a combination of economic crisis, market saturation, and the advent of illegal downloads caused the CD market to crash in the mid-2000s. As a result, Kleikamp had to change Pan Records' marketing strategy, ultimately undertaking many fewer CD releases (Kleikamp 2018, 1).

References

Anonymous. 1997. Review of *Naxi Music from Lijiang: The Dayan Ancient Music Association* (Monmouth, UK: Nimbus, 1997) and *Dongjing Music: Where Confucian, Taoist and Buddhist Culture Meet* (Leiden, Netherlands: Pan Records, 1998). In *CHIME* 10/11: 210–11.

Body, Jack. 1995. "Zhang Xingrong on His Fieldwork among Minorities in Southern China: 'One of Yunnan's Most Unique Features Is Its Music.'" *CHIME* 8: 59–66.

Bryson, Megan. 2017. *Goddess on the Frontier: Religion, Ethnicity, and Gender in Southwest China*. Stanford, CA: Stanford University Press.

Chang, Jung-a. 2017. "From 'Folk Culture' to 'Great Cultural Heritage of China': The Aporia of the Quest for the Essence of Chinese Culture." In *Intangible Cultural Heritage in*

Contemporary China: The Participation of Local Communities, edited by Khun Eng Kuah and Zhaohui Liu, 112–36. London: Routledge.

Davis, Sara. 1999. "Singers of Sipsongbanna: Folklore and Authenticity in Contemporary China." PhD dissertation, University of Pennsylvania.

———. 2004. Review of *South of the Clouds: Instrumental Music of Yunnan*, vols. 1 and 2 (Auckland, New Zealand: Ode Record Company, 2003). In *Ethnomusicology* 48 (2): 308–9.

Du Yaxiong. 1992. "Recent Issues in Music Research in the People's Republic of China." *Association for Chinese Music Research Newsletter* 5 (1): 9–12.

Fei Hsiao Tung (Fei Xiaotong). 1981. *Toward a People's Anthropology*. Beijing: New World Press.

Harrell, Stevan. 1990. "Ethnicity, Local Interests, and the State: Yi Communities in Southwest China." *Comparative Studies in Society and History* 32 (3): 515–48.

———, ed. 1995. *Cultural Encounters on China's Ethnic Frontiers*. Seattle: University of Washington Press.

Jairazbhoy, Nazir. 1991. "The First Restudy of Arnold Bake's Fieldwork in India." In *Comparative Musicology and Anthropology of Music*, edited by Bruno Nettl and Philip V. Bohlman, 210–27. Chicago: University of Chicago Press.

Jones, Stephen. 2003. "Reading between the Lines: Reflections on the Massive *Anthology of Folk Music of the Chinese Peoples*." *Ethnomusicology* 47 (3): 287–337.

Kleikamp, Bernard. 2018. "The First Years of Pan Records' 'Ethnic Series' and Dr. V. M. Shchurov's Involvement into Its Shaping." Unpublished manuscript.

Kurin, Richard. 1997. *Reflections of a Culture Broker: A View from the Smithsonian*. Washington, DC: Smithsonian Institution Press.

Lam, Joseph. 2003/2004. Review of *South of the Clouds: Instrumental Music of Yunnan* (Auckland, New Zealand: Ode Record Company, 2003). In *Asian Music* 35 (1): 155–59.

Lau, Frederick. 2000. Review of *Dongjing Music: Where Confucian, Taoist and Buddhist Culture Meet* (Leiden, Netherlands: Pan Records, 1998). In *Yearbook for Traditional Music* 32: 239.

Li, Jing. 2013. "The Making of Ethnic Yunnan on the National Mall: Minority Folksong and Dance Performances, Provincial Identity, and 'The Artifying of Politics' (*Zhengzhi Yishuhua*)." *Modern China* 39 (1): 69–100.

Lobley, Noel. 2014. "Sound Galleries: Curating the Experience of Sound and Music in and beyond Museums." *Music in Art* 39 (1/2): 243–55.

Merriam, Alan. 1964. *The Anthropology of Music*. Evanston, IL: Northwestern University Press.

Mullaney, Thomas S. 2011. *Coming to Terms with the Nation: Ethnic Classification in Modern China*. Berkeley: University of California Press.

Nannyonga-Tamusuza, Sylvia, and Andrew N. Weintraub. 2012. "The Audible Future: Reimagining the Role of Sound Archives and Sound Repatriation in Uganda." *Ethnomusicology* 56 (2): 206–33.

Proschan, Frank. 2001. "Peoples of the Gourd: Imagined Ethnicities in Highland Southeast Asia." *Journal of Asian Studies* 60 (4): 999–1032.

Rees, Helen. 2000. *Echoes of History: Naxi Music in Modern China*. New York: Oxford University Press.

———. 2009. "Use and Ownership: Folk Music in the People's Republic of China." In *Music and Cultural Rights*, edited by Andrew N. Weintraub and Bell Yung, 42–85. Chicago: University of Illinois Press.

———. 2012. "Intangible Cultural Heritage in China Today: Policy and Practice in the Early Twenty-First Century." In *Music as Intangible Cultural Heritage: Policy, Ideology, and Practice in Preservation of East Asian Traditions*, edited by Keith Howard, 23–54. Farnham, UK: Ashgate.

———. 2016. "Environmental Crisis, Culture Loss, and a New Musical Aesthetic: China's 'Original Ecology Folksongs' in Theory and Practice." *Ethnomusicology* 60 (1): 53–88.

Reinhard, Kurt, and George List. 1963. Liner notes to LP set *The Demonstration Collection of E. M. von Hornbostel and the Berlin Phonogramm-Archiv/Die Demonstrationssammlung von E. M. von Horbostel und dem Berliner-Phonogramm-Archiv*. New York: Ethnic Folkways Library FE 4175.

Seeger, Anthony. 1991. "Creating and Confronting Cultures: Issues of Editing and Selection in Records and Videotapes of Musical Performances." In *Music in the Dialogue of Cultures: Traditional Music and Cultural Policy*, edited by Max Peter Baumann, 290–301. Intercultural Music Studies 2. Wilhelmshaven, Germany: Florian Noetzel.

Seeger, Anthony, and Shubha Chaudhuri, eds. 2004. *Archives for the Future: Global Perspectives on Audiovisual Archives in the 21st Century*. Calcutta: Seagull Books.

Shennan, Jennifer, Gillian Whitehead, and Scilla Askew, eds. 2015. *Jack! Celebrating Jack Body, Composer*. Wellington, New Zealand: Steele Roberts.

Taylor, Timothy D. 2012. "World Music Today." In *Music and Globalization*, edited by Bob W. White, 172–88. Bloomington: Indiana University Press.

Thram, Diane. 2018. "IASA Research Grant Report: Pilot Project in Re-Study and Repatriation (Digital Return) of the International Library of African Music's Hugh Tracey Field Recordings." *IASA Journal* 48: 49–56.

Tingey, Carol. 1989. "The Nepalese Field-Work of Dr. Arnold Adriaan Bake." In *Ethnomusicology and the Historical Dimension: Papers Presented at the European Seminar in Ethnomusicology, London, 20–23 May 1986*, edited by Margot Lieth Philipp, 83–88. Ludwigsburg, (West) Germany: Philipp Verlag.

Touma, Habib Hassan. 1985. Review of LP set *The World Collection of Recorded Folk Music* (Geneva: AIMP, 1984). In *World of Music* 27 (3): 85–86.

Wu, Ben. 1998. "Music Scholarship, West and East: Tibetan Music as a Case Study." *Asian Music* 29 (2): 31–56.

Wu, David Y. H. 1990. "Chinese Minority Policy and the Meaning of Minority Culture: The Example of the Bai in Yunnan, China." *Human Organization* 49 (1): 1–13.

Yunnan cidian bianji weiyuanhui [Yunnan dictionary editorial board], ed. 1993. *Yunnan cidian* [Yunnan dictionary]. Kunming, China: Yunnan renmin chubanshe.

Yunnan yishu xueyuan yinyue xi [Music department of Yunnan Art Institute], ed. 1962. *Lancang Lahuzu Zhang Laowu xiao sanxian quji* [Anthology of pieces for small three-string plucked lute by Mekong Lahu Zhang Laowu]. Kunming, China: Yunnan yinyue wudaojia xiehui (mimeograph).

Zhang Xingrong, ed. 1986. *Dianxi minzu minjian qiyue quxian* [Anthology of ethnic folk instrumental music of western Yunnan]. Kunming, China: Yunnan minzu chubanshe.

———, ed. 1990a. *Yunnan minzu qiyue huicui* [Highlights of Yunnan national instrumental music]. Kunming, China: Yunnan renmin chubanshe.

———, ed. 1990b. *Yunnan yueqi wangguo de chuanshuo* [Legends from the musical instrument kingdom of Yunnan]. Kunming, China: Yunnan minzu chubanshe.

———. 1997. "A New Discovery: Traditional 8-Part Polyphonic Singing of the Hani of Yunnan." Translated by Helen Rees. *CHIME* 10/11: 145–52.

———. 1998. *Yunnan dongjing wenhua—ru dao shi sanjiao de fuhexing wenhua* [Dongjing culture in Yunnan: a cultural crossroads of Confucianism, Taoism and Buddhism]. Kunming, China: Yunnan jiaoyu chubanshe.

———. 2006. *Yunnan yuanshengtai minzu yinyue* [Original ecology ethnic music of Yunnan]. Beijing: Zhongyang yinyue xueyuan chubanshe.

———. 2016. *Yuehe, changxing yong: Zhang Xingrong zizhuan* [The musical journey of Zhang Xingrong: The autobiography of Zhang Xingrong]. Special issue (no. 253) of *Minzu yinyue* [National music (sic)].

Zhang Xingrong and Helen Rees. 2016. "Changyang Yunnan, xin de shengyin shijie: dianzan Xinxilan zuoqujia Jieke Bodi" [Wandering through Yunnan, a new soundworld: remembering New Zealand composer Jack Body]. *Minzu yishu yanjiu* [Ethnic art studies] 2016 (1): 42–49.

Zhongguo Renmin Gongheguo guojia tongjiju [National Bureau of Statistics of China]. 2012. "2010 nian Yunnan sheng di liu ci quanguo renkou pucha zhuyao shuju gongbao" [Bulletin of important data on Yunnan province from the sixth national population census, 2010]. Accessed January 28, 2018. http://www.stats.gov.cn/tjsj/tjgb/rkpcgb/dfrkpcgb/201202/t20120228_30408.html.

Zhou Heping, Wang Wenzhang, and Zhang Xu, eds. 2007. *Di yi pi guojiaji feiwuzhi wenhua yichan minglu tudian (shang, xia)* [An illustrated register of the first series of national-level intangible cultural heritage, 2 vols.]. Beijing: Wenhua yishu chubanshe.

Recordings (in Chronological Order)

1991 *Bake Restudy 1984*. Van Nuys, CA: Apsara Media for Intercultural Education. DVD with accompanying monograph. Film by Nazir Ali Jairazbhoy and Amy Catlin, incorporating historical field footage by Arnold Bake.

1995 *Baishibai: Songs of the Minority Nationalities of Yunnan*. Leiden, Netherlands: Pan Records, 2038 CD. CD. Field recordings by Zhang Xingrong and Li Wei.

1998 *Dongjing Music: Where Confucian, Taoist and Buddhist Culture Meet*. Leiden, Netherlands: Pan Records, 2058 CD. CD. Field recordings by Zhang Xingrong and Helen Rees.

1999 *Bamboo on the Mountains: Kmhmu Highlanders from Southeast Asia and the U.S.* Washington, DC: Smithsonian Folkways Recordings, SFW CD 40456. CD. Field recordings by Frank Proschan.

2001 *From China's S.W. Borders: Minority Dances, Songs, and Instrumental Music of Yunnan*, vols. 1 and 2. Van Nuys, CA: Apsara Media for Intercultural Education. 2-DVD set. Field footage by Li Wei and Zhang Xingrong.

2003 *South of the Clouds: Instrumental Music of Yunnan*, vols. 1 and 2. Auckland, New Zealand: Ode Record Company, CD Manu 2019/2020 and 2021/2022. 4-CD set. Field recordings by Zhang Xingrong and Li Wei.

2004 *Alili: Multi-part Folksongs of Yunnan's Ethnic Minorities*, parts 1 and 2. Leiden, Netherlands: Pan Records, 7012/7013. 2-CD set. Studio recordings, and field recordings by Zhang Xingrong, Li Wei, and Tian Libao.

2005 *Nanwoka: Multi-part Folksongs of Yunnan's Ethnic Minorities*, parts 3 and 4. Leiden, Netherlands: Pan Records, 7014/7015. 2-CD set. Field recordings by Zhang Xingrong and Li Wei.

2017   *Bai Opera: Only the Mountain Echo Responds.* Leiden, Netherlands: Pan Records, 2120. CD. Field recordings by Ito Satoru, directed by Zhang Xingrong.
2017   *Dai Opera: A Song Wafts into the Heart.* Leiden, Netherlands: Pan Records, 2121. CD. Studio recordings, and field recordings by Zhang Xingrong and Ito Satoru.

As of the time of writing (2018), the CDs and DVDs listed above may be obtained from the following sources:

>Apsara Media for Intercultural Education: www.apsara-media.com
>Ode Record Company: www.marbecks.co.nz
>Pan Records: www.panrecords.nl, or www.discogs.com
>Smithsonian Folkways: https://folkways.si.edu

HELEN REES is Professor of Ethnomusicology at the University of California, Los Angeles. Since the late 1980s, her field and archival research has focused on ritual and other traditional musical genres of southwest China and Shanghai. She also interprets and presents for Chinese artists at major European and US arts festivals. She is author of *Echoes of History: Naxi Music in Modern China* and editor of *Lives in Chinese Music.*

Glossary of Selected Chinese Terms and Phrases

Note: The terms and phrases below are alphabetized according to their first syllable, followed by their second syllable, and so on, regardless of whether the term or phrase appears as one word or multiple words separated by spaces. Mongolian and Korean terms are listed as they appear in the chapters, followed here by a transliteration of their Chinese equivalent in parentheses. Chinese terms that themselves are transcriptions of terms from other languages are also noted.

Abag (Abaga) Banner	阿巴嘎旗
Abao	阿宝
Abao xianxiang	阿宝现象
Alasha/Alxa (Alashan)	阿拉善
Alashan min'ge xiehui	阿拉善民歌协会
Alili (Chinese transcription of Naxi-language song title)	阿里里
Axi	阿细/阿西
Ayitula	阿依吐拉
A You Duo	阿幼朵
aihaozhe	爱好者
Altantsetseg (Alatanqiqige)	阿拉坦其其格
Anhui huagudeng	安徽花鼓灯
Bai	白
Bai Bingquan	白秉权
baihuayuan	百花园
Baimao nü	白毛女
Baishibai (Chinese transcription of Lisu-language term for a song genre)	摆时摆
Bain Delger (Baoyin Delige'er)	宝音德力格尔
Bao'an	保安
baohu	保护
baohu yu fazhan	保护与发展

Baoshan	保山
Barga (Ba'erhu bu)	巴尔虎部
Beijing daxue geyao zhengjichu	北京大学歌谣征集处
Beipingshi sili pingmin daxue	北平市私立平民大学
benti	本题
bi	比
Bi Fujian	毕福剑
bilangmudao (Chinese transcription of Dai-language term)	毕朗木叨
bisai	比赛
bixing	比兴
biyu	比喻
bianjiang wu	边疆舞
Bianjiang yinyue wudao dahui	边疆音乐舞蹈大会
bianle	变了
Botolt (Boteletu, aka Yang Yucheng)	博特乐图
Bu He	布赫
bu kexue	不科学
Caidie fenfei	彩蝶纷飞
caifeng	采风
caiji fengyao	采集风谣
Cai Yuanpei	蔡元培
caoyuan gequ	草原歌曲
changdiao	长调
Chaoji nüsheng	超级女生
chengxian qihou	承先启后
Choe Seung-hui (Cui Chengxi)	崔承喜
Chongqing	重庆
Chuxiong	楚雄
chuanbashi	串把式
chuanchengren	传承人
chuantong	传统
chuantong yinyue	传统音乐
chuangzao	创造
chuangzuo zuopin	创作作品
cucao	粗糙
Cui Miao	崔苗

Glossary of Selected Chinese Terms and Phrases

Dali Baizu Zizhizhou Baijutuan	大理白族自治州白剧团
dasai	大赛
Datong	大同
Datong River	大通河
Dayanjing bukan ge wole	大眼睛不看个我了
dazhong	大众
Dai	傣
Dai Ailian	戴爱莲
daibiaoxing chuanchengren	代表性传承人
daibiaozuo	代表作
Dedema	德德玛
Dehong Zhou Daijutuan	德宏州傣剧团
difangzhi	地方志
Di si jie quanguo shaoshu minzu wenyi huiyan	第四届全国少数民族文艺会演
dianxing	典型
dianxingxing	典型性
diaoyan	调演
Ding Ling	丁玲
Dolan (Daolang)	刀郎
Dongbei yangge	东北秧歌
Dongfang hong	东方红
Dongfang wu	东方舞
dongjing	洞经
dongjinghui	洞经会
Dongxiang	东乡
Du Rongfang	杜荣芳
Du Zhusheng	杜竹生
duandiao	短调
duanzhuang	端庄
Dunhuang	敦煌
Ejinai (Ejina) Banner	额济纳旗
erhu	二胡
fayang	发扬
fazhan	发展
Fang Kun	方堃

Fangxianzhe yaozhi ge shoupa	纺线者要织个手帕
fengge	风格
fengge secaiqu	风格色彩区
feng jiao xue	风搅雪
fu	赋
gamei	尕妹
Gansu Liangzhou de hao mianhua	甘肃凉州的好棉花
Gansu minguo ribao	甘肃民国日报
Gansu minzu chubanshe	甘肃民族出版社
Gao Jingye	杲景业
ge fenghuang	歌凤凰
geming gequ	革命歌曲
gewutuan	歌舞团
Geyao yanjiuhui	歌谣研究会
Geyao zhoukan	歌谣周刊
Gu Jiegang	顾颉刚
Guangming ribao	光明日报
guobiao wu	国标舞
Guofeng	国风
Guomindang	国民党
Guo Moruo	郭沫若
Guo Zhengqing	郭正清
Hani	哈尼
Halh (Ka'erka)	喀尔喀
Han	汉
Hanhua	汉化
Han-Tang	汉唐
Hanzu minjian wu	汉族民间舞
He Yaozu	贺耀组
Hoshud (Heshuote)	和硕特
Honggehui	红歌会
hong haizi	红孩子
Honghe	红河
hoomii (humai)	呼麦
Horchin (Ke'erqin)	科尔沁

Glossary of Selected Chinese Terms and Phrases | 159

Hulunbuir (Hulunbei'er)	呼伦贝尔市
Huabei	华北
hua'er (song genre)	花儿
hua'er (speech)	话儿
Hua'er de jiaxiang	花儿的家乡
hua'er de wenxue yiwei	花儿的文学意味
Hua'er de yanjiu guocheng	花儿的研究过程
Hua'er houxu	花儿后序
Hua'er ji	花儿集
Hua'er jingxuan	花儿精选
hua'er wang	花儿王
Hua'er xu	花儿序
Hua'er xuan	花儿选
Hua'er yu shaonian	花儿与少年
Hua'er zaixu	花儿再序
Huanghe	黄河
Huanghe zhi sheng	黄河之声
Hui	回
huiyan	汇演
Idanjab (Yidanzhabu)	伊丹扎布
Ih-Juu (Yikezhao) League	伊克昭盟
jicheng	继承
jicheng yu fayang	继承与发扬
jicheng yu fazhan	继承与发展
jida chengzhe	集大成者
Jidazhaizhu	冀达斋主
Jirim (Zhelimu) League	哲里木盟
jiage	家歌
Jiarong	嘉绒/嘉戎
Jia Shuying	贾舒颖
Jia Zuoguang	贾作光
jianzhi	剪纸
Jiaozhou	胶州
jie wu	街舞
jiezi (Chinese transcription of Lisu-language term)	洁资

Jin Hao 金浩
jinghua 精华
Jingju 京剧
jingshen shiliang 精神食粮
Jiuqu (song title) 酒曲
jiuqu dasai 酒曲大赛
juelie (Chinese transcription of Lisu-language term) 诀咧

kang 炕
Kangba'erhan 康巴尔汗
Ke Yang 柯杨
Kemu 克木
kexuehua 科学化
kuaican 快餐
Kuaile nansheng 快乐男声
Kunqu 昆曲

Lahu 拉祜
Lasurong 拉苏荣
Lanzhou 兰州
Lanzhou chengli bing bianle 兰州城里兵变了
laobaixing 老百姓
laodong gaizao 劳动改造
Lei dandan pao zai shahaohao lin 泪蛋蛋抛在沙蒿蒿林
Lhajau (Hazhabu) 哈扎布
Li Chuanxin 李传新
Li Dexian du hua'er 李德贤读花儿
Li Fu 李富
Lisu 傈僳
Li Wei'er (aka Li Wei) 李薇儿 (李薇)
Li Yang 力杨
Li Yu 李雨
Li Yusheng 李玉生
Li Zhengfei 李政飞
Lianhe chubanshe 联合出版社
Liang Lun 梁伦
Lintao 临洮

Glossary of Selected Chinese Terms and Phrases | 161

ling	令
Liu Gaiyu	刘改鱼
liupai	流派
Liu Xicheng	刘锡诚
Lu Badma (Lu Badema)	鲁·巴德玛
luohou	落后
Luoluo	倮倮
Ma Guoguo	马国国
Ma Wenhui	马文惠
manhandiao	漫瀚调
Maomaoyu	毛毛雨
Menggu fengge	蒙古风格
Menggu weidao	蒙古味道
Menggu wu	蒙古舞
Meng-Han diao	蒙汉调
Mengxiang Zhongguo	梦想中国
Mengzi	蒙自
Miao	苗
Miao Meng	苗萌
min'ge	民歌
min'ge wang	民歌王
min'ge wangzi	民歌王子
minjian	民间
minjian wu	民间舞
minjian yiren	民间艺人
minzu changfa	民族唱法
minzu minjian wu	民族民间舞
minzu wudao	民族舞蹈
minzu xingshi	民族形式
Modeg (Modege)	莫德格
Modegema	莫德格玛
morin huur (matouqin)	马头琴
Nashunhutu	那顺呼图
Naxi	纳西
Nanwoka (Chinese transcription of Dai-language song title)	南硪卡

Neimenggu yinyue chuancheng zhan	内蒙古音乐传承站
nengge shanwu	能歌善舞
Ni man hua'er wo dahua	你漫花儿我答话
Nisu	尼苏
nongcun yinyue	农村音乐
nü Abao	女阿宝
Oirat (Wala/Weilate)	瓦剌/卫拉特
Ordos (E'erduosi)	鄂尔多斯
paoqi	抛弃
pengyou jiushi caifu	朋友就是财富
pingfan	平反
pingmin xuexiao	平民学校
qiben (Chinese transcription of Lisu-language term)	其奔
Qi Fulin	奇富林
Qiang	羌
Qiao Jianzhong	乔建中
qingge	情歌
qingsihua zuo dianwang	情丝化作电网
Quanguo nongcun yeyu yanchu diaoyan	全国农村业余演出调演
Quanguo nongmin yishu diaoyan	全国农民艺术调演
Quanguo qingnian geshou dianshi dajiang sai	全国青年歌手电视大奖赛
Quanguo qingnian geshou shengyue bisai	全国青年歌手声乐比赛
Quanguo shaoshu minzu shengyue dasai	全国少数民族声乐大赛
quanmu	全牧
quanxin Shaanbei fengge zuhe	全新陕北风格组合
qunzhong	群众
Renmin huabao	人民画报
Renmin ribao	人民日报
Renmin yinyue chubanshe	人民音乐出版社
Ruili	瑞丽
Salar (Sala)	撒拉
Sani	撒尼
Sanguo yanyi	三国演义

Glossary of Selected Chinese Terms and Phrases

san jie	三杰
Shaanbei min'ge wang	陕北民歌王
Shandandan kaihua hongyanyan	山丹丹开花红艳艳
shan'ge	山歌
shaonian	少年
shaoshu minzu	少数民族
shaoshu minzu wudao	少数民族舞蹈
shehui jinbu	社会进步
shequ	撷取
Shenmu	神木
shengzhan	圣战
Shi'er yue	十二月
Shijing	诗经
Shilingol (Xilinguole) League	锡林郭勒盟
Shi Zhanming	石占明
shouji	收集
Shoujie Zhongguo nanbei min'ge leitaisai	首届中国南北民歌擂台赛
Silu hua yu	丝路花雨
Siqintariha	斯琴塔日哈
Si xiaomen shangle suole	四校门上了锁了
sucai	素材
Sulian guoli minjian wudaotuan	苏联国立民间舞蹈团
suibu	碎步
Sun Zhikuan	孙志宽
Taiyuan	太原
taizhuzi	台柱子
Taohuajiang	桃花江
Taomin	洮岷
Tao River	洮河
tese	特色
texing	特性
Teng Xiaotian	腾晓天
Tian Qing	田青
Tonghai	通海
Tongliao City	通辽市
Tongque ji	铜雀伎

tongsu weir	通俗味儿
tongsu yinyue	通俗音乐
Torghud (Tu'erhute)	土尔扈特
tu (rustic)	土
Tu (Monguor)	土
tudi (disciple)	徒弟
Tumed (Tumote)	土默特
Ujumchin (Wuzhumuqin)	乌珠穆沁
Ulanji (Wulanjie)	乌兰杰
wajue	挖掘
waiguo de	外国的
Wang Duanshu	王端淑
Wang Erni	王二妮
Wang Jingzhi	王景志
Wang Kun	王昆
Wang Luobin	王洛宾
Wang Pei	王沛
Wang Xiangrong	王向荣
Wei	魏
weidao	味道
Wei Quanming	魏泉鸣
Weiwu'erzu wu	维吾尔族舞
wengongtuan	文工团
wenhua fazhan	文化发展
Wenhua fuwushe	文化服务社
wenhua renmin	文化人民
wenhua yichan	文化遗产
Wen Shilong	文世龙
Wo yao shang chunwan	我要上春晚
Wo yi Lintao hao	我忆临洮好
Wudao (journal title)	舞蹈
wudaojia	舞蹈家
Wudao tongxun	舞蹈通讯
Wudao xuexi ziliao	舞蹈学习资料
wudao yishu	舞蹈艺术

wudao yishu gongzuozhe	舞蹈艺术工作者
Wugengqu	五更曲
Wulanjie (Chinese transcription of Ulanji)	乌兰杰
wulanmuqi	乌兰牧骑
wutaihua	舞台化
Wu Xiaobang	吴晓邦
wuzhe	舞者
Wu Zhen	吴镇
Xibei minjian geyao yanjiu zhi yi: Hua'er ji	西北民间歌谣研究之一·花儿集
Xibei ribao	西北日报
Xibei shan'ge hua'er ji xulun	西北山歌花儿集叙论
Xibei wenhua xiehui	西北文化协会
Xibu gewang	西部歌王
Xibu min'ge dianshi dasai	西部民歌电视大赛
Xi Huimin	郗慧民
Xining	西宁
xiqu	戏曲
Xiyang de	西洋的
Xia River	夏河
xiandaihua	现代化
xiandai wu	现代舞
Xianju	仙居
xiangsheng	相声
Xiaohuaxi	小花戏
Xiao Mei	萧梅
Xiao Shenyang	小沈阳
Xin Lisheng	辛礼生
Xinsheng shudian	新生书店
Xintianyou gewang	信天游歌王
xinxing wudao	新兴舞蹈
Xinzhou	忻州
xing	兴
Xing'an/Hinggan League	兴安盟
Xingguang dadao	星光大道
Xu Lingxiao	徐凌霄
xushi hua'er	叙事花儿

xueyuanpai	学院派
xueyuanpai minjian wu	学院派民间舞
Xun shang ge dalu zou ba	寻上个大路走吧
Ya Hanzhang	牙含章
Yan'an	延安
Yankan gamei xin bianle	眼看尕妹心变了
Yang Cui	杨璀
Yang Dehong	杨德宏
yangge	秧歌
Yang Hui	扬晖
Yangjiajiang	杨家将
Yang Yucheng	杨玉成
yecao	野草
yequ	野曲
Yi	彝
yiri yiduo hua'er	一日一朵花儿
Yi shan'ge jie shan'ge	以山歌解山歌
Yishu pinglun	艺术评论
Yinyue zhoubao	音乐周报
Yugu/Yugur	裕固
Yulin	榆林
Yumiti	玉米提
Yuzhong	榆中
Yuan Fuli	袁复礼
yuanshengtai	原生态
Yuanshengtai chongji qing ge sai	原生态冲击青歌赛
yuanshengtai min'ge	原生态民歌
yuanshengtai wudao	原生态舞蹈
yuanshengtai zuhe	原生态组合
yuansu	元素
yuanweir	原味儿
Yuefu	乐府
Yunnan huadeng	云南花灯
Yunnan yishu xueyuan	云南艺术学院
Zahua hua'er	杂话花儿
Zange	赞歌

Glossary of Selected Chinese Terms and Phrases | 167

Zangzu wu	藏族舞
zaopo	糟粕
Zhanshi Gansu xinwen jianchachu shangxiao chuzhang	战时甘肃新闻检查处上校处长
Zhang Junren	张君仁
Zhang Laowu	张老五
Zhang Lin	张林
Zhang Shaochun	张少淳
Zhang Taiyan	章太炎
Zhang Xingrong	张兴荣
Zhang Yaxiong	张亚雄
Zhang Yiwu	张一悟
Zhao Zongfu	赵宗福
Zheng	郑
zhengli	整理
zhengmai (Chinese transcription of Dai-language term)	整迈
zhengtao (Chinese transcription of Dai-language term)	整涛
Zhongguo balei	中国芭蕾
Zhongguo getan	中国歌坛
Zhongguo gewuju yishe	中国歌舞剧艺社
Zhongguo gudianwu	中国古典舞
Zhongguo minjian gequ jicheng	中国民间歌曲集成
Zhongguo minzu minjian yinyue jicheng	中国民族民间音乐集成
Zhongguo wudao	中国舞蹈
Zhongguo xiandai wu	中国现代舞
Zhong wan wu	盅碗舞
Zhongyang minzu gewutuan	中央民族歌舞团
Zhongyang ribao	中央日报
Zhou Jinping	周金平
Zhu Zhonglu	朱仲禄
zhuanji	专辑
zhuanyehua	专业化
zixu	自序
Ziyou zhi hua	自由之花
Zizhou	子洲
Zuoquan	左权

Index

Note: Italicized page numbers represent figures (f) and tables (t). In the subentries, the *Anthology of Hua'er Folksongs* is abbreviated as *Anthology*.

Abao (b. 1969, real name Zhang Shaochun): and album of "Chinese Rural Music," 54; as competition judge, 53; earnings of, 58n3; iconic performance of, 50, 51; rise to fame, 47–49; with Shi Zhanming and Liu Gaiyu, 55; as song king, 59n10
agency: in celebrity culture, 48; creative agency, 102–3; individual, 2, 7–9, 10, 11, 99; through freedom and identification, 9
AIMP (Switzerland), 126
"Airs of the States," 103
Alasha Folksong Society, 32
Alasha region (Inner Mongolia): about, 26; Badma as heritage ambassador in, 31–32; Dedema and, 20–21; musical culture of, 26–29, 30, 34; urban influences on culture in, 27–28. *See also* Altantsetseg; Lu Badma; Yang Yucheng
Alili (Pan, 2004) (Yunnanese CDs), 129, 137, 140, 141, 143, 152
All-China National Young Singers' Television Competition, 42, 49
Altangaole, 21
Altantsetseg (b. 1955), 30–31
anthologies: canonization of singers in, 57; erotic songs in, 120n17; as genre and pedagogy, 100–101, 110; intertextual and communal nature of, 95, 99, 101; methods used to create, 103; and nationalism, 101–2; proliferation of, 104, 119n13; singers' names in, 115–16; as sites of tradition, 1; as structuring structures, 101–2, 111–12; of Yunnanese folk music, 128, 148n8
"Anthology of Chinese Music" project, 28
Anthology of Hua'er Folksongs (*Hua'er ji*): and *Book of Songs*, 103–4; as collection of flowers, 95–96; contents and character of, 107–9, 112; contributors to, 106, 110; as cultural history, 117–18; "Hua'er Afterword," 106, 114; intertextuality of, 96; motivation for, 109–10; organization and editing of, 111–12; publication of, 95, 105, 106–7, 108; references to other texts and people in, 115–17, 119n3
archival musical knowledge, 10, 144
archival-quality recordings, 29
Atwood, Christopher, 25, 26
authenticity, 24, 49, 77–80
authoring of tradition, 80, 84
awards in competitions, 11, 41, 54–56
Ayitula (b. 1940), 80
A You Duo (b. 1977), 50

Badma. *See* Lu Badma
Bai Bingquan, 51
Bain Delger (b. 1945), 26–27
Bai Opera (Pan, 2017) (Yunnanese CD), 129, 137, *138f*, 139, 141, 153
Bai Opera and Dai Opera CD project, 137–40, *138f*, *139f*
Baishibai (Pan, 1995) (Yunnanese CD), 127, 129, 140, 141, 152
Bake, Arnold, 144–45
Bake Restudy 1984 (Jairazbhoy and Catlin, 1991) (DVD), 152
Bamboo on the Mountains (Smithsonian Folkways, 1999) (CD), 152
Baranovitch, Nimrod, 21
Bauman, Richard, 1, 43, 44, 45, 48, 57, 102, 117–18
"The Beautiful Grasslands Are My Home," 20, 21
Beijing Folksong Research Society, 95, 105
Benedict, Barbara, 101

169

Bi Fujian, 48
biographies, 3, 7–8
Body, Jack: about, 148n9; "From Yunnan," 143; interest in anthology project, 128–29; and language and transliteration decisions, 136–37; promotion of CDs, 142; work on liner notes, 132–34, 133f
Bohlman, Philip, 42
Boltz, Judith, 130
Book of Songs (Shijing), 103, 107, 114, 119n14, 120n17
Botolt. *See* Yang Yucheng
Bourdieu, Pierre, 9, 18, 43, 46, 101
bricoleurs, 11, 99
Bronner, Simon, 9
Bruin, Joost de, 42
Brunt, Shelley, 42–43
Bu He, 74–75
Butterflies Fluttering About (Caidie fenfei) (film), 84

Cashman, Ray, 5, 11, 99
Catlin, Amy, 144–45, 147n3
CCTV-MTV (China Central Television–Music Television) Music Awards, 43
CCTV Spring Festival Gala, 54
CCTV Western China TV Folksong Competition, 47, 49, 53
CD albums: and access to cultural heritage, 144; and canonization of style, singer, and repertoire, 57; commercialization of, 140–42; and refiguring of public understanding of performers and tradition, 6–7; of Shi Zhanming's performances, 56; as symbolic sites of tradition, 1, 2; as tool to transmit cultural heritage, 28, 36–37. *See also* "Great Masters Series"; *On the Vast and Fertile Plains of Alasha* (Lu Badma); Yunnanese CDs
celebrity culture: achieved and attributed celebrity, 48; and competition judging, 53, 58–59n6; and singers' earnings, 58n3
Central Daily News (Zhongyang ribao) advertisement for *Anthology*, 110
Central Nationalities Song and Dance Troupe (Zhongyang minzu gewutuan), 21
Chen Jie, 49
Chen Yaping, 79–80
China. *See* People's Republic of China (PRC)
China Central Conservatory National Music Ensemble, 77
China Dancers Association, 68
Chinese classical dance, 66, 72, 73, 76, 80, 83–84, 88
Chinese Communist Party (CCP), 104, 105
Chinese dance: basic materials in, 75, 76; categories of, 65–66; as cumulative process and product, 77, 78, 88; development of, 65; distinctive characteristics and type/typicality in, 75–76; ethnic dance, 3; goals in, 76; inheritance in, 87; leaders in development of, 68; modern/traditional dichotomy in, 66; national forms in, 64, 65; style and flavor in, 75–76; training for, 65, 68, 81, 86. *See also* Dai Ailian; dynamic inheritance; Liang Lun; Siqintariha
Chinese ethnomusicology, 146
Chinese Federation of Literature and Art Circles, 109
Chinese Folk Literature Movement, 95
Chinese Nationalities Folk Music Collection series, 104–5
Chinese religious music, 130–31
Choe Seung-hui (aka Sai Shōki/Choi Seunghee, 1911–1969), 83; "The Future of Chinese Dance Art," 73
choreographers: and problem of creation, 74–75; recognition of, 88; as representatives of new interpretations, 10; and use of basic materials, 75
Ci, Jiwei, 9
A Collection of Alasha Mongolian Folksongs, 32
collector-editors: creative agency of, 102–3; intertextual and communal nature of, 95, 99–100; practices of, 99; source of term, 102; Zhang Yaxiong as model of, 118. *See also* Zhang Yaxiong
color regions, 32, 36, 38n8

Comaroff, John and Jean, 8–9
commercialized "fast food" musical options, 7, 36
Confucian canon, 103
Confucian values and hua'er folksongs, 114
Confucius, 119n6, 120n17
conservatory training: and authenticity, 31; Chinese attitudes toward, 23; incorporation into long song technique, 32–33, 34; and shift in China's recording interest, 140
creation process in dance, 71–77, 72t
creativity and tension with tradition, 102
Cui Miao (b. 1986), 50, 51, 56
cultural brokers, 6, 44, 47–48, 146
cultural heritage: access to, 144; documentation of, 2, 17–18, 34–35, 72–73, 144, 149n19; importance of folksong in, 104; preservation of, 18, 24, 26–29, 34, 35, 77–79; role of individual creativity in, 67; tourism based on, 22; valorization of regional folk artists, 22. See also *Anthology of Hua'er Folksongs* (*Hua'er ji*); "Great Masters Series"; individuals and traditions; Lu Badma; Yunnanese CDs
cultural production: arbiters in Inner Mongolia, 34–35; in China, 19; legitimacy in, 46; "making a mark" on the field of, 11–12
cultural transmitters (*chuanchengren*), 22, 25, 29, 31, 35, 38n7, 142, 143
culture, reconception of, 8
"Cup and Bowl Dance" (*Zhong wan wu*), 81, 82f, 83–86, 87
cup and bowl dance techniques, 85f, 86f
Cup-Bowl-Chopstick, 85
curation of recordings: choice of sounds in, 130–31; expectations in, 146; goals of, 145; languages and romanization, 136–37, 139–40, 148n14; liner notes and accuracy, 132–34, 133f, 138–39, 140; and presentation of ethnic minorities, 134–36; process in, 129, 132, 148n10, 148n12; Zhang Xingrong's concept for opera CDs, 137–38

Dai Ailian (1916–2006): about, 68; choreography of, 69–70, 80, 89n7; and invented tradition, 79; methodology of dynamic inheritance, 71–72; "The First Step in Developing Chinese Dance" (1946), 68–70; view of Chinese dance, 70
Dai Opera (Pan, 2017) (Yunnanese CD), 129, 137–40, 153
Dali Bai Autonomous Prefecture Bai Opera Troupe, 137
dance, modern *versus* traditional, 3. See also Chinese classical dance; Chinese dance
dance artists, 72, 87, 89n5
Dancers of the Tongque Stage (*Tongque ji*) (Sun Ying, 1985), 76, 80, 87
Dedema, 20–21, 25
Dedema Art School, 86f
Dégh, Linda, 5
Dehong Prefecture Dai Opera Troupe, 138, 140
DeMare, Brian, 67
Ding Ling, 46
Dongjing Music (Pan, 1998) (Yunnanese CD), 129, 130–31, 131f, 140, 141, 148n11, 152
Du Chunmei, 23
Dunhuang school, 66, 76
Durham Oriental Music Festival, 77
Du Zhushen, 106
dynamic inheritance: artistic methodology of, 71–77, 72t, 81; and authoring of tradition, 80; concept of, 66–67, 88; dual nature of, 76; emergence of, 67–68; leaders in use of model, 68–71; use of methodology in "Cup and Bowl Dance," 83–84; use outside of China, 87

The East Is Red (1964), 20, 84
Edwards, Louise, 48
Ejinai Mongols, 25
English, James F., 52
ethnic minorities: Bai and Dai groups, 135–36, 148n15; in China, 19–20, 21; contribution to Chinese dance, 80; cross-border migration of, 135; and dance, 66, 72, 73; description in CD liner notes, 134–35; dongjing music, 130–31; Kemu

ethnic minorities (*cont.*)
   minority, description of, 135; Mongol identity, 25, 38n5; musical styles of, 128; recognition for, 17, 18; and transitions from pop to folksong, 49; in Yunnan Province, 147n4. *See also* hua'er songs; indigenous performances; Mongols; Shaanxi folksongs; Yunnanese CDs; Zuoquan folksongs
ethnographers, dance artists as, 72–73
ethnographic recordings, 1, 128, 145–46, 147n1, 147n3, 149n20. *See also* "Great Masters Series"; Yunnanese CDs
ethnographies, view of individuals in, 3, 7–8, 13n4
ethnomusicology, 3, 146
European art music, 24
European Foundation for Chinese Music Research (CHIME), 126, 141
Eurovision Song Competition (ESC), 42
excavation process in dance methodology, 72–73, 75

faces of tradition, double meaning of, 6, 10
Fang Kun, 77, 78–79
Flowers and Rain on the Silk Road (*Silu hua yu*) (1979), 76, 80
"folk," concept of, 65
folklore and folk culture: mandates to study, 67–68; modern studies of, 120n15; revival of, 94; transformation through anthologizing, 102; value of, 24, 64. *See also* cultural heritage
folklorists, 94
folk music artists: careers of, 142; as featured in "Great Masters" series, 28–29; kings/queens, 22, 26–27, 31, 53, 120n23 (*see also* Abao; Lu Badma; Shi Zhanming; Sun Zhikuan; Wang Xiangrong); and pathways for, 37; residencies for, 28; skills of, 23; visibility of, 144
folksingers, professional: celebrity status of, 44; competitions and careers of, 41–42, 57, 58n3; and cultural identity, 43. *See also* Abao; Cui Miao; Liu Gaiyu; Li Yu; Lu Badma; master-disciple relationships among singers; Qi Fulin; Shi Zhanming; Sun Zhikuan; Wang Erni; Wang Xiangrong
Folksong Collection Office (Peking University), 104
folk song collections, 19, 32, 37n1. *See also* anthologies
Folksong Weekly (*Geyao zhoukan*), 104
Fourth National Minorities Arts and Culture Festival, 85
From China's S. W. Borders (Aspara Media, 2001) (DVDs), 152
Frontier Music and Dance Meeting, 69–70
Fung, Anthony, 43

Gansu Nationalities Press, 117
Gansu Province, 94, 100, 105–7, 115
Gansu Provincial Arts and Literature Conference, Second, 107
Gansu Republican Daily News (*Gansu minguo ribao*), 106
Gao Jingye, 94, 119n8
Glassie, Henry, 5
Gower, Herschel, 4, 5, 7
grassland pastoralism, 27–28, 35, 37n5
Graves, Alfred Perceval, 100–101
"Great Masters Series" ("Inner Mongolia Ethnic Music Classics—Great Masters Series"): circulation of, 37; as documentation of heritage, 18, 24, 35–36; and focus on individual artists in, 28–29; and future of musical preservation in Inner Mongolia, 34; purpose of, 17
groupings of success, 52–54
Gu Jiegang (1893–1980), 104
Guo Moruo, 103
Guo Zhengqing, 116, 120n20

Hafstein, Valdimar, 102
Han Chinese: cultural influences of, 27–28; folk dance of, 65–66, 69, 72; and *yuanshengtai* folksongs, 49
Handler, Richard, 6
Hani, polyphonic folksongs of, 143
Han-Tang school, 66, 76, 87–88
Harris, Rachel, 59n9

Hasan-Roken, Galit, 102
Hellier, Ruth, 5, 8
Hockx, Michel, 52
Hohhot (Inner Mongolia), 27
Holm, David, 87
horse-head fiddle, standardization of, 33
"Horse Race," 21
house songs, 113
Huabei University Dance Team, 89n7
hua'er genre of folksongs: about, 97, 98–99, 119n10; importance of *Anthology* to, 117; lyrics that characterize, 113; as national tradition, 100; redefinition of, 95–96; solidification of, 97–98
hua'er performance practice, 112
hua'er songs: about, 95, 113, 119n5; importance of, 111; key questions about, 117; king of, 120n23; linking mechanisms in, 98–99; lyrics of, 113, 114, 115; metaphor in, 114–15; national attention to, 95; publications and recordings on, 117; research on, 94; terms for, 97, 119n7–8; as voice of Northwest China, 114. *See also* Zhang Yaxiong
hua'er studies, 6–7, 97, 119n3
Hui Xiao, 43
Huun Huur Tu, 23

ICH. *See* Intangible Cultural Heritage (ICH) (UNESCO)
Idanjab (b. 1955), 17
Idols shows, 42
imagined tradition, 100, 119n10
indigenous performances, 65, 68–69, 70–71, 72. *See also* hua'er songs; long song; *yuanshengtai*; Yunnanese CDs
individual agency: complexity in, 11; and intentionality, 8–9; and refiguring of culture, 8, 10; and tradition, 2
individuals and traditions: approaches to understanding, 4–8; interconnectedness of, 2, 3, 12; mutual transformation of, 4, 5–6, 78; and overlooked contributions of individuals, 3–4; scholars' framing of, 6–7. *See also* individual agency

inheritance, metaphor of, 87. *See also* dynamic inheritance
Inner Mongolia: energy for transmission of heritage in, 36; folk music of, 17; musical reformers in, 32–33; pastoral zone of, 26; representative songs and singers in, 19–22. *See also* "Great Masters Series"; Lu Badma
Inner Mongolia Cultural Work Troupe, 74
Inner Mongolia Musical Heritage Inheritance Station, 28, 35
Inner Mongolia Song and Dance Ensemble, 81, 83
Inner Mongolia University Art College, 17, 28, 29, 33, 37, 86
instrumentalists, 142, 144. *See also* Lu Badma
instrumental music, 130
Intangible Cultural Heritage (ICH) (UNESCO): China's embrace of, 18, 22, 143; and documentation of tradition, 35; projects of, 28; and recognition for artists and scholars, 18, 38n7; social change and loss of heritage, 35
Intangible Cultural Heritage of Humanity (UNESCO), 95, 118, 119n4
intentionality, problems of, 8
International Phonetic Alphabet (IPA), 136–37
intertextuality: in anthologies, 95, 96, 99, 101, 107; in hua'er songs, 98–99
"I Want to Be on the Spring Festival Gala," 54

Jairazbhoy, Nazir, 144–45, 147n3
Japanese War, effect on Zhang Yaxiong, 110, 111
Jeffreys, Elaine, 48
Jia Shuying, "'Original Ecology' Hits the Youth Song Competition," 23
Jia Zuoguang, 83, 84
Jin Hao, 76
Jones, Stephen, 37n1, 58n4, 59n14, 126, 149n19
judges of performances: and continuity and change of traditions, 12, 46; and master-disciple relationships, 52–54; roles of, 44, 45; and traditionalization of performances, 44, 45

Kangba'erhan (1914–1994), 80, 89n9
Ke Yang (1935–2017), 94
Kleikamp, Bernard, 129, 137, 142, 148n11, 149n21

"Lamp Dance," 83, 84
languages and romanization, 136–37, 139–40, 147n2
Lasurong, 20, 21, 25, 38n6
Lau, Frederick, 130
Lévi-Strauss, Claude, 11
Lhajau (1922–2008), 26
Liang Lun (b. 1921), 68, 71–72; "Marco Polo Bridge Call and Answer Dance," 71; "The Problem of Making Dance Chinese" (1947), 70–71
Linnekin, Jocelyn, 6
Liu Gaiyu, 54, 55
Li Wei'er (aka Li Wei, b. 1945): communication with Yunnan residents, 136; discovery of Hani polyphonic folksongs, 143; and dongjing music, 148n11; expertise of, 127; promotion of CDs, 142; video recordings of, 128, 147n3; and Yunnanese field recordings, 125, 146. See also Yunnanese CDs; Zhang Xingrong
Li Yu ("female Abao"), 50, 51
Li Yusheng, 144
Li Zhengfei (b. 1980), 51, 53, 59n14
long song: collections of, 32; genre and artists of, 26–28; importance of, 54; influence of conservatory training on, 32–33; and Lasurong, 38n6; queen of, 31; sounds of Alasha in, 36; technique in, 20. See also Lu Badma
Lord, Albert B., 4, 5
love songs, 98
Lu Badma (b. 1940): as authentic cultural transmitter, 30, 31–32, 36; celebration of Alasha heritage, 26; horse-head fiddle technique of, 30, 33; as minority in government heritage project, 17–18, 30; role in promotion of Alasha, 26, 33; singing technique of, 30, 33; tribute concert to, 33. See also *On the Vast and Fertile Plains of Alasha* (Lu Badma)
lyric songs, 98

Ma Guoguo, 142
Mandarin-language pop songs, 20
manhandiao, 41, 56, 58n1
Mao Zedong: on art and folk culture, 18, 64; cultural policies of, 19–20, 37n1; on folk forms, 87; and principles of Chinese culture, 71
Marshall, P. David, 50
Marxist socialist realism, 19–20
master-disciple relationships among singers, 52–54
Ma Wenhui, 96, 119n6
May Fourth movement, 95
mechanisms of traditionalization, 3, 6, 9–12, 57. See also anthologies; CD albums; ethnographic recordings; representative works; singing competitions; traditionalization of performances
media and documentation of heritage, 2, 10. See also CD albums; ethnographic recordings
Merriam, Alan, 144
Ministry of Culture, 55, 127
minorities. See ethnic minorities
Modeg (b. 1930), 17
Modegema (b. 1941), 83, 84
Moiseyev, Igor, 88
Mongol dance, 83–86, 90n13
Mongol folk musicians, 17
Mongols: identities of, 19, 20, 25; Ordos Mongols, 25, 84; stereotypes of, 21–22, 24
Mongol stylistic flavors, 21
Mould, Tom, 5, 11, 99
mountain songs, 97, 113. See also Yunnanese CDs
MTV competitions, 42
musical restudies, 144–45
Music of the Bai Opera and the Dai Opera in Yunnan Province (Pan, 2017) (Yunnanese CDs), 137–40

Nanwoka (Pan, 2005) (Yunnanese CDs), 129, 137, 140, 141, 152
narrative strategies in fieldwork, 7
Nashunhutu, 84, *85f*

National Chinese Folksong Competitions, 49, 54, 55
national culture, construction of, 67–68, 87, 88
national dance forms, 79
National Folk Dance Ensemble of the Soviet Union, 88
National Intangible Cultural Heritage Protection Center, 59n17
nationalism: and dance, 65, 71; folksong and, 100, 104, 110–11; and identity through anthologies, 102
Nationalist Party (KMT) nationalism, 79
National Minorities Song Competition, 30
National Selection of Rural Amateur Performers (1980), 42
National Young Singer's Competition, 30
native performance practice. *See* indigenous performances
New Zealand art music composition, 143
Nimbus (UK), 126
Northwest Daily News (*Xibei ribao*), 106
Noyes, Dorothy, 6

Ocora (France), 126
Ode Record Company, 128–29, 141, 143, 149n16
On the Vast and Fertile Plains of Alasha (Lu Badma), 24–25, 29–30
Ordos drink bowl dance, 83
Ordos Mongols, 25, 84
organization in dance methodology, 73–74, 76
original ecology. See *yuanshengtai*
Ortner, Sherry B., 8, 9

Pan Records (Netherlands), 126, 129, 140, 141, 149n16, 149n21
peasant masses, learning from, 111, 120n21
Peng Song (b. 1916), 69
People's Republic of China (PRC): access to cultural research in, 2; aesthetic preferences in, 19, 141, 147–48n7 (see also *yuanshengtai*); anthologies in, 111–12; classification of ethnic minorities in, 134, 135–36; cultural heritage policies of, 18–19, 22–25, 24; funding for heritage projects, 28, 35; individual agency in, 9; musical reformers in, 32; national singing style in, 21; Northwest China (*see* hua'er songs); outstanding folk genres of, 54; recognition of regional folk artists, 22, 144, 149n19; recordings of folk genres of, 125–27 (*see also* Yunnanese CDs); revolutionary culture of, 64; sound preservation in, 18, 28; stereotypes of Mongols in, 21; and study of folk culture, 67
performance traditions: branding in, 50–51, 52; Chinese scholarship on, 2; continuity and change in, 1, 43, 77–79 (*see also* dynamic inheritance); and impact of singing competitions, 56–57; refiguring of, 43, 50
performers as faces of tradition, 1. *See also* individuals and traditions
Picard, François, 126
place: and attention to regions, 47; repositioning of, 54–56. *See also* Alasha region; Gansu Province; hua'er studies; Inner Mongolia; Qinghai Province; Shaanxi Province, northern region of; Yunnan Province
poetry, native place of, 114
Porter, James, 4, 5, 7
PRC. *See* People's Republic of China
preservation of cultural heritage, 18, 24, 26–29, 34, 35, 77–79. See also *Anthology of Hua'er Folksongs*; dynamic inheritance; "Great Masters Series"; Lu Badma; Yunnanese CDs
professionalism, 21, 31
Provine, Robert, 77–78

Qiao Jianzhong: on *Anthology*, 107; coining of term "color regions," 38n8; definition of "original ecology folksongs," 23; on important folksong genres, 54; and May Fourth folksong movement, 104; and pioneering work recording Chinese folk music, 126; and singing competitions, 7, 53; on Zhang Yaxiong, 117

Qi Fulin: awards presentation ritual of, 41, 56; contest preparation of, 56; validation as singer, 46
Qinghai Province, 107, 108, 113, 119nn7–8, 120n23

Red and White Song Contest (Japan), 43
Red Song Contest (China), 44–45, 52, 53
Rees, Helen: and bifurcated approach in focus on individuals, 3; on China's cultural heritage policies, 22; on judges for singing competitions, 53; on survival of traditional performing arts, 24; and YST folksongs, 23. See also curation of recordings; Yunnanese CDs
representational stance, 8
representative transmitters. See cultural transmitters
representative works: in dance, 80–81, 88; as inspiration for future work, 11; qualities of, 81; of singers, 57; status of Yunnanese CDs, 142; as symbolic sites of tradition, 1, 2. See also Anthology of Hua'er Folksongs (Hua'er ji); "Cup and Bowl Dance"
revolutionary song, 19
Rhenen, Jan van, 148n11
Rice, Timothy, 7, 13n4
Robertson, Jeannie, 7
Rojek, Chris, 48
Ruskin, Jesse, 7, 13n4

Satoru, Ito, 137, 140
Schechner, Richard, 44
Schimmelpenninck, Antoinet, 3
scholars: and approaches to individuals and traditions, 4; and dance discourses, 67; debate over authenticity and tradition, 77–79; influences of, 6–7; roles in competitions, 11; support for regional singers from, 55
Seeger, Anthony, 147n1
selection and discernment in dance methodology (absorb/abandon), 73, 76
Shaanxi Province, northern region of: bringing attention to, 47, 54, 56; ethnographic studies of, 48; folksingers from, 41, 46–47, 50–51, 53–54, 56, 58n3, 59n16; folksongs of, 46, 47, 49, 50, 51; hybrid song genres of, 58n1.
Shanxi Province, 41, 53–54, 55. See also Zuoquan County
Shay, Anthony, 3, 88
Shijing. See Book of Songs (Shijing)
Shi Zhanming (b. 1973), 52, 53–55, 59n16
Shukla, Pravina, 5, 11, 99
singers: and cultural identity, 43; and impact of awards, 11. See also folksingers, professional
singing competitions: and assistance to singers, 47–48; and branding of singers and traditions, 50–51, 52; and career advancement, 44–45, 52–54; and celebrity culture, 47, 48, 53, 58–59n6, 58n3; effect on professional singers, 41–42; emergence of, 42, 58n4; "making a mark" through, 43; and master-disciple relationships, 52–54; and repositioning of place, 54–56; as symbolic sites of tradition, 1; talent, hype, and social network in, 48; traditionalization of performances through, 43, 45, 46–50. See also folksingers, professional; judges of performances; performance traditions
Sing Singapore, 42
Siqintariha (b. 1932), 81, 82f, 83, 85f, 86, 86f, 87; "From 'Lamp Dance' to 'Cup and Bowl' Solo Dance," 83–84
Smithsonian Folkways recordings, 135, 148n13. See also Bamboo on the Mountains (Smithsonian Folkways, 1999) (CD)
socialism, art in service to, 19–20, 43, 64, 71
South of the Clouds (Ode, 2003) (Yunnanese CDs), 152; challenges of project, 132; curation process in, 132–33; genesis of, 128–29; impacts of, 142, 143; and shift in Zhang Xingrong's aesthetic views, 147n7; success of, 149n16
Soviet models, 68
Stalin, Joseph, 64, 68
Starlight Highway, 47, 50, 53, 56
Stern, David, 100

Stillman, Amy Kuʻuleialoha, 43
Stock, Jonathan, 3, 4, 8, 79
style and flavor in dance, 75–76
Sun Ying, 87
Sun Zhikuan (b. 1958), 51
Super Girl TV competition, 43
"Survey of Chinese Music" (1964), 28

Tai-Nüa language, 140
Taiwan, dance in, 79–80
Taoist texts, 130
"Tears Fall on the Desert Brush," 51
"Ten Greatest Song Kings," 54
textual anthologies as symbolic sites of tradition, 1
Thompson, Stith, 8, 9
Three Saintly Graces of Alasha (Lu Badma), 31
Tian Qing, 7, 55, 59n17
"Top Ten Northern Shaanxi Song Kings," 53
tradition: authoring of, 87; Chinese *versus* Western notions of, 77; as collective body of works and practices, 100; continuity and change in, 1, 43, 77–79; and creativity, 120n23; fluidity of, 6; imagined tradition, 100, 119n10; influence of social change on, 35; invented tradition, 79; as process and resource, 99. See also cultural heritage; folklore and folk culture; mechanisms of traditionalization; preservation of cultural heritage
traditionalization of performances: judges' role in, 44, 45; of singers and singing styles, 2, 46–50; in singing competitions, 43, 45
translations. See curation of recordings
Traveller tradition, 5
Trippner, Josef, 119n8

Ulanmuchir (local troupe), 19–20, 30
Uyghur dance, 80

Victoria University, 143

Wang Duanshu, 120n17
Wang Erni (b. 1985), 50, 51, 52, 54, 58n3

Wang Jingzhi, 85
Wang Kun (1925–2014), 52
Wang Luobin (1913–1996), 59n9
Wang Xiangrong (b. 1952), 46–47, 52, 53, 58–59n6, 59n8
Wartime Gansu News Inspection Department, 107
Wen Shilong, 51
Wheeler, Nicholas, 128
"The Wild Lilies Bloom a Brilliant Red," 47, 50, 51
Williams, J. Lloyd, 100–101
women: contribution to Chinese dance, 80; representation as dignified, 84
World Festival of Youth and Students, 84
Wu, David Y. H., 79
Wudao on "Cup and Bowl Dance," 81
Wudao on Inner Mongolia Song and Dance Ensemble, 83
Wu Xiaobang (1906–1995), 68, 72–73
Wu Zhen (1721–1797): "Ten Poems on My Good Recollections of Lintao," 106

Xiaobing Tang, 67
Xiaohuaxi dramas, 55
Xiao Mei, 103
Xiao Shenyang, 51
Xi Huimin, 119n8
Xinjiang folk songs, 59n9
Xin Lisheng, 55
Xu Lingxiao (1882–1961), 106

Ya Hanzhang (1916–1989), 106, 116, 120n20
Yan'an "national forms" movement, 87
Yang Cui, 59n8
Yang Dehong, 144
Yang Hui, 109
Yang Yucheng (Professor Yang, aka Botolt), 6–7, 28, 29, 35, 36. See also "Great Masters Series"
Yellow River (*Huanghe*) (1988), 76, 80
YST. See *yuanshengtai*
Yuan Fuli (1893–1987), 106, 120n19
yuanshengtai (YST, or "original ecology"): and Alasha region, 26; and credibility of artists, 31; and dance, 65; folksong

yuanshengtai (cont.)
  recordings, 140; and future in the city, 34; growth in status of, 49; original ecology folk bands, 23–24; preserved by Badma, 30; YST folksongs, 23–24
Yulin Folk Arts Troupe, 46
Yumiti (b. 1987), 80
Yunnan Art Institute, 125, 127, 147n2, 149n17
Yunnanese CDs: aspirations for, 141; as baseline for future studies, 145; as communal project, 125, 146; genesis of projects, 127–29; historical timing and, 144, 145–46; impact on folklore studies, 125; influence of Pan and Ode CDs, 140–44, 149n16; reviews of, 131, 144, 148n14; role of researcher in, 127; significance of, 145, 149n18. See also *Alili*; *Bai Opera*; *Baishibai*; curation of recordings; *Dai Opera*; *Music of the Bai Opera and the Dai Opera in Yunnan Province*; *Nanwoka*; *South of the Clouds*
Yunnan Province, 54, 126*f*, 147n4

"Zange" (Song of praise), 20
Zhang Laowu (1932–c. 1998), 142, 149n17
Zhang Lin, 107
Zhang Taiyan (1869–1936), 112
Zhang Xingrong (b. 1941): agreement to record music collected by, 128–29; CD project proposal of, 127; communication with Yunnan residents, 136; digitization project of, 144; discovery of Hani polyphonic folksongs, 143; and festival performances, 142–43; field recordings of, 125, 146; future studies of, 145; juxtaposition of state and folk performances in CDs, 137–38; liner notes for CDs, 129, 130, 131; promotion of CDs, 142; recognition from project, 143; shift in aesthetic understanding of, 128, 147n7; and video recordings, 147n3. *See also* Yunnanese CDs
Zhang Yaxiong (1909–1989): biographical information about, 105–7, 120n18; classification work of, 98; and collection within a community, 96, 117; creative agency of, 102–3; as father of hua'er studies, 94–95, 97, 118; "Hua'er Afterword" (1936), 106, 114; "Hua'er: A Preface" (Hua'er xu) (1931), 106, 113, 116; impact of work, 114; imprisonment of, 117; on metaphor in hua'er songs, 114–15; motivation for anthology, 109–10; and tradition of collecting and publishing, 100; and use of structuring structures, 101; and Ya Hanzhang's hua'er work, 116, 120n20. *See also under* hua'er
Zhang Yiwu (1895–1951), 105–6
Zhou Jinping, 52
Zhu Zhonglu (1922–2007), 117, 120n23
Zipes, Jack, 101
Zuoquan County (Shaanxi Province), 54, 55–56
Zuoquan folksongs, 54, 55
Zwaan, Koos, 42

www.ingramcontent.com/pod-product-compliance
Lightning Source LLC
Chambersburg PA
CBHW030655230426
43665CB00011B/1101